The Tyndale Old Testament Commentaries

General Editor:
PROFESSOR D. J. WISEMAN, O.B.E., M.A., D.LIT., F.B.A., F.S.A.

JOB

JOB

AN INTRODUCTION AND COMMENTARY

by

FRANCIS I. ANDERSEN, M.A., B.D., M.SC., PH.D., D.D.
Research Fellow, The Australian Institute of Archaeology

INTER-VARSITY PRESS
LEICESTER, ENGLAND
DOWNERS GROVE, ILLINOIS, U.S.A.

Inter-Varsity Press
38 De Montfort Street, Leicester LE1 7GP, England
P.O. Box 1400, Downers Grove, Illinois 60515, U.S.A.

© *Inter-Varsity Press, Leicester, England*

*Inter-Varsity Press, England, is the book-publishing division of the Universities and Colleges
Christian Fellowship (formerly the Inter-Varsity Fellowship), a student movement linking
Christian Unions in universities and colleges throughout the United Kingdom and the Republic
of Ireland, and a member movement of the International Fellowship of Evangelical Students.
For information about local and national activities in Great Britain write to UCCF, 38 De
Montfort Street, Leicester LE1 7GP.*

*InterVarsity Press, U.S.A., is the book-publishing division of InterVarsity Christian Fellowship,
a student movement active on campus at hundreds of universities, colleges and schools of
nursing in the United States of America, and a member movement of the International
Fellowship of Evangelical Students. For information about local and regional activities, write
Public Relations Dept., InterVarsity Christian Fellowship, 6400 Schroeder Rd., P.O. Box 7895,
Madison, WI 53707-7895.*

Text set in Great Britain
Printed in the United States of America ∞

UK ISBN 0-85111-831-3 (paperback)
Library of Congress Catalog Card Number: 76-12298
USA ISBN 0-87784-869-6 (cloth)
USA ISBN 0-87784-263-9 (paperback)
USA ISBN 0-87784-880-7 (set of Tyndale Old Testament Commentaries, cloth)
USA ISBN 0-87784-280-9 (set of Tyndale Old Testament Commentaries, paperback)

27   26   25   24   23   22   21
05   04   03   02

GENERAL PREFACE

THE aim of this series of *Tyndale Old Testament Commentaries*, as it was in the companion volumes on the New Testament, is to provide the student of the Bible with a handy, up-to-date commentary on each book, with the primary emphasis on exegesis. Major critical questions are discussed in the introductions and additional notes, while undue technicalities have been avoided.

In this series individual authors are, of course, free to make their own distinct contributions and express their own point of view on all controversial issues. Within the necessary limits of space they frequently draw attention to interpretations which they themselves do not hold but which represent the stated conclusions of sincere fellow Christians. The book of Job, with its profound discussion of the mystery of personal suffering, is here commented upon by a scholar who knows something of the problem. Professor Andersen writes also from his experience as a teacher of Hebrew and cognate Semitic languages and literatures in which his reading is wide and up-to-date. He faces the many problems of the difficult text of this ancient book clearly and fairly and at the same time brings fresh insights and interpretation to a commentary which reflects not a little of his personality, life and work and so should help all modern Jobs and their would-be comforters.

In the Old Testament in particular no single English translation is adequate to reflect the original text. The authors of these commentaries freely quote various versions, therefore, or give their own translation, in the endeavour to make the more difficult passages or words meaningful today. Where necessary, words from the Hebrew (and Aramaic) Text underlying their studies are transliterated. This will help the reader who may be unfamiliar with the Semitic languages to identify the word under discussion and thus to follow the argument. It is assumed throughout that the reader will have ready access to one, or more, reliable rendering of the Bible in English.

Interest in the meaning and message of the Old Testament continues undiminished and it is hoped that this series will thus further the systematic study of the revelation of God and His will and ways as seen in these records. It is the prayer of the editor and publisher, as of the authors, that these books will help many to understand, and to respond to, the Word of God today.

D. J. WISEMAN

CONTENTS

AUTHOR'S PREFACE

IT is presumptuous to comment on the book of Job. It is so full of the awesome reality of the living God. Like Job, one can only put one's hand over one's mouth (40:4). But God has revealed Himself, preserving at the same time the inaccessible mystery of His own being. So we must attempt this impossible thing which He makes possible (Mk. 10:27). However forbidding, He fascinates us irresistibly until, by 'kindness and severity' (Rom. 11:22), He brings us in His own way to Job's final satisfaction and joy. The story of Job is an invitation and a guide to discoveries like his. It is especially the book for any who find themselves in 'Job's sick day'[1] as a result of some shattering experience.

This commentary has taken shape in turbulent times. It was begun in Jerusalem, against a background of wars whose horrors have awakened the cries of Job again. It was continued in Africa and New Guinea, where the struggle for subsistence has its own misery. Finally Berkeley, California, provided a convulsive background of moral protest against war, poverty and racism.

The book of Job is about the unchanging human realities – war, destitution, sickness, humiliation, bereavement, depression. Also the unchanging goodness of God, who transforms our human agony into justice, kindness, love and joy. It is about 'the terror of the Lord' (2 Cor. 5:11) and His great tenderness (Jas. 5:11). It is the story of one man who held on to his life in God with a faith that survived the torments of utter loss and expanded into new realms of wonder and delight.

The author is indebted to more persons that he can name. A generous research grant from the Australian Institute of Archaeology made it possible to complete the final revision. With a full heart I thank God for the unfaltering love of my wife Lois. The completion of this book is also a tribute to the Dean of Auckland, the Very Reverend John O. Rymer, and his wife, Joyce, who brought the love of God to us in a dark hour. Everything is a gift, suffering the holiest of all; and the

---

[1] John Donne, *From the Litany*.

9

healing of all hurts is found in the Body of One who was broken, the only *pharmakon athanasias*.

Saint Andrew's Day, 1974   FRANCIS I. ANDERSEN

CHIEF ABBREVIATIONS

11QtgJob	The Qumran Targum of Job (see p. 55, n. 1).
AASOR	*Annual of the American Schools of Oriental Research.*
AB	*The Anchor Bible.*
AJSL	*American Journal of Semitic Languages.*
ANEP	*The Ancient Near East in Pictures* edited by James B. Pritchard, 1954.
ANET	*Ancient Near Eastern Texts relating to the Old Testament²* edited by James B. Pritchard, 1955 (³1969).
AS	*Anatolian Studies.*
ATANT	*Abhandlungen zur Theologie des Alten und Neuen Testaments.*
ATD	*Das Alte Testament Deutsch.*
BASOR	*Bulletin of the American Schools of Oriental Research.*
BJRL	*Bulletin of the John Rylands Library.*
BWL	*Babylonian Wisdom Literature* by Wilfred G. Lambert, 1960.
BZAW	*Beihefte zur Zeitschrift für die alttestamentliche Wissenschaft.*
CAD	*Chicago Assyrian Dictionary.*
CB	*Cambridge Bible* (for schools).
CBQ	*Catholic Biblical Quarterly.*
COCR	*Corpus Reformatorum: Calvini Opera.*
DOTT	*Documents from Old Testament Times* edited by D. Winton Thomas, 1958.
EI	*Eretz Israel.*
HAT	*Handbuch zum Alten Testament.*
HTR	*Harvard Theological Review.*
HUCA	*Hebrew Union College Annual.*
IB	*The Interpreter's Bible.*
ICC	*International Critical Commentary.*
IDB	*Interpreter's Dictionary of the Bible.*
JAOS	*Journal of the American Oriental Society.*
JBL	*Journal of Biblical Literature.*
JCS	*Journal of Cuneiform Studies.*
JEA	*Journal of Egyptian Archaeology.*
JNES	*Journal of Near Eastern Studies.*

JQR	*Jewish Quarterly Review.*
JSS	*Journal of Semitic Studies.*
JTS	*Journal of Theological Studies.*
KAT	*Kommentar zum Alten Testament.*
K–B	*Lexicon in Veteris Testamenti Libros* by L. Koehler and W. Baumgartner, 1953.
NBCR	*The New Bible Commentary Revised,* 1970.
NCB	*New Century Bible.*
OTMS	*The Old Testament and Modern Study* edited by H. H. Rowley, 1951.
OTS	*Outtestamentische Studien.*
RB	*Revue Biblique.*
SBT	*Studies in Biblical Theology.*
SBT²	*Studies in Biblical Theology,* second series.
SVT	Supplements to *Vetus Testamentum.*
TOTC	*Tyndale Old Testament Commentaries.*
UF	*Ugarit-Forschungen: Internationales Jahrbuch für die Altertumskunde Syrien-Palästinas.*
WMZANT	*Wissenschaftliche Monografien zum Alten und Neuen Testament.*
ZA	*Zeitschrift für Assyriologie.*
ZAW	*Zeitschrift für die Alttestamentliche Wissenschaft.*
ZDMG	*Zeitschrift der deutschen Morgenländischen Gesellschaft.*

Texts and Versions

AV	Authorized Version (King James).
JB	Jerusalem Bible.
LXX	The Septuagint (pre-Christian Greek version of the Old Testament).
Moffatt	A New Translation of the Bible by James Moffatt.
MT	Massoretic Text.
NAB	New American Bible.
NEB	New English Bible.
RSV	Revised Standard Version.
RV	Revised Version.
TEV	Today's English Version.
Vulg.	The Vulgate (Jerome's Latin version of the Bible).

Commentaries

(referred to by author's name and page number)

Bickell	*Das Buch Hiob* by G. Bickell, 1894.
Budde	*Beiträge zur Kritik des Buches Hiob* by K. Budde, 1876.
Davidson	*The Book of Job* by A. B. Davidson (*CB*), 1884.
Delitzsch	*Job* by F. Delitzsch (*Biblical Commentary on the Old Testament*), 1866.
Dhorme	*A Commentary on the Book of Job* by E. Dhorme, translated by H. Knight, 1967.
Driver–Gray	*A Critical and Exegetical Commentary on the Book of Job* by S. R. Driver and G. B. Gray (*ICC*[2]), 1950.
Duhm	*Das Buch Hiob* by Bernhard Duhm (*Kurzer Hand-Commentar zum Alten Testament*, XVI), 1897.
Fohrer	*Das Buch Hiob* by G. Fohrer (*KAT*, XVI),
Gordis	*The Book of God and Man: A Study of Job* by Robert Gordis, 1965.
Guillaume	*Studies in the Book of Job* with a new Translation by A. Guillaume, edited by John Macdonald (Supplement II to the Annual of Leeds University Oriental Society), 1968.
Hölscher	*Das Buch Hiob* by G. Hölscher (*HAT*), 1952.
Jones	*The Triumph of Job* by E. Jones, 1966.
Pope	*Job: Introduction, Translation and Notes*[3] by Marvin H. Pope (*AB*), 1973.
Rowley	*The Book of Job* by H. H. Rowley (*NCB*), 1970.
Tur Sinai	*The Book of Job: A New Commentary*[2] by N. H. Tur Sinai, 1957.
Weiser	*Das Buch Hiob* by A. Weiser (*ATD*[2]), 1956.

INTRODUCTION

I. THE STORY OF JOB

THE book of Job tells the story of a good man over-whelmed by troubles. He is stripped of his wealth, his family, his health. He does not know why God has done this to him. Only the reader knows that God is trying to prove to the Devil that Job's faith is genuine. Three friends come to console him in his misery, and the four engage in a long discussion. The friends try to explain what has happened by connecting Job's sufferings with his sins. Job rejects their theory. Instead of accepting their advice to repent and so make peace with God, Job insists on his own innocence and questions the justice of God's treatment.

At this point a new character, Elihu, appears and makes four speeches which he thinks will solve the problem; but this does not seem to make any difference. Eventually the Lord Himself addresses Job. These speeches change Job's attitude, for he responds with contrite submission. In the end God declares Job to be in the right and restores his prosperity and happiness.

Upon this simple plot an unknown writer of superlative genius has erected a monumental work. The most persistent questions of the relationship of men to God have been given powerful theological treatment in verse whose majesty and emotion are unsurpassed in any literature, ancient or modern.

II. THE STUDY OF THE BOOK OF JOB

The Old Testament book about Job is one of the supreme offerings of the human mind to the living God and one of the best gifts of God to men. The task of understanding it is as rewarding as it is strenuous. For his help, the modern student has a rich legacy from the labours of the past. It is a tribute to the greatness of the book that the work of interpreting it is never finished. After each fresh exploration the challenge to scale the heights remains. One is constantly amazed at its audacious theology and at the magnitude of its intellectual achievement. Job is a prodigious book in the vast range of its

15

ideas, in its broad coverage of human experience, in the intensity of its passions, in the immensity of its concept of God, and not least in its superb literary craftsmanship. It reaches widely over the complexities of existence, seeking a place for animals as well as men in God's world. It plumbs the depths of human despair, the anger of moral outrage, and the anguish of desertion by God. From one man's agony it reaches out to the mystery of God, beyond all words and explanations. It is only God Himself who brings Job joy in the end. And, when all is done, the mystery remains. God stands revealed in His hiddenness, an object of terror, adoration and love. And Job stands before him 'like a man' (38:3; 40:7), trusting and satisfied.

The study of these great questions as they are raised by the book of Job has produced a huge literature, only a fraction of which can be indicated in this commentary. Ultimately such work must go back to the Massoretic Text (MT). Translators agree that the Hebrew text of Job presents more problems than most other parts of the Old Testament. The commentary will make use of many versions, including such ancient translations as the Septuagint (LXX). Comparison of one with another shows that we are still in the dark as to the exact meaning of the Hebrew text in many places. There is not room in this commentary for detailed examination of all the textual and philological questions encountered in the book, and even the technical literature is still a long way from reaching final answers. We shall have to be content with such uncertainty for the time being; but the incomplete state of our research should not be permitted to diminish our respect for the integrity of the Hebrew text. On the contrary, the difficulties we encounter are themselves a tribute to the fidelity of the Jewish scribes, who reverently preferred to copy an obscure text exactly rather than attempt to clarify it by an emendation. In this they were more modest, and more scientific, than many modern critics. In the hey-day of the criticism that reached its peak at the turn of the century, scholars were quick to infer that a passage which they could not understand must be corrupt. They then proceeded to 'correct' it. Some problems have been solved in this way, for even the Massoretic Text is not without its blemishes; but more often than not rewriting the text does not solve the problem. It merely destroys the evidence.

Recent research has made text critics more cautious. Numerous discoveries, especially those derived from archaeology, now enable us to make sense of the text as it stands. Many of the ingenious reconstructions of a previous generation of scholarship must now be abandoned as uncalled for. Yet, in spite of great progress, many passages in Job remain problematical. They must be attacked with all the apparatus of contemporary learning: the latest advances in the analysis of the spelling of words in ancient Hebrew, of the meanings of rare words (which are abundant in Job), of grammatical constructions, of the forms of Hebrew poetry, of the kinds of literature incorporated into the design of this book. Job is a little encyclopedia of life in the ancient Near East; so its cultural milieu and sociological background help to explain many passages.

No one book can now hope to embrace such a many-sided task, let alone review the vast labours of the past; and intricate technicalities would be out of place in this series.[1] Several of the larger works happily complement each other. For textual matters Édouard Dhorme's monumental commentary[2] is indispensable. The commentary begun by S. R. Driver[3] gathers up the main results of the older higher criticism. But the death of Professor Driver before it was finished left Dr Gray at a disadvantage in unifying the material. In any case, much of their philological work has now been superseded by subsequent linguistic discoveries. Of the continuing stream of commentaries and special studies on Job only a few will be mentioned here. The lifelong studies of Naphtali H. Tur Sinai (H. Torczyner) have bequeathed a wealth of provocative philological observations.[4] The recovery

[1] Copious bibliography up to 1953 is given by C. Kuhl, 'Neuere Literaturkritik des Buches Hiob', *Theologische Rundschau*, XXI, 1953, pp. 163–205, 257–317, and 'Vom Hiobbuche und seinen Problemen', *ibid.*, XXII, 1954, pp. 261–316. This may be augmented by the references in commentaries published since then. See the list in *Chief Abbreviations* (p. 13, above), and particularly Georg Fohrer, *Das Buch Hiob* (*KAT*), pp. 59–68.

[2] *Le Livre de Job* (1926); English translation by H. Knight, *A Commentary on the Book of Job* (1967).

[3] S. R. Driver and G. B. Gray, *A Critical and Exegetical Commentary on the Book of Job Together with a New Translation* (*ICC*[2], 1950).

[4] His great three-volume analysis, *Hallāšôn wᵉhassēper* (1950, 1954, 1955) and *Sēper 'Iyyôb* (1954) were followed by a summary of revised results in English: *The Book of Job: A New Commentary*[2] (1957), which highlights the Aramaic features of the language. See the review by W. F. Albright in *BASOR*, CXLIV, 1956, p. 39.

of a body of old Canaanite literature in the language of the city of Ugarit has opened up a whole new phase of research, whose benefits can be seen in Marvin Pope's contribution to *The Anchor Bible*,[1] and in the continuing work of Mitchell Dahood.[2] Robert Gordis has written a fine appreciation of the book as a literary whole in the best traditions of theistic humanism.[3] The commentaries of G. Hölscher (*HAT*, 1952), Artur Weiser (*ATD*[2], 1956) and H. H. Rowley (*NCB*, 1970) may also be mentioned.

The reflections of earlier thinkers on this great book still have much to offer, especially when it comes to theological understanding. A number of teachers and preachers of the early church made use of Job, but little of their work survives, except in the *catenae* of later students. The commentary of Gregory the Great[4] dominated later centuries. The works of Albert Magnus and Thomas Aquinas gave expression to a more scientific approach. But for a thousand years the church had generally preferred the methods of allegorical, typological, moral and spiritual interpretation to the literal meaning of Scripture. The Reformation rehabilitated grammatico-historical exegesis and produced the greatest exposition of Job ever given, in the one hundred and fifty-nine sermons of John Calvin on this book.[5]

The immensity of the theme and the numerous technical problems presented by the book of Job should not be allowed to intimidate the general reader. The impact of this story is not impeded by our continuing puzzlement over various textual and linguistic mysteries. It is on the level of human experience that the artistic and theological greatness of this writing can be powerfully felt. The disgust expressed in Job's remark that '*ryr ḥlmwt* is tasteless' (6:6) can be appreciated, even though we still do not know what that substance is. The rigorous study of the text by every available scientific means is an essential preliminary to sound exegesis. But Rabbi Gordis

[1] Marvin H. Pope, *Job: Introduction, Translation, and Notes*[3] (*AB*, 1973).

[2] See Anton C. M. Blommerde, *Northwest Semitic Grammar and Job* (*Biblica et Orientalia*, No. 22, 1969).

[3] *The Book of God and Man: A Study of Job* (1965).

[4] *Expositio in librum Job, sive Moralium libri XXXV*, Migne, *Patrologia Latina*, LXXV, cols. 500ff.

[5] *Calvini Opera: Corpus Reformatorum*, Vols. XXXIII–XXXV. A selection of twenty of these sermons, translated by Leroy Nixon, is available in English: *Sermons from Job* (1952).

has wisely advanced beyond this groundwork to insist that it is the literary effect of the whole book, at once aesthetic and intellectual, that is the medium of its theology. Reading it in this way then becomes the occasion, or at least the opportunity, for any person to recapitulate Job's dramatic encounter with the living God.

As a Christian, the present writer recognizes in Job ideas which point beyond the Old Testament, especially in Job's reiterated longing for a mediator and his desperate hope for personal resurrection. This hope finds its fulfilment in Jesus, the Messiah. Already in this older part of His self-revelation, the God who pardons and saves can be seen behind the Creator and Judge, and Job is ready to meet his Redeemer.

III. THE DESIGN OF THE BOOK OF JOB

The plan is readily grasped. By a simple arrangement of corresponding materials in balancing positions, a scheme is built up in which the episodes of the story are easy to follow. The massive speeches that make up the bulk of the book have been incorporated into the narrative framework with a symmetry that effects artistic harmony. At the same time there is a development in the tempo that leads from climax to climax, until the final resolution. The speeches are assembled in cycles through which tension is built up from stage to stage. Thus the second interview with the Satan is more drastic than the first, and Yahweh's second address to Job is more tremendous than the first. The exchanges between Job and his friends become more and more heated as round follows round. But the drama does not move steadily upwards to its peak and then down through the dénouement to the end. Job's crowning speech is set off by using a beautiful poem on Wisdom (chapter 28) as an interlude after the three main cycles are finished. The tranquillity of this meditation contrasts with the turbulence before and after it, and provides needed relief for the reader. By a similar device the two most stupendous moments in the book – Job's final intrepid challenge (chapters 29–31) and Yahweh's overwhelming reply (chapters 38–41) – are kept apart by the speeches of Elihu (chapters 32–37), whose very slowness of movement creates an interval of suspense against which the words of the Lord become all the more majestic.

The plan can be shown as follows.

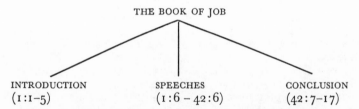

THE BOOK OF JOB

INTRODUCTION   SPEECHES   CONCLUSION
(1:1–5)   (1:6 – 42:6)   (42:7–17)

The Introduction shows Job in his original happiness; the Conclusion paints a similar picture of his final contentment. All of the action in between takes the form of words rather than deeds. The speeches have the same kind of architectonic balance.

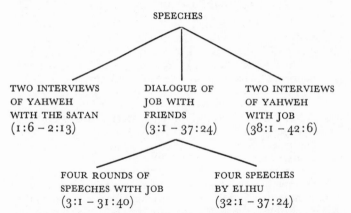

SPEECHES

TWO INTERVIEWS   DIALOGUE OF   TWO INTERVIEWS
OF YAHWEH   JOB WITH   OF YAHWEH
WITH THE SATAN   FRIENDS   WITH JOB
(1:6 – 2:13)   (3:1 – 37:24)   (38:1 – 42:6)

FOUR ROUNDS OF   FOUR SPEECHES
SPEECHES WITH JOB   BY ELIHU
(3:1 – 31:40)   (32:1 – 37:24)

The similarity in form between the opening scene, in which God talks twice to the Satan, and the closing scene, in which God talks twice to Job, is important as a mark of the artistic integrity of the treatment. It suggests deliberate planning and unity of authorship. But many scholars assign these episodes to the 'Prologue' (identified as 1:1 – 2:13) and 'Dialogue' (3:1 – 42:6) respectively, and ascribe them to different authors. We admit that the inner structure of these two double interviews is different. The final confrontation between Yahweh and Job is quite simply recounted. It consists of two cycles in each of which the Lord makes a long speech and Job makes a brief reply. But this part of the story is told in the same epic style as 1:6 - 2:13, by using the same stereotyped formula to introduce the speakers in each round. Thus both speeches of Yahweh are made 'out of the whirlwind', just as each interview with the Satan takes place in the divine assembly with almost identical introductions to each occasion. The section 1:6 – 2:13 does, of course, include more than the two interviews with the Satan. Each of these is followed by the Satan's action and Job's response. The similarity of the development has the balance of a classical musical composition.

Round 1	*Round* 2
Interview with the Satan (1:6–12)	Interview with the Satan (2:1–7a)
The disasters (1:13–19)	The affliction (2:7b, 8)
Job's reaction (1:20–22)	Job's reaction (2:9–13)

What we have called Job's reaction to his illness is more complex than his simple response to the first disasters. For now his wife and his friends come into the story, and this material is transitional to the main dialogue which follows. But, by way of compensation, the tale of disasters in the first round is more elaborate than the simple stroke of 2:7b. Furthermore, the reports of the destruction of Job's household are brought by four messengers, an artificial pattern which reveals a propensity of the author for the number four which is found throughout the book. Thus Elihu makes four distinct speeches, even though they come all together. And the dialogue with the three friends actually involves four cycles of speeches, even though Job is the sole speaker in the last of them.

We have already observed that the poem on Wisdom (chapter 28) and the speeches of Elihu (chapters 32–37) serve special purposes as interludes between other, more important, speeches by Job and Yahweh. Leaving these aside, we see that the remaining speeches made by Job and his three friends are also arranged in a symmetrical pattern like the one we have already met in the book as a whole and in the speeches as a whole.

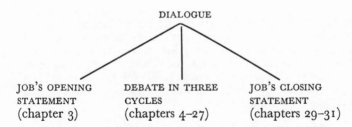

		DIALOGUE		
JOB'S OPENING STATEMENT (chapter 3)		DEBATE IN THREE CYCLES (chapters 4–27)		JOB'S CLOSING STATEMENT (chapters 29–31)

There is a real correspondence between Job's opening curse (chapter 3) and his closing auto-imprecation (chapter 31). But it is not clear how the several speeches are to be grouped in the three cycles. By separating off chapter 3 as an opening statement, we leave Eliphaz to commence the debate in chapter 4. Job replies to this, and so it goes on. This implies that the dynamics of the dialogue is a succession of attacks by Job upon the statements of his friends, rather than criticisms of Job's words by each of his friends in turn.[1] But it would over-simplify the matter and create serious problems for interpretation to look on each successive speech as a logical reply to the one immediately preceding it. The dialectic is not as closely woven as that.

While Job speaks in alternation with each of the friends in turn, the three cycles are not identical.

		Cycle 1	*Cycle* 2	*Cycle* 3
Eliphaz	chapters	4–5	15	22
Job		6–7	16–17	23–24
Bildad		8	18	25
Job		9–10	19	26
Zophar		11	20	?
Job		12–14	21	27

It will be noticed at once that Zophar does not make a speech in the third cycle. Many attempts have been made to

---

[1] The latter approach is taken by W. E. Hulme in *Dialogue in Despair* (1968).

explain this, and we shall look more closely at some of them in section VII below.

There are other ways of looking at the total structure of the book. One system which has been widely used by scholars distinguishes an opening Prologue (1:1 – 2:13) and a closing Epilogue (42:7–17), both in prose, from the intervening Dialogue, in poetry. The dialogue falls into three parts as the speakers change. First Job talks with his three friends (chapters 3–31); then Elihu makes four speeches, without discussion (chapters 32–37); finally Yahweh addresses Job twice (chapters 38 – 42:6).

IV. THE LITERARY BACKGROUND OF THE BOOK OF JOB

A book like Job was not written in a vacuum. Only God creates out of nothing. His creatures use the materials He gives them, and the work of the mind is done with what flows into a man's life from his own experience and from the culture of his people. If he is well-educated, he feeds on other people's ideas. The author of Job was not only sensitive and intelligent; he was experienced and cultivated. We can only guess at the community that nourished his thought. We do not know how much he learnt from reading, from discussion of the kind he portrays in his own book, or from travel. We do not know if he could read other languages besides Hebrew, and so draw directly on the literature of neighbouring countries.

Whatever the stimulus, his art is unique. But not isolated. In the first place, it stands in the tradition of his own people. It is Israelite in spirit and distinctively Israelite in theology. At the same time it is universal in its humanism, and is a sample of the kind of literature from the ancient world which was most cosmopolitan in character – the literature broadly called 'Wisdom'.

This term covers a wide variety of literary forms, from simple sayings of the common folk to the learned discourse of philosophical minds. All Israel's neighbours had their own store of Wisdom literature, which has survived in varying amounts. While there are local peculiarities, there is much of it which expresses the common experiences of men, beyond all differences of race, nation or culture. The Old Testament contains a considerable quantity of Wisdom literature, not only in entire works such as Job, Proverbs and Ecclesiastes, but also in smaller adages, riddles, poems, scientific lists and meditations on cosmological or ethical questions scattered through other biblical writings. The New Testament also has its share of Wisdom materials.[1]

Many similarities have been observed between Job and other writings from the ancient world, particularly the Wisdom literature of Mesopotamia and Egypt. These other works supply valuable background and help to interpret many parts of Job. They also raise the question of how much of such literature the author of Job actually knew, and perhaps used as a source of his ideas or even of quotations.

In studying this problem, two extremes should be avoided. Nothing is gained by contending so energetically for the uniqueness of Israel's life, especially its religion, as the product of special revelation, that the people of God are cut off from the rest of the world. Some scholars have not been prepared to recognize much affinity between the Old Testament and 'pagan' writings, and insist on interpreting the Bible solely in terms of itself. At the other extreme, the culture of the ancient Near East is sometimes viewed as if it were uniform from the Persian Gulf to the upper reaches of the Nile. 'Comparative' studies of myths and rituals have highlighted similarities between the gods and institutions of the peoples of the region; and the impression is sometimes given that the Israelites invented nothing of their own, but borrowed everything, just as they borrowed the alphabet, from one or other of their neighbours. The book of Job is then seen as a cosmopolitan work, a miscellany of 'wisdom' garnered by some bookish Israelite from the libraries of other peoples.

There is some truth in each of these positions; but neither is true if stated alone. Job shows a certain resemblance to other works here and there. How far that resemblance goes can be found out only by detailed comparison of Job with each such companion piece. This research will also show the extent to which Job is *sui generis*.

So far as *plot* is concerned, it is curious that the only story which, as a story, is said to be like Job, is one for which any

---

[1] G. von Rad, *Wisdom in Israel* (Eng. tr. 1972) is the most valuable general recent study.

historical connection is quite improbable. The Indian legend of Hariś-candra[1] has been compared with Job.[2] The hero is introduced as an ideal king in whose realm prosperity, justice and contentment prevail. The claim of some Western scholars that the gods decide to test his virtue by suffering is not borne out by reading the story. While coming to the aid of a woman in distress, the king is brought to an avowal of his piety by professing his duty to give alms, especially to brahmans, to protect the fearful and to make war with enemies. Having extracted this admission, the brahman puts Hariś-candra's ethics to the test by requesting all his possessions – his entire kingdom, in fact – excepting his wife, his son, his body and, of course, his inalienable rectitude. All these the righteous king gives up without a murmur, and leaves his domain as a penniless beggar.

But he had omitted the fee for the Raja-súya sacrifice, and no longer had means to pay it. He does not deny his obligation to keep the promise, and is granted time to do it. Visvámitra is unrelenting in his demand, which Hariś-candra's continued destitution renders impossible. Finally, at the last minute, he sells his wife and child for the fee, and ekes out his own subsistence in utter degradation as worker in a burial-ground. The son dies, and when his mother brings his body to the cemetery, the parents resolve to immolate themselves on his funerary pyre. Then Indra intervenes; the boy is restored to life and Hariś-candra's unflinching virtue is rewarded as the reunited family ascends to heaven.

There is very little resemblance to Job in this story. Hariś-candra's misery is the result of voluntary renunciation. He is submissive and uncomplaining. The background of ethics and theology is totally different from that in the Bible. R. K. Harrison thinks that it is possible that such a story is a late corruption of much earlier Mesopotamian material.[3] But, if so, it has travelled so far and so long that any connection with the Near East cannot be demonstrated. The few simi-

---

[1] *The Mārkaṇḍeya Purāṇa*, translated by F. Eden Pargiter (*Bibliotheca Indica*, Vol. 125, 1904), pp. 32–61. (Reprinted by Indological Book House, Delhi-6, 1969.)

[2] P. Volz, *Hiob und Weisheit* (1921), pp. 8f.; P. Bertie, *Le poème de Job* (1929), p. 54; Adolphe Lods, *Histoire de la littérature hébraïque et juive* (1950), pp. 691f.; E. G. Kraeling, *The Book of the Ways of God* (1939), pp. 187ff.

[3] R. K. Harrison, *Introduction to the Old Testament* (1970), p. 1027.

larities are merely coincidences that are only to be expected in such common experiences of life.[1]

In this context we should say decisively that Job has nothing in common with the vulgar stories of wagers between celestial beings over the corruptibility of some conspicuously good human. The agreements between Yahweh and the Satan are not bets (see commentary on Jb. 1:11).

Nearer the Israelite homeland a comparison can be made with the Ugaritic story of Keret,[2] a good king who is bereaved of all his family (seven sons!) and whose fortunes turn after ritual prayers. But the story goes on to end quite differently from Job, and the questions raised in the Bible are nowhere discussed.

The suggestion that an Akkadian work entitled *Ludlul Bêl Nêmeqi* could be called 'The Babylonian Job' was first made in 1906.[3] Evidence for the text has gradually accumulated.[4] The work is actually a hymn of thanksgiving to Marduk for recovery from an illness. Form-criticism of prayers of lamentation and songs of gratitude has shown a close affinity between such compositions, in spite of their totally opposite moods of grief and jubilation. For in each the sufferer recounts his plight, in the first to arouse the pity of the gods, in the second in thankful reminiscence. Each tells the story of the poet's sufferings, although from a different point in time.[5] The so-called 'Babylonian Job' belongs to this genre,

[1] Hölscher (p. 3) suspects that the Indian story has been contaminated somewhat from the biblical one.

[2] A full bibliography of Keret studies is given by George Saliba in his (unpublished) Master's dissertation submitted to the University of California (Berkeley) in 1969. Among many available English translations of *Keret* see *ANET*, pp. 142–149 or *DOTT*, pp. 118–124.

[3] M. Jastrow, Jr., 'A Babylonian Parallel to the Story of Job', *JBL*, XXV, 1906, pp. 135–191.

[4] The first fragments published are documented in *ANET*, p. 434. The first extensive text was published by S. H. Langdon, *Babylonian Wisdom* (1923), Plates I–V; translation pp. 35–66; see also *Babyloniaca*, VII, 1923, pp. 131ff. The text of the Istanbul copy was published by R. J. Williams, 'Notes on some Akkadian Wisdom Texts', *JCS*, VI, 1952, pp. 4–7. Sultantepe has provided more evidence: W. G. Lambert and O. R. Gurney, 'The Sultantepe Tablets: III. The Poem of the Righteous Sufferer', *AS*, IV, 1954, pp. 65–99. English translations in *ANET*, pp. 434–437 and *BWL*, pp. 21–62. Updated translation in *ANET³*, pp. 596–600.

[5] On the use of similar imagery in both types see H. H. Rowley, *OTMS*, p. 174. S. Mowinckel points out the affinity between psalms of this kind and 'Wisdom' literature: *The Psalms in Israel's Worship*, translated by D. R. Ap-Thomas (1962), Vol. II, pp. 31–52.

and here the resemblance to the biblical work ends. The worshipper reviews his ordeal of a horrible and unaccountable disease, and, while there are passages in Job in which Job describes his symptoms with equally gruesome details, a piece such as the Babylonian composition properly belongs after Job's deliverance, where no such song of thanksgiving is provided. Thus, while a story lies behind the Mesopotamian poem, it is only a monologue and lacks the elaborate dramatic form of Job. Furthermore, Babylonian polytheism could never approach the questions raised by Job. Gratitude to the gods for the return of good health is a universal theme, and it is remarkable that the book of Job says nothing about the cure of Job's dreadful ailment, unless this is covered by the statement in 42:10 that 'the Lord restored the fortunes of Job'.

An even older work from Mesopotamia is a Sumerian poem which attains more narrative development. Samuel Noah Kramer has called it 'the first "Job" '.[1] It is, however, not a story or a dialogue, but an edifying tract intended to encourage a person in affliction to keep on glorifying his personal god (a minor deity), and by bitter wailing, whose volume should be increased by the assistance of his friends and the hiring of professionals, to move the god to pity.[2] The point is made by citing a specific case, and here there is some resemblance to Job's experience, including the happy ending. There are also similar expressions of misery, but these are quite conventional. While the Sumerian poem shares with Job a tragic sense of the burden of sin, the justice of the gods is never questioned. It is not even assumed. All a man can do is weep. The simplistic advice of the Sumerian sage is just like the discreditable theology of Job's friends. While there can be no question of direct influence from a work more than a thousand years older than Job, the Sumerian poem shows how ancient is the theory that guilty man's only hope is to move God to compassion.

So far as the *form* of Job is concerned, its prominent dialogue invites comparison with the extensive 'contest' literature of

---

[1] S. N. Kramer, *History Begins at Sumer*[2] (1961), pp. 167–171.

[2] S. N. Kramer, 'Man and his God: A Sumerian Variation on the "Job" Motif', *Wisdom in Israel and in the Ancient Near East*, edited by M. Noth and D. Winton Thomas, *SVT*, III, 1960, pp. 172–182. English translation in *ANET*[3], pp. 589–591.

the ancient Near East. This gives a clue as to how the debate works. It does not proceed, by closely-woven dialectic, to confute an opponent by irresistible logic; it is intended rather to impress an audience by brilliant rhetoric. A well-known example is the insertion into 1 Esdras of the elocution contest between three courtiers of King Darius (1 Esdras 3–4). Another is the submission to Absalom of the contradictory advice of Ahithophel and Hushai (2 Samuel 17). These situations make clearer the role of Elihu, and later of Yahweh, as adjudicator in the debate between Job and his three friends.

A popular variant of such disputation comes down in numerous fables which deal with such riddles as which is sweeter, sugar or salt, or which argue about which tree is most serviceable to man.[1] The debate between the tamarisk and the date palm[2] is an ancient example to which Jotham's fable (Judges 9) offers a resemblance.

The ancients also debated more serious subjects, including the problem of divine justice in a world of suffering. A work of this kind from Mesopotamia has been called 'The Babylonian Theodicy',[3] or the Babylonian Ecclesiastes. The poem is probably earlier than 1000 BC. Like Job it is highly artificial in structure. It consists of twenty-seven stanzas, each of eleven lines. In each stanza all the lines begin with the same cuneiform sign, and the twenty-seven signs constitute an acrostic which contains the name of a priest who could have been the author. Although no speakers are identified, it is clear from the content, as well as from the changes of the acrostic, that the complaints of a sufferer are answered in the alternating stanzas, whether by one or several friends. Not only is his problem like Job's, but many passing phrases remind one of expressions in Job. Yet W. G. Lambert is emphatic that there is no direct connection between the two works.[4] Since there is no story, the debate is more abstract than Job, and also more inconsequential, since it lacks the foundation of Israelite

---

[1] S. N. Kramer, *History Begins at Sumer*[2] (1961), chapter 18, *Logomachy*.

[2] English translation in *BWL*, pp. 151–164 and *ANET*[3], pp. 592–593.

[3] English translations in *DOTT*, pp. 97–103 (selections); *BWL*, pp. 63–91; *ANET*[3], pp. 601–604 (superseding the translation by R. H. Pfeiffer in *ANET*[2], pp. 438–440, where it is called 'A Dialogue about Human Misery').

[4] *DOTT*, p. 97; also *BWL*, p. 27. A full comparison, with ample quotations, is given by S. Terrien in *IB*, III, pp. 878–884 and also by M. H. Pope, *AB*, XV, pp. LVI–LXXI.

moral monotheism. Yet the two works stand in the same tradition, and Albright, from the analogous case of Ahiqar, thought that the author of Job might have been acquainted with some such Babylonian wisdom materials through Aramaic translations.[1]

The dialogue form was also used in Egypt for quasi-philosophical discussions. A story called *The Protests of the Eloquent Peasant*[2] has been compared to Job. The similarity begins with its superficial structure, for this composition, from the early second millennium BC, consists of nine semi-poetic speeches enclosed in a prose prologue and a prose epilogue. This in itself proves nothing, except the widespread use of the familiar design of Introduction, Middle, Conclusion for a literary work. Thus the Code of Hammurabi is a corpus of laws in prose framed by an introduction and conclusion in poetry. Such evidence has some value in Job studies in pointing to the integrity of the A–B–A design, at least negatively. That is, a mixture of prose and poetry in an ancient work is not evidence for composite authorship.[3] Of more interest is the dialogue in the Egyptian work. It consists of a series of appeals by a misused peasant for justice, with replies by the magistrate. The similarity to Job is slight. The central issues are entirely different. The peasant complains about untrustworthy crafts-men; Job's protest against injustice is levelled against God, not men. For the same reason Job cannot be placed alongside such 'protest' literature as the *Admonitions of Ipu-Wer*,[4] which complains about the collapse of public morality at the end of the Old Kingdom (late third millennium BC). This work consists of six poems which deplore the disappearance of the good old ways, but find no theological significance in the social convulsions of the times. It is the familiar voice of political reaction. The reversal of the status of rich and poor, which in the Old Testament is celebrated as a great and characteristic act of God, is bemoaned, but questions of right and wrong are not raised.

The speeches of Job have also been compared with the soliloquies met in the literature of pessimism. Despair over

[1] W. F. Albright, *From the Stone Age to Christianity*[2] (1956), p. 331.

[2] English translation in *ANET*, pp. 407–410.

[3] See further, section VII below, where the common opinion that Job consists of prose plus poetry plus prose will be rejected.

[4] Translation, with bibliography, in *ANET*, pp. 441–444.

the chaos in society is expressed in another Egyptian work from the late third millennium BC. Again the composition begins as prose, switches to poetry, and ends as prose. This *Dispute over Suicide*[1] has the artificial form of a debate of a despondent man with his own soul. He maintains that self-destruction is the best solution to the problems of life. A poignant longing for death is expressed in words which invite comparison with chapter 3 of Job. But here similarity ends.[2] Weariness with life is a common enough theme. But Job is far beyond the self-pity of the Egyptian. The latter does not struggle through to the ultimate issues. He dismisses life as meaningless; Job resolutely searches. The Egyptian does not question the gods; Job insists on an answer from the Lord Himself. Although Job sometimes soliloquizes, he is mainly engaged in a debate with his friends, that is, with established ideas. And Job never contemplates suicide. On the contrary, he rejects death by passionately demanding fulfilment in life. Job is hurt and angry; but he is never sour or cynical.

Different again from Job's moral outrage and the futile bad temper of the last two Egyptian works mentioned is the genteel meditation on death found in *A Song of the Harper*.[3] Since no-one has ever returned to tell us what death is like, the best we can do is to enjoy this life while it lasts. These sentiments remind us more of the hedonism of Ecclesiastes than the tough-minded arguments of Job.

Some pessimistic writings from Mesopotamia also take the form of dialogue. The one nearest to Job is a discussion of a master with his slave on the emptiness of life.[4] Scholars have not been sure whether to take this work seriously or whether to regard it as satire.[5] Lambert acknowledges that there is a humorous strain in it.[6] Its lack of moral earnestness keeps it apart from Job. The problem is boredom, not suffering. The effete and languid master knows nothing of Job's agony.

---

[1] *ANET*, pp. 405–407; *DOTT*, pp. 162–167.
[2] T. W. Thacker (*DOTT*, p. 163) admits the parallels, but concludes that there is no connection between the two works.
[3] *ANET*, p. 467.
[4] 'A Pessimistic Dialogue between Master and Servant', *ANET*, pp. 437–438; *BWL*, pp. 139–149.
[5] E. A. Speiser, 'The Case of the Obliging Servant', *JCS*, VIII, 1954, pp. 98–105. Compare Gordis, pp. 58ff.
[6] *BWL*, p. 139.

There is no real debate, since the slave merely echoes (mockingly?) his master's sentiments.

According to the book of Proverbs, it was the task of the 'wise' to teach others, particularly the young, the right way to conduct themselves in the world. The *content* of Job includes a lot of such material, and it is not surprising that parallels to its ethical teachings can be found elsewhere. On the theory that Job was primarily didactic, Hölscher (p. 4) finds affinities with such Egyptian instruction manuals as *The Sayings of Amenemope*.[1] That this work is connected somehow with the book of Proverbs cannot be denied, but the exact relationship between them has been vigorously debated.[2] Hölscher assumes that instruction in the form of dialogue in this work and in *The Instruction of Ani*,[3] a similar work, casts Job's 'comforters' in the role of teachers. But by no stretch of the imagination can Job be compared with a pupil in a Wisdom classroom.

In order to be called another 'Job' any similar work should resemble the biblical book in plot, form and content. A passing similarity here or there is not enough. To call every story of human suffering a 'Job' creates a false impression and obscures the uniqueness of the Israelite composition. Suffering is universal, and discussion of the reasons for it is sure to arise in any reflective culture. The human response ranges from vehement protest through agonized perplexity to placid resignation.

The literature of the ancient Near East has not yielded another 'Job'. There is a considerable list of writings from this region, and a few from further afield, which remind one of Job in this way or that. But none comes close to Job when each work is examined as a whole. Each shows more differences than similarities, and not one can be considered seriously as a possible source or model for Job.[4] The doleful Israelite in the

[1] Translation in *ANET*, pp. 421–425; *DOTT*, pp. 172–186.

[2] In addition to the bibliography attached to the translations in the preceding note, see the review of the question by Derek Kidner in *Proverbs* (*TOTC*, 1964), pp. 23–24. He admits that the balance of evidence favours borrowing from Egypt. But K. A. Kitchen refers to an unpublished study by J. Ruffle that seems to call for continued reservation (*Ancient Orient and Old Testament* (1966), p. 88, n. 3). See also B. J. Peterson, 'A New Fragment of *The Wisdom of Amenemope*', *JEA*, LII, 1966, pp. 120–128.

[3] *ANET*, pp. 420–421.

[4] R. H. Pfeiffer, *Introduction to the Old Testament*[2] (1952), pp. 683f.

grip of calamity did not have to read a Mesopotamian or an Egyptian work to raise the question of why God sends such experiences to men. The closest parallels are sufficiently explained by the common background of Wisdom tradition, without implying direct borrowing. The parallels can, however, be used piecemeal with real advantage to throw light on the individual verses in Job which they resemble.

Job stands far above its nearest competitors, in the coherence of its sustained treatment of the theme of human misery, in the scope of its many-sided examination of the problem, in the strength and clarity of its defiant moral monotheism, in the characterization of the protagonists, in the heights of its lyrical poetry, in its dramatic impact, and in the intellectual integrity with which it faces the 'unintelligible burden' of human existence. In all this Job stands alone. Nothing we know before it provided a model, and nothing since, including its numerous imitations, has risen to the same heights. Comparison only serves to enhance the solitary greatness of the book of Job.

V. THE LITERARY CHARACTER OF THE BOOK OF JOB

It is not easy to study a book which is the only one of its kind. Two distinct questions arise concerning its literary character.

The modern discipline of form-criticism takes up the task of classifying a piece of literature. It recognizes that there are many different kinds of literary composition, and that these are put to various uses in the community for which they are produced. Each work has some social function and, even if the form is conventional, it is recognizable in its proper place in the life of the people. Words are spoken in ceremonies, ranging from the simple exchange of greetings by friends meeting in the street or visiting in the home to the grand liturgies of national worship. Any event in private or public life – funeral, wedding, coronation, law-suit – is likely to be accompanied by appropriate speeches.

The content of such speeches serves as a clue as to when and where they would be used. When the context is actually given, as when David makes a warrior's boasting speech prior to combat with Goliath, the interpretation is not in doubt. But imaginative literature is able to make use of a conventional form in an alien context. Thus Isaiah is able to recite a dirge, not to console the bereaved, but to predict in derision the downfall of a great city (Is. 14). Mockery and satire can transform the meaning of a poem.

The book of Job is an astonishing mixture of almost every kind of literature to be found in the Old Testament. Many individual pieces can be isolated and identified as proverbs, riddles, hymns, laments, curses, lyrical nature poems. Some of these, particularly the hymnic material, might have their proper location in the cult; but it would be wrong to infer from this that the book as a whole was ever presented as a religious ritual. Since there is a sense in which Job is on trial, the speeches accusing him of sin and his responses in self-defence (especially his great 'negative confession' in chapter 31) are the kind of thing that one would hear in the law-courts. But this abundant use of quasi-juridical rhetoric for artistic purposes does not mean that the book as a whole is a law-suit. While the tools of form-criticism can be applied with profit to the interpretation of many individual passages, they have not been able to answer the question of what the book of Job itself is.

Having failed to find any comparable work in the ancient Near East, some scholars have turned to Greek literature. There is no evidence that the Israelites had anything in their culture resembling the theatre. Even the cultus was devoid of dramatic representations of either theological stories (such as Creation) or national history (such as the patriarchal saga). The celebration of the Passover was the only ritual re-enactment of a past event, but only a small part of the story (the meal) was actually performed. Similarly the annual festival of living in 'booths' was more a reminder than a drama.[1] In any case, by word and mime, these ceremonies were intended to renew the nation's participation in these events; they were not presented as a spectacle for an audience, whether for entertainment or edification.

The Song of Songs is a cycle of love lyrics. Attempts have been made to find a narrative thread that unifies them into a drama in which the poems are speeches spoken by members of a cast. If the work was intended for performance in this fashion, stage directions are completely lacking. The same

---

[1] Long ago D. B. Macdonald expressed the opinion that the Israelites had no drama in their literature; 'The Drama in Semitic Literature', *Biblical World*, n.s. Vol. V, 1895, pp. 16–28.

goes for Job. The alternating speeches give the impression of dramatic interchange, but there are no suggestions that it was ever produced as a drama. On the contrary, the form established in the opening and closing sections is that of classical Hebrew narrative.

The idea that Job is some kind of play has often suggested itself.[1] The dramatic quality of Job can be recognized without calling it a drama in the strict sense.[2] A serious attempt to recognize Job as a Jewish imitation of Greek drama was made by H. M. Kallen.[3] A grave problem of dating is involved in this theory. So far as history knows, the first Jewish drama was written by a Hellenistic poet called Ezekiel(-os) in the second century BC. He chose the Exodus as his theme. More serious is the very idea of tragedy, as developed by the Greeks.[4] In spite of a deep sense of guilt before God, the Israelite, Job included, could never regard life as ultimately tragic. The Greeks had already felt the burden of the moral indifference of a closed universe, once more pressing on the soul of modern secularized man. Man was the helpless, pitiable victim of ineluctable fate, or, even worse, of the implacable malevolence of the gods, particularly Zeus as in the most moving of all tragedies, Prometheus. It is quite wrong to compare Job's attitude of questioning with the *hybris* of the Greek.

In the Shakespearean tradition, tragedy is the outworking of a fault of character or of an error in judgment. Shakespeare's human world is already secular. God is absent, whereas in Job He is all-important. Belief in the goodness of creation, in the justice of God, and in the ever-available possibility of

[1] Reflected in such translations as G. H. B. Wright, *The Book of Job* (1883), pp. 1–3. Also J. Owen, *Five Great Skeptical Dramas of History* (1896), pp. 107–167; P. Forbes, 'Is "Job" a Problem Play?' *Nineteenth Century and After* (1906), pp. 414–426; J. S. Flory, *Dramas of the Bible: A Literary Interpretation of the Book of Job and the Song of Solomon* (1923), pp. 11–162; R. Balmforth, 'The Drama of Job', *The Ethical and Religious Value of the Drama* (1925), pp. 11–40; W. H. Stubbs, 'The Drama of Job', *London Quarterly Review*, October 1930, pp. 213–219.

[2] W. H. Green, 'The Dramatic Character and Integrity of the Book of Job', *Presbyterian and Reformed Review*, VIII, 1897, pp. 683–701; H. Gaertner, *Der dramatische Charakter des Buches Hiob und die Tendenz desselben* (1909).

[3] H. M. Kallen, *The Book of Job as a Greek Tragedy Restored* (1918); see review by C. G. Montefiore in *HTR*, XII, 1919, pp. 219–224.

[4] G. Murray, *Aeschulus: The Creator of Tragedy* (1940). Kallen traced Job to Euripides. A valuable feature of Pope's work (*AB*) is the numerous quotations from Greek drama which express ideas similar to those met in Job.

redemption made tragedy impossible within biblical thought. This is the reason for the much misunderstood 'happy ending' of Job, which, far from spoiling the book, which certainly does not end as a tragedy, is essential for the vindication of Job and for the vindication of God.

The great pioneer in the modern study of Hebrew poetics, Bishop Lowth, already examined in the eighteenth century the question of whether Job was a drama. He applied Aristotelian criteria, and found it lacking for want of 'action'.[1] He admitted, however, that it could be called a dramatic poem.[2]

But, if Job is not a drama,[3] the dramatic dialogue has suggested to some that it is the Israelite counterpart of a Greek symposium.[4] As we shall see by studying the dialectical relationships between the various speeches in the commentary itself, the book of Job completely lacks the tightly-woven logical texture of philosophical argument. The suggestion made by Fries, following Oscar Holtzmann, that Job is an imitation of a Platonic dialogue[5] is a false scent.

It would seem that the rabbis were not sure how to classify the book of Job. This is reflected in the fact that it never acquired a fixed position in the list of canonical books, although they associated it with Psalms and Proverbs in the third division of the Canon – the 'Writings'. This location befits its poetic character. Christian lists show a greater variety, since questions of date and historicity enter into consideration.[6]

---

[1] R. Lowth, *De sacra poesi Hebraeorum*[2] (1768), pp. 706–717; English translation, *Lectures on the Sacred Poetry of the Hebrews* (1829), pp. 273–293; or (1847), pp. 372–381.

[2] The justice of this observation is borne out by the fact that the biblical text has actually been staged. Coleman's bibliography of plays based on biblical materials lists nearly twenty examples of renditions of Job into more explicitly dramatic form, some with a minimum of changes in the biblical text, others with imaginative revisions or modernizations. E. D. Coleman, *The Bible in English Drama: An annotated list of plays including translations from other languages from the beginnings to 1931* (1931). Most notably since 1931 should be added Alexander MacLeish's famous *J.B.* and H. Ehrenburg, *Hiob – der Existentialist* (1952).

[3] G. G. Bradley, *Lectures on the Book of Job*[2] (1888), pp. 14–15.

[4] M. Jastrow, Jr., *The Book of Job: Its Origin, Growth and Interpretation* (1920), pp. 174–181.

[5] C. Fries, *Das philosophische Gespräch von Hiob bis Plato* (1904).

[6] Full details in Dhorme, chapter 1.

The opinion of Resh Lachish (second century AD) is often quoted to the effect that Job never existed, but was a *māšāl*, 'proverb', a term which must be interpreted broadly in this context to mean a piece of instructive fiction. We have already noted Lowth's observation that there is not much action in the book. The same point is made even more emphatically by Gordis, who says that Job 'is characterized by a total lack of plot' (p. 4). Dhorme says more cautiously that the literary *genre* is ambiguous (pp. xiii, cxiii) because the prose narrative should be classified with the historical books while the poetic dialogue belongs with Wisdom writings. He implies that the book falls short of achieving a real unity.

We disagree with this opinion. Job is a well-wrought story that stands in the main stream of classical Hebrew narrative. The artificial form of the speeches should not blind us to the realism of the plot. There is a lot of action, even if much of it is talk. Speech, often poetic, and often with 'Wisdom' touches, is found through all Hebrew historical narrative. In *genre* Job stands closest to the epic history of early Israel, which found its golden expression in the patriarchal stories, the saga of the Exodus, the career of David, the tale of Ruth. If it does not actually come from the time of the united monarchy, in which such literature reached its greatest heights, at least it seems to imitate such writings. Job resembles this corpus in four distinctive features of the writer's craft. First, an economy in relating the essential facts which gives the false impression that the plot is sparse. Secondly, as a more specific aspect of this brevity, an objectivity in describing people's actions without psychological analysis of either their motivations or their emotions. By contrast the modern novel is for ever telling us what is going on in the hero's mind. The feelings of Job and of the others are not described by the author as part of the story; they are expressed by the protagonists in their speeches. Thirdly, the authors are remarkably detached; they refrain from moral comment. For example, the motivation of the author of the incomparable story of Absalom's insurrection (2 Samuel) is impossible to detect; he simply tells the story. We have exactly the same problem in trying to find out why the story of Job was written as it was. Fourthly, and this is the key point, just as the interest in the stories in Genesis, Samuel, *etc.*, lies mainly in the speeches, which occupy a high proportion of the space, which tend to be poetic and which express the enduring human interest we find in the characters, so the story of Yahweh and Job is told chiefly through the speeches.

The book of Job can thus be called 'epic' in the same way as the stories of Abraham, of Joseph or of Moses deserve this epithet. M. H. Pope has made the point that its atmosphere is reminiscent of the book of Ruth.[1] The point could be carried much further. Jacob M. Myers, in a study of the literary form of the book of Ruth, has shown how much of it is actually in poetic form.[2] What he does not sufficiently indicate is that poetry dominates the dialogue, while most of the connective narrative is prose. The same is exactly the case with Job. Contrary to the common statement that Job is a poem, we might say that Job is written entirely in prose, except that the speeches are in verse.

VI. THE POETRY OF THE BOOK OF JOB

Since most of Job is composed in verse, some understanding of Hebrew poetry is necessary for its interpretation. The detailed work of poetic appreciation is best done in the commentary itself. Here we will make a few general observations and explain the use of a few terms.

Poetry is not easy to define. It is artistry with words in which the properties of language, especially its sounds, are exploited for aesthetic purposes. The rhymes and rhythms of the Hebrew original cannot be discussed in a commentary on an English translation, but fortunately the main features of Hebrew prosody are preserved in other versions. The structure of Hebrew verse survives translation (the more literal the better) because it depends mainly on the juxtaposition of ideas, on the balancing of one thought with another.

Compared with the strict rules of classical poetry that have been the norm for European civilization for centuries, Hebrew poetry, on first encounter, seems very irregular or ill-formed. Compared with the westerners from Homer onwards, it has been judged 'primitive', or redeeming features have been sought in its exotic 'oriental' flavour, such as the use of a different kind of imagery. But once the conventions of Hebrew poetry are properly recognized, it will be seen as an instrument

[1] *IDB*, II, p. 917.
[2] J. M. Myers, *The Linguistic and Literary Form of the Book of Ruth* (1955).

just as demanding on the intellectual ingenuity of the poet as the most exacting rules of the classicists, and just as pleasing to the taste when some genius brings the rules in subjection to his aims. The writer of Job was such a genius – a Homer (for epic quality), a Shakespeare (for human and dramatic interest), a Pushkin (for mastery of a variety of moods), above all a Milton (for the majesty of his treatment of the highest of all themes – the ways of God with men).

There are several kinds of unit in Hebrew poetry. We shall use the term 'verse' to refer to the sections into which the text has now been divided by modern editors. Their labelling with numbers enables a place to be found by chapter and verse, but these often have no value as a guide to poetic structure.

The smallest unit can be called a 'line' or 'stich(-os)' or 'colon'. A 'period' is a unit of one or more such colons which is grammatically or semantically complete. The commonest period is a 'bicolon'. In its simplest form a bicolon says the same thing twice in different words. Such a rhyming thought is usually called 'synonymous parallelism'. Job 27:4 provides an example:

(A) Not will-speak	(B) my-lips	(C) falsehood
1 2–3–4̇–5	6–7–8̇	9–1ó

And- (B′) my-tongue	(A′) not will-utter	(C′) deception
1–2–3–4̇	5 6–7̇	8–9–1ó

Each colon has four words in Hebrew, and each has ten syllables. Since the word translated 'not' is not accented, there are three stresses in each colon. There is thus a quantitative balance between the paired lines, whether measured as syllables, as words, or as stresses. The last word in each colon ends with the sound -*â*, so there is rhyme as well as rhythm. Not all Hebrew bicolons are as well-formed as this. Furthermore, unlike European verse, which prefers to compose each poem out of the same kind of 'feet', for example, iambus (short–long or unstressed–stressed), the scansion of each colon in the above example is quite different. The second stress falls on the eighth syllable in the first colon, on the seventh syllable in the second. If it is in order to look for feet in Hebrew verse, then there is quite a mixture. Three are anapaests; the rest are all different.

The real interest in Hebrew poetry is found more in the

ideas than in the sounds. The two colons that make up the period in Job 27:4 are almost synonymous. Except for 'and' in verse 4b, all the vocabulary comes in pairs of words.

verse 4a	*verse 4b*
not	not
will-speak	will-utter
falsehood	deception
my-lips	my-tongue

The pair may be a repetition ('not') or synonyms ('speak' = 'utter'; 'falsehood' = 'deception') or complements ('lips' and 'tongue' are not synonyms, but together they constitute the organs of speech). It is such use of complementary vocabulary in successive lines that binds them into a single period. It is not quite exact to describe verse 4a and 4b as complete clauses of identical meaning in parallel.

Another rhetorical feature binds the two colons together. The literal translation given above shows a cross-over of the parallel items A // A' and B // B'. This pattern

$$\text{A B} \dots$$
$$\text{B' A'} \dots$$

is called chiasm(-us). Sometimes more extended patterns of introversion, such as A B C D C' B' A', are used.

The intricate beauty of the one bicolon we have now looked at gives only a slight idea of the complexity of Hebrew versification. Numerous patterns of parallelism are possible and they were developed by Israelite poets to a high degree of sophistication. Unfortunately, limited space prevents detailed examination of the fine verbal texture which, throughout the book of Job, marks it out as poetry of the highest excellence.

The bicolon is not the only form of the period used in Hebrew verse. A single colon can be used as a unit; and it is a mistake to say, as the older critics so often did, that the second part of a bicolon must have fallen out by scribal error when an apparently lonely line is met. As we shall see, an isolated colon is often a vital signal to the rhetorical structure of a longer passage, such as a strophe.

A tricolon is also used quite often. Once more the dogma that Hebrew poetry was written exclusively in bicolons has led quite unnecessarily to the belittling of the tricolon as a period. Many critics do not accept some tricolons, but convert them to bicolons by removing one line to leave two only. It is supposed that the unnecessary duplicate crept into the text when a scribe treated an alternative reading of a colon as authentic. Another explanation is that an original four lines (two bicolons) have become three, the third being an authentic line whose partner has been lost and cannot be restored. Three colons in parallel present even more complicated possibilities for developing interlacing patterns. While periods of four, five or more colons are sometimes used, they are less common. We prefer not to use the word 'stanza' for such periods, for this term suggests a design, familiar in European poetry, in which each stanza has the same number of lines throughout an entire poem. Few Hebrew poems display this kind of regularity.

A group of periods often constitutes a unit which may be called a 'strophe'. Again there is no room here to discuss the vast question of strophic structure in long Hebrew poems. We shall make observations about strophic patterns in Job in the commentary itself as we go along. Here we shall simply observe that strophes come in all sizes and that each is unified by a common theme as well as by various structural and rhetorical devices.

We shall use the term 'poem' to describe a composition of distinct character which is complete enough to stand alone. The author of Job has incorporated many individual poems into his work. We have already noticed in the gross structure of the book a series of speeches by the various characters. In some cases the speech may be a single poem. Quite often the speech comprises more than one distinct poem, either a series of poems one after the other whose connection in the speech we may find it hard to trace, or a set of related poems which are arranged to give a coherent effect to the total speech.

The structure of Hebrew poetry is thus hierarchical. The largest single unit in Job is a speech, which may consist of one or more poems. Each poem consists of one or more strophes. A strophe is made up of one or more periods, and each period consists of one or more 'lines'. A period of two or more colons usually exhibits some kind of parallelism. However, parallelism is met, not only in lines in immediate succession, but also in lines which may be separated by a considerable quantity of intervening material. Critics have often taken the liberty of moving such passages around so as to bring them physically nearer to a related idea. For example, Job 3:16 is sometimes shunted in between 3:11 and 3:12 so as to assemble all the references to birth in the same place. We believe that such reorganization of the text is misguided and unnecessary. Indeed it does harm, for the removal of 3:16 deprives it of its vital function as a pivot in between the two balancing strophes on the bliss of death, as we shall attempt to show in our commentary on that verse.[1]

VII. THE COMPOSITION OF THE BOOK OF JOB

No sources for the book of Job have been found. Fragmentary parallels to other parts of the Old Testament or to passages in the surviving literature of the ancient Near East (see section IV, above) cannot be considered as documents incorporated into or quoted in the book of Job and which therefore existed before it. The book could have been written all at once by one person, or it could have passed through several stages of composition under the hands of more than one author. The complexity of the final product has been explained by many scholars as the result of a long and complicated literary development.

Study of the structure of the book as it now is has raised a number of questions, including the following. What is the relationship between the prose Prologue and Epilogue and the poetic Dialogue? Are the Yahweh speeches an integral composition, or is there more than one distinct document in them? Are they original to the work, or were they added later? Are the Elihu speeches original? Is the poem on Wisdom (chapter 28) a later addition? Does the lack of a third speech by Zophar mean that the original cycle has suffered damage in transmission, or is it intentional? And so on.

Each scholar has answered these questions in his own way, so that the number of opinions expressed in the literature on this subject is almost countless. Here only a brief survey of the problem can be given and only some of the proposed solutions can be examined.

No answer can be supplied from outside the book of Job itself. There is nothing in the doctrine of the divine inspiration

---

[1] These few remarks may be augmented by the felicitous introduction to Hebrew poetry in Derek Kidner, *Psalms 1–72 (TOTC, 1973)*, pp. 1–4.

of Holy Scripture that requires that each biblical book must have been written by only one person within a brief space of time. God can create something in a moment and He can inspire someone to produce a book in a single spurt of creativity. God can also make things slowly by processes of growth through historical conditions. A book produced as the result of the successive work of several people over a considerable period of time is not disqualified by such a literary history from being part of the Word of God. The way in which the book of Job was put together can be discovered only from evidence within the book itself; and, by the nature of the evidence, certainty on many of the problems involved may not be possible to attain.

Nevertheless, the question of the unity of Job is very important when it comes to its interpretation. If, for example, as many critics hold, the Elihu speeches do not really belong in the book as it was originally planned, but were added by some misguided and inferior later writer, then it makes quite a difference if we remove them and study as the 'real' book of Job only what remains. If Job is the work of one man, or even if its over-all structure was organized by one final editor, one should try to discover the plan he had in mind, and interpret the book as a whole in terms of this scheme. If, however, a number of successive authors, each with a different point of view, have reworked the book so as to change its character with each new edition, then the state of the book at each stage of its growth should be recovered as precisely as possible, and the point of view of each different author, if this can be ascertained, will serve as a guide to the particular form he gave to the work. Here it must be admitted that the wide variety of opinions, some quite contradictory, among scholars who have tried to trace the growth of the book through several stages does not encourage us to believe that their work rests on very secure methodological foundations. In spite of these reservations, however, we shall give in what follows an outline of results which have been fairly generally accepted. While some theories are more complicated than others, seven supposed stages in the development of the book are commonly recognized.

Stage 1

Scholars who deny that the unity of the book in its present

form is original divide it into at least two parts – an original prose story about Job and the poetic dialogue added later. The seed of the work is said to be an old folk-tale[1] about a patriarch who was tested by misfortune, maintained his faith and was rewarded by God. Attempts to retrieve this original simple story have led to the most divergent results. Some identify it as chapters 1, 2 and 42:7–17. But this creates all kinds of problems.

It has been pointed out that the present Prologue and Epilogue do not constitute a complete story. Job 42:7–9 refers to the discussion with the three friends, who are quite silent in chapter 2, and so presupposes some kind of dialogue in the original. By the same token, some kind of response from God is needed before 42:7. It is supposed, then, that an original discussion in the folk-idiom of the surviving Prologue and Epilogue was later replaced by the grander poetry of the present work.[2] But such a theory, by recognizing the need of some kind of dialogue within the framework of the Prologue and Epilogue, is really an argument for the unity of the work as it now stands. Why should not the present Dialogue be original?

But the evidence of 42:7–9 has been accounted for in another way. Since it obviously refers to the present Dialogue, it has been explained as a later editorial addition to join the earlier story, which survives in 42:10–17, to the later poetic materials of chapters 3 – 42:6.

Some scholars have found problems within the prose story (Prologue plus Epilogue) as it now survives. Apart from the question of joining the (later) Dialogue to the earlier story[3] either by the author of the Dialogue himself, or by some later redactor, there are apparent inconsistencies and alleged contradictions within the narrative framework.

[1] It was Duhm (p. vi) who first suggested that the present Prologue and Epilogue were fragments of a *Volksbuch*.

[2] On this basis Duhm suggested that 38:1 is also a fragment of the original.

[3] To show that almost every imaginable theory seems to have been tried out by someone or other, we note the suggestion of W. Irwin in the new *Peake's Commentary on the Bible* (1962), §§339e, 340b, that, while there was an old folk-tale that inspired the book of Job, it is not what we now have in the present Prologue and Epilogue. Rather the latter were written *after* the Dialogue as its necessary framework, and the idiom of a folk-story was deliberately imitated. This theory does not seem to have appealed to many scholars.

Thus it has been pointed out that the Satan, so prominent in the opening scenes, is never heard of again. It is presumed that a third and final interview in the divine council is needed to round things off, and to prove that Yahweh was correct after all. But we have no right to tell the author how he should end his story. And scholars who have remarked on the fact that Job's wife is also not heard of again seem to have overlooked the necessity for Job's later children to have a mother. Instead of these characters, whom we have already met in the Prologue, the Epilogue brings in for the first time Job's friends and relations (42:11).

From another point of view, the role of the Satan has been viewed as secondary, mainly because the idea of such a being is considered to have developed far too late in Israelite thought to have been part of the original story. But the *mise en scène* of the divine council is very ancient in Hebrew tradition, and the relaxed, informal dialogue would not have come easily to a post-exilic Jew who had developed a demonology side by side with increasingly transcendent ideas of God. In any case, it is hard to see how the story could get going without this glimpse behind the scenes. It is essential for the book that the reader knows (as Job does not know) that his troubles came from God, but were not provoked by any fault on his part, but were, in fact, a consequence of his virtue and were intended to prove and enhance his righteousness.

Without going into details, we note that the unity of the Prologue itself, the unity of the Epilogue and the unity of both together have been questioned in various ways. The supposed inconcinnities have been accounted for as the result of the compilation of this little tale from several distinct sources, or as due to its successive modification in several editorial stages. Thus Fohrer[1] goes so far as to find five stages of development in the Prologue plus Epilogue: (i) a pre-Israelite legend; (ii) a pre-exilic Israelite version of this which imitated patriarchal stories; (iii) a retouching of the story during the exile to bring out the idea of Job as a righteous intercessor; (iv) post-exilic revision which betrays influences from priestly, Wisdom and Persian sources; (v) final redaction to blend with the Dialogue. Arguments in terms of internal consistency have been supported by analysis of the

[1] G. Fohrer, *Introduction to the Old Testament*, translated by D. Green (1968), p. 325.

vocabulary, especially for purposes of tracking down the affinities to the proposed layers of tradition.

The *reductio ad absurdum* of this critical methodology can be seen in the fact that the more rigorously it is applied, the more ridiculous the results become. In detecting a 'priestly' hand at one point along the way, it is fallacious, or at least utterly incapable of proof, to assert that, because P (the so-called 'priestly' source in the Pentateuch) is the only Israelite document now known that used a certain expression, when a similar expression turns up in Job the author must have taken it from P.

But, taking for granted, or at least as not disproved, the unity of the Prologue plus Epilogue, the rest of the book (the Dialogue) is said to be quite different. The most obvious contrast, poetry versus prose, we believe to be, on the contrary, a powerful argument for the unity of the whole. Quite apart from other ancient works, of indubitable unity, which have such an A–B–A pattern, we have already pointed out that the casting of speeches into poetic form is a general feature of Hebrew narration, even in the historical books which are usually described as being written entirely in prose. The alleged poetic substratum in the patriarchal narratives is found mainly in reported speech. Such dialogue blends harmoniously with the more prose-like descriptive material that comes between speeches.

Furthermore, the contrast between poetry and prose carries with it a difference in vocabulary which cannot be used as an argument for different authors. Two different media were available, and one person could use them both in the same work as he switched from prose narration to poetic speeches.

The alleged contrast between the theology of the story and of the Dialogue has been largely exaggerated. Indeed, before going any further, we should sound a caution about this kind of generalization. As will become clearer from the details of the commentary, the Dialogue itself is far from homogeneous, in either language or thought. It is a collection of diverse materials, with a variety of styles and a wealth of ideas in which there is often a clash of opinion. That is part of the debate, and part of the author's technique. But it has been maintained, in a general way, that in the original prose story God, whose name is Yahweh, is a simple anthropomorphic folk-deity; in the poems His name is El, Eloh or Shadday.

While His power and justice are not questioned, He is not understood, at least by Job. He is silent, inscrutable, with a hint of the demonic. In the prose, Job is a simple, good man; in the poems he is a tempestuous thinker whose radical questioning leads him to the most daring heterodoxy. In the Prologue the Satan instigates Job's troubles; but he is mentioned nowhere in the poems.[1] In Job 1:5 Yahweh is propitiated by sacrifice; but this is not considered elsewhere as a remedy for Job's ills, unless in 22:27, and its performance is not mentioned in the list of Job's virtues in chapter 31. Job's final prosperity as the reward of righteousness is said to be a glaring contradiction of the main point in the debate in which Job consistently and correctly denies any such connection. We are told, in effect, that the sophisticated, mature theology of the Dialogue contrasts with the naïve, unreflective ideas of the folk-tale.

The present commentary assumes the unity of the book and will try to show that the theology is consistent from beginning to end. But, even if this exposition succeeds in displaying the theological unity of the book, this feature as such cannot settle questions of literary history. A succession of authors might bring a work through several stages to a reasonable unity at the end, while a single author might produce a muddled piece of writing. Modern readers with a western education will unconsciously apply formal canons of consistency; they might, for instance, treat all the statements about God as a set of propositions, each of which is intrinsically true and all of which are consistent with one another, because they are doctrine revealed by God. If such a cerebral approach succeeds, it may harmonize all the ideas in the book into a unity that the author did not intend, and miss the unity he actually had in mind. Just as God is given a variety of names, so all the things said about Him are not the same. There is argument and disagreement. This is the way the book is written, and such features cannot be taken as evidence that the book is a mixture of the differing theologies of several contributing authors. But, by the same token, the 'teaching' of the book is not the sum total of all its accumulating statements. The 'meaning' of the book will be found in its culmination, in the resolution of the problems it deals with,

---

[1] Note the resolution of this problem by ascribing the Satan passages to one of the latest redactors.

including the rejection of inadequate answers. This meaning will be found in the total structure of the book, and in the functions of the individual speeches within that structure. The unity of Job will be dramatic rather than conceptual; it will be found in what God does to him, rather than in what his friends say to him.

Stage 2

If we concede, for the sake of discussion, that the present book of Job looks as if an original story, which now survives in chapters 1 and 2 and in 42:7–17, was expanded and transformed by the insertion of the poetic Dialogue, the question arises, how much poetic material was added at this second stage?

Many critics would identify the dialogue proper between Job and his three friends as a single composition now found in chapters 3–31, with the exclusion of chapter 28, which is a special problem (see Stage 5). The editorial remarks in 3:1 and 31:40b mark the boundaries of this major supplement. So the second edition of Job was essentially chapters 1–31 and 42:7–17.

The arrangement of the discussion in a scheme consisting of three cycles of speeches with opening and closing statements by Job has already been noted. Although this section contains many kinds of poetry, with contrasts in style, language and theology, the unity of this block of material has not been seriously doubted, except for minor changes which might have occurred later on (Stages 6 and 7).

Before isolating chapters 3–31 from the remaining poems – Wisdom (chapter 28), Elihu (chapters 32–37), Yahweh (chapters 38–41) – we ask whether the differences *within* the main dialogue, which are not considered as evidence of composite authorship, are any greater than the differences *between* it and the other poems, which are considered as evidence of diverse authorship.

Belief that Job 1–31 and 42:7–17 constitute a finished work rests heavily on the statement in 31:40b that Job had completed his speeches. This leaves no room for any further remarks, either from a completely new character, like Elihu, or for a fresh discussion (on what sounds like an entirely fresh topic, namely, God's power in nature) between God and Job. The story moves at once to its simple conclusion. Yahweh declares Job to be in the right; He does not participate in the debate Himself, but merely adjudicates on the discussion in chapters 3–31. Note that 42:7a must be removed to secure a smooth transition.

Stage 3

Scholars who think that the original dialogue ended at 31:40 suppose that, in a third edition of the work, additional speeches by Yahweh Himself were added to remove from the book the intolerable implication that God is silent except for His announcement of the final verdict, as an attempt to provide a more effective answer to the inconclusive debate of chapters 3–31.[1] But this interpolation is said to have spoiled the natural transition from the dialogue to the dénouement when 31:40 is followed immediately by 42:7b, as in Stage 2.[2] It is not just that the extra material delays the end of the story; it changes its character completely, by taking the discussion on to quite new ground.

Here we confront one of the most urgent and baffling questions in Job studies. What *are* the Yahweh speeches doing in the book? Far from providing a better answer to Job's questions than anything to be found in the speeches of his friends, the words of the Lord are, on first impressions, not addressed to Job's problem at all. They are, in fact, a series of additional questions. These nature poems have been rejected as irrelevant to Job's moral questionings, and are said to have had no original place in the book at all.

But it mutilates the book when the Yahweh speeches are removed. Readers who are sensitive to their poetic power generally recognize that here is the highest point of the book, as if the author had concentrated his best gifts on their composition. Can we suppose that the superb theologian who wrote these chapters was also a bungler who missed and obscured the real point of the story of Job? But, if the Yahweh speeches properly follow the dialogue in chapters 3–31 and, indeed, are demanded by the inconsequential end of the discussion on the human level; if, in fact, they are the climax of the book and contain the resolution of the whole matter, then such a vital connection between chapters 38–41 and

---

[1] Scholars who maintain that the Yahweh speeches are a later addition include Volz, Baumgärtel and Kuhl.
[2] W. E. Staples, *The Speeches of Elihu* (1925), and others since.

chapters 3–31 does not have to be the work of a later reviser. It might just as readily be seen as part of the plan of the author of the main dialogue.

It is generally admitted that the Yahweh speeches are written in the same language and style as the discussion between Job and his friends, allowing, of course, for the different subject-matter and the more elevated tone. We have already pointed out the similarity between the double exchange between God and Job at this stage and the double interview between God and the Satan at the beginning.

The unity of this concluding dialogue with Job has been widely recognized, but some scholars think that at first this section was shorter than it now is. Apart from minor questions, such as the originality of the poem on the ostrich (39:13–18), which happens to be absent from LXX, two distinct problems are involved. Hölscher (p. 1) suggests that originally there was only one speech by God with a single response by Job.[1] Another theory accepts the two rounds of speeches, but removes either or both of the long concluding poems on Behemoth (40:15–24) and Leviathan (chapter 41), considering either that the development of this part of the book in Stage 3 was a complex process with its own inner history, or that additional poems were incorporated bodily later on (Stage 5). Here critical opinions seem to be at their most subjective. While some find the poems on these two monsters flamboyant and tedious, ruining 40:6–14 as an excellent final statement by God when it is followed at once by 42:1–6, others reserve their highest praise for these compositions. It is worth pointing out that the cycle of individual poems on the various creatures which constitutes the Yahweh speeches advances from terse questions in a line or two in the realm of cosmology (38:1–38) to longer and longer poems until we reach the rhapsody on Leviathan, a fit crescendo that overwhelms Job at the last.

Stage 4

In spite of the problems that have just been reviewed, the coherence of Job 1–31 and 38–42 is widely recognized. The simplest explanation of its unity is that it was all written by the same person. The speeches of Elihu, however, found in chapters 32–37, are a different matter. They are commonly

[1] Among others with a similar point of view see K. Fullerton, 'The Original Conclusion to the Book of Job', *ZAW*, XLII, 1924, pp. 116–135.

rejected as no part of the original. Their addition represents the fourth and last major stage in the formation of the book as we now have it.

It is supposed that, some time after the book had reached Stage 3, a later writer, with a different theological perspective, and using a somewhat different kind of Hebrew, was so dissatisfied with the inconclusive nature of the arguments that he ventured to supply a better answer to Job than the three friends, or even the Lord Himself, had done. This essay is then the first commentary on the 'real' book of Job, and in it we hear the voice of orthodoxy at its safest. In order to bring about what is, in result, a major revision of the book, this last author has invented a completely new character, of whom the rest of the story knows nothing.[1]

This well-meaning writer has been castigated for his meddling, and condemned as an inferior thinker and second-rate poet who has spoilt the book with his dull theology and turgid style. On the other hand, he has been greatly praised for his excellent review of the preceding debate and for the positive contribution he makes. Some have even found in his remarks, rather than in the speeches of Yahweh, the high point of the book and the central message that the author – the single author of the whole – intended to convey. It is certainly surprising, if the speeches of Elihu are so ruinous as some have said, that this debased version succeeded in ousting the superior original, which must already have attained some measure of canonicity.

The reasons for rejecting the Elihu speeches as an unwarranted interpolation are structural, theological, stylistic and linguistic. It is astonishing how divided scholars are in their evaluation of these arguments. Opinions are so diverse that many of them cancel the others out. We do not have space to line up the names of scholars on this side or that of this question.

In terms of the over-all design of the book, Elihu comes in abruptly and, when he has finished speaking, is never heard of again. He claims to have been present during the preceding dialogue, but no-one has noticed him or appealed for his opinion. He claims to have the true solution to the problem;

[1] S. B. Freehof, *Book of Job* (1958), compares Elihu with a stage-struck young man who comes into an empty theatre and pretends to take part in a drama after all the actors have gone.

but, when God speaks the final word in chapter 42, He commends Job, condemns his three friends, and ignores Elihu. So it seems as if Elihu is never really part of the story, which is quite complete without him. These arguments from structure are not compelling. They misunderstand the role of Elihu as a protagonist, rather than as an adjudicator. He is the first of two who record their impressions of what has been said in chapters 3–31. Elihu gives the human estimate; Yahweh gives the divine appraisal. There is no need for the Lord to comment also on Elihu's summing up; His silence on this point is no more a problem than the absence of any final show-down with the Satan at the end.

The theological content of the Elihu material has been given a low rating by some scholars.[1] Others have esteemed it highly as a needed complement to the rest of the book. Once more we encounter highly subjective impressions which should not be allowed the decisive word on questions of literary authenticity.

Style is also a quality whose assessment can be highly subjective. The poetry of Job 31–37 is said to be inferior to the rest of the book.[2] The prolixity of the first speech (32:7–22) is a common target of complaint. But other readers have found in this laboured and pompous utterance the psychological characterization of this young man which has been deliberately and cleverly done. A good author does not make all the people in the story talk in exactly the same way, so the different mode of the Elihu speeches is not evidence of a different hand. The last human word on the question, which is intentionally weak and turgid, in spite of its pretentious claims, contrasts with the final word from God, for which our author reserves his best talent.

The linguistic features of Job 32–37 have been brought as evidence both for and against its unity with the rest of the book. Impressive names can be lined up on both sides of this question. Larger commentaries supply lists of words and idioms shared with the rest of the book (evidence for unity) and similar lists of items found only in this section (evidence of disunity). It is further alleged that there are more Ara-

[1] As one illustration, see the scathing remarks of R. H. Pfeiffer, *Introduction to the Old Testament*[2] (1952), p. 673.
[2] H. H. Nichols is particularly severe in her criticism of the composition, in *AJSL*, XXVII, 1910–11, pp. 97ff.

maisms in this part of Job than elsewhere, suggesting a later date. But these may be explained simply as another means used by the author to give Elihu a different character from the others.

There is another reason for suspecting that the Elihu speeches were written after the rest of the book, and as a response to it. When we are studying chapters 3–31, and try to follow the course of the debate, we shall be surprised that each speaker in turn does not seem to refer more explicitly to what the others have said. But when we come to the Elihu speeches, we find that they are full of quotations from and allusions to chapters 3–31.[1] Furthermore, he is said to quote earlier material like the reader of a book, not like a listener to the debate. But this dependence of the Elihu speeches on the other dialogue could be part of the original author's plan, and does not prove that another person wrote them later on.[2]

Stage 5

Whether written by one or several persons, whether the result of one act of creation or of a long process of growth, the book of Job was essentially complete at Stage 4. Some scholars think that other, smaller changes have taken place in it since then. Such alterations belong to the history of the transmission rather than to the history of the composition of the book, even though there is no agreement as to whether a person who makes a substantial change should be called a reviser or an editor.

The most important opinion in this regard is that three major poems, on Wisdom (chapter 28), on Behemoth (40:15–24) and on Leviathan (41:1–34), were not part of the original work. And, unlike the Elihu speeches, which were deliberately composed for incorporation into the previously existing work, these are suspected of being independent compositions, added rather loosely, and not properly belonging where they now are. They were attached because of their literary similarity to the rest of Job.

[1] D. N. Freedman, 'The Elihu Speeches in the Book of Job', *HTR*, LXI, 1968, pp. 51–59.
[2] Among recent votes in favour of the authenticity of chapters 32–37, and therefore of the unity of the whole book, we may note N. H. Snaith (*The Book of Job: Its Origin and Purpose, SBT*[2], XI, 1968, pp. 72–75), Gordis (pp. 104–116) and W. F. Albright (*EI*, IX, 1969, p. 44). All agree that the chapters are a later insertion by the original author, but they differ in the reasons given for the changes.

We have already expressed the opinion that the two longer concluding nature poems are integral to the Yahweh speeches. Chapter 28 is more often thought to be an intrusion because it fits badly. Although embedded in the words of Job, who is the only speaker identified from chapter 26 to the end of 31, it does not sound well on his lips. Its calm and detached mood contrasts with the frenzy of Job's closing speeches, and it expresses a contentment with the inscrutability of the ways of God, and the sufficiency of human reverence and integrity as wisdom (28:28) which Job has not yet attained. Its didactic posture and the artistic patience with which it develops its sustained figures create a restful interlude within the turbulence of Job's peroration. Its admiration for man's ingenuity contrasts with the poor opinion of mankind found elsewhere. Yet its language and form are not unlike the rest of the book, and we have already seen that the author has incorporated all kinds of poetry (not all of which he necessarily wrote himself) into the dialogue. Chapter 28 is best explained as a kind of coda between the main dialogue and Job's final word, but not as a part of Job's own thought at this stage. It is a comment by the author, and the speaker is the person telling the story, not one of the characters in the story.

Stage 6

For hundreds of years the book of Job was copied by hand. During this transmission, two kinds of changes could have taken place. Many scholars think that the book suffered at least one major accident at the hands of the scribes. It is a curious fact that in the third cycle Zophar makes no speech, and Bildad's speech is quite short. On the other hand, Job's concluding response is extraordinarily long (chapters 26–31), with new beginnings marked by the opening words of chapters 26, 27 and 29. We have already recognized that chapter 28 might not have been spoken by Job himself. His three speeches, which become successively longer, serve in turn to complete the third cycle (chapter 26), to round off the whole dialogue (chapter 27), and then, after the interval of chapter 28, to take the initiative again in the middle section.[1] But this is not the main problem in this part of the book.

---

[1] Viewed in this way, Job in chapters 29–31 is the counterpoise to Elihu in chapters 32–37.

Some of the ideas expressed by Job in chapters 26 and 27 seem to be quite contrary to what he says elsewhere. They are more like the opinions of the three friends, opinions which Job has been steadfastly opposing all through the preceding debate. There is no indication that they have won him over to their point of view, for his final speech expresses even more defiant rejection of their case. To account for all this, some scholars have suggested that the speeches in the third cycle have fallen into disarray. Either Zophar's third speech has been lost, or some of it at least has got mixed up in the words of Job. Attempts have been made to retrieve this missing speech, but the difficulty of the task is revealed in the wide variety of solutions offered. Snaith[1] lists two dozen schemes, omitting many more whose complexity defies simple statement. Often 27:13–22 is identified as (part of) Zophar's missing speech. If Job is saying this, he is not necessarily expressing what he thinks himself; he could be representing his friends' point of view sarcastically, or for purposes of refutation. (In the commentary we arrive at a different result: *q.v.*)

There is no reason why the last round of speeches should have the same design as the first two. Bildad's desultory words (chapter 25) and Zophar's complete silence after the end of chapter 26, when it would have been his turn to speak, could be the author's way of showing that the debate had collapsed.[2] In the light of 32:1 this breakdown might show, not that Job had reduced them to silence, but that they had given up in exasperation over Job's seeming intransigence.

Other less drastic displacements of shorter passages or single verses have been suspected here and there, and some modern translations have moved these sections back to what are considered to be their original positions. For example, 31:35–37 is thought to be a better ending for Job's final speech than 31:38–40a.

Stage 7
Other changes which take place in the transmission of a text include the alteration (modernization or normalization) of spelling, the (sometimes misguided) correction of a suspected

---

[1] *SBT*[2], XI, Appendix I.
[2] Davidson sees in Zophar's silence 'a confession of defeat' (pp. xi, 27).

mistake, the loss or addition of an occasional word or phrase – in short, all the familiar errors made by scribes in copying ancient manuscripts, with the result that no two exemplars are ever quite the same. It is obvious that the gross changes hinted at under Stage 6 and the trivial variations of the text in Stage 7 could both occur at the same time.

The translation of Job into other languages is another part of its literary history. The versions, especially the Greek Septuagint (LXX), are valuable evidence. But LXX is considerably shorter, and sometimes quite different from the Massoretic Text.

At this distance in time the details of the complex process of literary growth and subsequent transmission of Job will never be known. Arguments for the disunity of the book are not conclusive, and, in spite of numerous difficulties, the Hebrew text is probably in pretty good shape. It is possible that the whole work is the product of a single mind, and insoluble textual problems need not prevent us from making sense of the book as a whole. At least that is what this commentary will attempt to do.

VIII. THE TEXT AND LANGUAGE OF THE BOOK OF JOB

For text criticism, Dhorme has sifted the versions so thoroughly that his apparatus makes a good point from which to continue such work. Since his day there have been some important studies of the Greek (LXX) text of Job, especially by Harry Orlinsky, and the extent to which the Greek translator betrays a theological bias has been warmly debated.

Most important evidence for the text of Job has come from the recovery, in Cave XI at Qumran, of a text of a Targum of Job which existed in the time of Jesus. The language suggests that the translation could have been made two hundred years earlier, making it the oldest known Targum. It is obvious that the value of such a document for the text criticism of Job is incalculable. Since it has only recently been published,[1] the effects of this discovery on Job studies have still to be felt. Here we will observe only that, like other evi-

---

[1] *Le Targum de Job de la Grotte XI de Qumran*, édité et traduit par J. P. M. van der Ploeg et A. S. van der Woude, avec collaboration de B. Jongeling (1972). This MS is referred to as 11QtgJob. There was also a small fragment in Cave IV.

dence from Qumran, the text generally agrees with the Massoretic Text, sometimes stands with LXX, thus enhancing the general value of the latter as an independent witness to a pre-Massoretic text type, but also presents peculiar readings of its own, reflecting a stage when a variety of recensions was already abroad, and none had yet won the day as definitive. This makes all the more significant its agreement with MT in its present state for chapters 24–27. This means that, if the changes in this part of the book described as Stage 6 in section VII above ever took place, they had already occurred by 200 BC. Modern speculative reconstructions thus remain unconfirmed by this new discovery.

The language in which Job is written presents many peculiarities. These have baffled scholars, who have attempted to account for them in several quite different ways. There are four main kinds of theory: the language of Job is either *a.* a dialect of genuine Hebrew; or *b.* an artificial literary language; or *c.* an admixture of Hebrew with some other language; or *d.* translation Hebrew.

a. The first question to be decided is whether the language of this book is a real sample of some variety of Hebrew or not. If it is Hebrew, it varies considerably from the standard of the language which dominates most of the Old Testament. The prestige of David's court established the dialect of Jerusalem under the united monarchy as a norm which controlled Israelite literature until the time of the Exile. Quite apart from the high incidence of unusual words (the book has about one hundred words not found anywhere else), Job deviates from the vocabulary of standard Hebrew in the area of ordinary words, and also in grammar, particularly morphology. To pinpoint the language of Job as a sample of a distinct dialect of Hebrew has a bearing on the date and location of the book, but until more specimens are found, we cannot say when or where such a dialect might have been in use.

b. The similarity of the language of the prose narrative to that used in the earliest Israelite story-telling has already been pointed out. Either they all have the same provenance, or the author of Job has deliberately imitated the early style. The poetic form of the Dialogue is more likely to embody a literary language than some vernacular. In this respect, however, it does not belong to the same tradition as the Psalter, making full allowance for the great diversity within the latter. In a general way, of course, most Hebrew poetry stands squarely on the foundation of the old Canaanite tradition, and here Job is no exception. Indeed, Job has more than its share of affinities with what little survives of this older literature.[1] The numerous Canaanisms in Job could be genuine, either genuinely ancient, or genuine survivals of ancient forms, although some might be due to later cultural contact with the Phoenicians.[2] The tendency of the text to preserve primitive spellings is quite marked.[3] This leans to an earlier date for its origin, and supports the authenticity of its archaisms. But the antique flavour could be cultivated (archaizing).[4] This could be the reason why such effects are not consistently secured. (But the same impression would be given if an old text were only partly modernized in transmission.) It is hazardous to infer anything about the date of the language from the morphology or orthography of the surviving text, for the data admit of several possible explanations. They do, however, make an exilic date unlikely, and a post-exilic date highly improbable, unless the alleged Aramaisms are felt to outweigh the Canaanisms in significance.

c. Many of the linguistic features in which the language of Job differs from standard Hebrew are found in one or other of the related Semitic languages. A simple example is found in the use of the suffix *-în* for masculine plural nouns. This is found in Arabic and Aramaic, whereas Canaanite, represented by Ugaritic or Phoenician, uses *-îm*. Both endings are found in Job. While *-îm* is standard in Hebrew, *-în* is occasion-

[1] L. R. Fisher (ed.), *Ras Shamra Parallels*, I (*Analecta Orientalia*, No. 49, 1973). The parallels with Job are on pp. 472–474 of the Index, and number more than 250. Moreover, they are found in every chapter of the book, another mark of its unity.

[2] There were several periods when such impact would have been felt more than usual – the age of Solomon, the reign of Ahab, and also in the burst of cosmopolitanism (accompanied by studied antiquarianism) prior to the Exile. But even if Hellenistic thought picked up a Phoenician tincture in passing through the coastal ports to inland Israel, a Hellenistic date for Job is altogether too late.

[3] D. N. Freedman, 'Orthographic Peculiarities in the Book of Job', *EI*, IX (Albright Volume), 1969, pp. 35–44.

[4] An analogy is found in the poetry of Spenser, whose diction abounds in genuine and spurious archaisms.

ally found in the Old Testament, apart from occurrences in Job. This variant cannot be attributed solely to late Aramaic influence, for it is found also in some ancient poems. And its use in the Mesha Inscription (Moabite) suggests that it was a dialectal variant within the South Canaanite languages spoken by the Israelite tribes and other closely-related peoples.

So, while such an alternate ending could have survived as a legitimate dialectal variant within Hebrew (*a.* above), many scholars consider it, and other similar features, to be the result of contamination of Hebrew by another language.

The trouble with this theory is that too many neighbouring languages are eligible as the source of this admixture, and more than one has to be invoked to explain everything. They include Aramaic, Arabic, Edomite, Phoenician (or some other form of Canaanite).

The idea that Job has an Edomite background is as old as the LXX, which equates Job with Jobab, king of Edom (Gn. 36:33). The theory that the book is an example of the world-famous, but otherwise lost, wisdom of the Edomites found its most serious modern supporter in R. H. Pfeiffer.[1] It has not found many takers, if only because we know practically nothing about this language and have no literature from this culture.

Since the recovery of the language of Ugarit in the Ras Shamra tablets, and the accumulation of a considerable body of Canaanite literature in this language, the question of the linguistic affinities of the language of Job, as distinct from its literary affinities, has taken on a new dimension. There can be no doubt that numerous problems in Job have been cleared up by evidence derived from Ugaritic.[2] This does not explain why Job is open to the application of such evidence. If it has more than its share of Canaanisms, this could be due either to the persistence of this background in some traditional streams of Israelite literature from early times, or due to a fresh infusion of such influence, most likely

[1] *Introduction to the Old Testament*[2] (1952), pp. 683f.

[2] Abundant use is made of such evidence in Pope's translation (*AB*). In addition to the literary and lexicographical parallels assembled in Volume I of *Ras Shamra Parallels* (see p. 57, footnote 1, above), numerous grammatical nuggets, of which Fr Mitchell Dahood has been the chief miner, have been gathered by A. C. M. Blommerde, *Northwest Semitic Grammar and Job* (*Biblica et Orientalia*, No. 22, 1969).

through Phoenician channels, at a later date. The question, already approached in *b.* above, is whether this produced a hybrid language in some community. Without going into the complex question of mixed languages, including creoles and pidgins, in bi-lingual or multi-racial societies, as distinct from the enlargement of vocabulary through heavy borrowing, we are forced to admit that all the deviations from standard Hebrew in Job cannot be explained as Canaanisms. In particular, Phoenician influence does not explain such non-Canaanite features as the *-în* ending and other apparent Aramaisms.

Whether the land of Uz is located in the north or in the south (see commentary on Jb. 1:1), Job's homeland is somewhere to the east of Israel proper. Israelites living in northern Transjordan would be more influenced by Aramaic than those living west of the river, especially since some of their territory was often under the control of Damascus. Those to the south, on the other hand, would be in contact with peoples speaking languages akin to ancestral Arabic. But in this direction, contact is less likely so long as the kingdoms of Ammon, Moab and Edom (who spoke South-Canaanite languages more closely akin to Hebrew and probably intelligible to Israelites) intervened between Israel and such ancient Arabian states as Dedan. We have every reason to suspect that the linguistic picture in Transjordan was very complex. Such an intermingling of peoples might have produced a community speaking a hybrid language, but we have no evidence that this occurred.[1] Hebrew itself has been described as a mix of languages.[2] This matter continues to be hotly debated, so that the special difficulties met in the language of Job are hard to relate to the larger question. A grave difficulty lies in the fact that the more Job is placed within the range of Phoenician culture, the less likely it is that it was similarly

[1] The dialect of the inscriptions of Panammuwa and Bar-rakib from Zincirli (called Yaudic by J. Friedrich) has been explained as an admixture of Old Aramaic with various Canaanisms, but the point has been energetically debated. The Mesha Inscription, similarly, which is not even internally consistent in spelling, morphology or (as the present writer has shown: *Orientalia*, XXXV, 1966, pp. 81–100) syntax, has been accounted for as regional Moabite infiltrated by Hebrew. But such texts are too small for safe inductions to be made about linguistic kinship.

[2] H. Bauer and P. Leander, *Historische Grammatik der hebräischen Sprache* (1922), p. 19.

nourished by contributions from the 'children of the East' (Qedemites) to whom Job himself belonged.

d. It is because this question of the actual existence of the language of the book of Job as a living dialect (whether a vernacular variety of Hebrew or a mixture of Hebrew with something else) cannot be settled that some scholars have turned to theories which explain the book as an imperfect translation from another language. Here there are two candidates, Arabic and Aramaic.

The idea that Job was first written in Arabic was expressed as long ago as Ibn Ezra and later by Jean Jacques Rousseau. The latter was prejudiced. He could not believe that the Jews were capable of producing anything so magnificent. More serious in modern times is the work of A. Guillaume, who asserted that 'the underlying language is Arabic'.[1] An abundance of suggestive etymologies (Hebrew and Arabic words with the same roots) supports the argument. The affinity of Job with Arabic is not unlike the much-argued problem of the linguistic classification of Ugaritic, whose kinship with Arabic, through closeness to ancestral Semitic, has been measured differently by different scholars. On the level of lexicography the rich vocabulary of Arabic can always reward the diligent seeker, and such evidence is a valid aid in the interpretation of the Hebrew word stock.[2] But it is a long shot to argue from this to an Arabic original. As with the Edomite theory, we know nothing of a community which developed literature in the Hijaz in the sixth century BC.[3] It is hard to believe that a work so thoroughly Israelite in spirit, standing in the traditions of biblical wisdom, was produced anywhere but in the Israelite homeland, and in Hebrew. The attempts of Guillaume to supply the historical background for his chosen location remain speculative.

From another direction, H. S. Tur Sinai has explained the numerous Aramaisms of the book as the result of a half-way translation from an Aramaic original. The theory is that once Aramaic had come into use as an international lingua

---

[1] Guillaume, p. 5.

[2] On the dangers of unskilful or over-skilful use of arguments from comparative Semitic philology to solve Old Testament problems see J. Barr, *Comparative Philology and the Text of the Old Testament* (1968).

[3] Guillaume, p. 6.

franca, and was taken up by many Jews as a second language, if not as their vernacular, the translator could safely leave in their original Aramaic form words and expressions which such Jews would understand. Tur Sinai developed his theory with vast learning and great ingenuity, and his numerous observations on the text bring much valuable light from the Aramaic quarter. Resemblances between Hebrew and Aramaic, as closely-related Semitic languages, are only to be expected. The influence of Aramaic on Hebrew became greater in later times with the ascendency of the former. But we think that Tur Sinai has overstated his case by inferring from the Aramaic component in the language of Job that the book was originally written entirely in that language.[1]

IX. THE DATE AND AUTHORSHIP OF THE BOOK OF JOB

We do not know who wrote the book of Job or when he lived. Nor do we know where. If several persons were involved, we still know nothing about them. Unless the author was a professional Wisdom teacher, we have no idea of his place in society. And even then, as a member of the intelligentsia, we cannot discover any institutional setting for the composition of such a work, whether the royal court, a shrine whose officers could read and had books, or, later, the synagogue.

A wide range of dates has been proposed, extending from the time of Moses to the Hellenistic period. The preceding discussion has already indicated how vexed this question can become. The options would be narrowed if we could place the language of the book in its right period in the historical development of Hebrew. On the one hand, its abundant archaisms and numerous parallels with old Canaanite literature suggest that it is early, with the age of Solomon as a real, but perhaps the earliest, possibility. But, if such features are

[1] We might add that N. H. Snaith, who discusses the question with some care and detail, concludes, 'We find virtually no Aramaisms at all' (*The Book of Job, SBT*[2], XI, 1968, p. 83). For a comprehensive study of the general question, with ample bibliography, see Max Wagner, *Die lexikalischen und grammatikalischen Aramaismus in alttestamentlichen Hebräisch (BZAW,* 96, 1966). His summary of the evidence in quantitative form, on p. 145, does not bear out the claim that Job is aramaized like post-exilic writings. It does show, however, that the Elihu speeches have more Aramaic features than the rest of the book. But they do not rise to the level of Esther, Ecclesiastes or the Song of Solomon.

explained as a later injection through Phoenician contacts, then the alleged Aramaisms can be marshalled to support a late, even a post-exilic, date. Freedman's study of orthography has now, however, in our opinion, made any date later than the seventh century hard to uphold.

Another way of tackling the date of Job is to work out where its ideas fit into the historical development of Hebrew thought. Here it is hard to find our bearings without a lot of *a priori* assumptions. Job does not refer to any historical events, not even those that were always in the mind of an Israelite – the call of Abram, the Exodus, the Conquest, the Exile. The awareness of living in covenant with the Lord who had guided His people through all this long history is focused so intensely in the experience of one man that all the historical background becomes a shadow. Nor does Job refer to any of the familiar institutions of Israel – the monarchy, the temple, the prophets. It is quite astonishing how detached from all these matters the book is. It has been supposed that, just as Job and his friends are not Israelites, so all this national background has been deliberately suppressed by the author so as to give his work a neutral or more universal setting in the gentile world. But his characters are not pagans, and it could be argued with equal cogency that the author has simulated the pre-Mosaic world of the patriarchs, and has succeeded in concealing his own day and age by avoiding detectable anachronisms.

Since the search for clues in concrete historical events or identifiable institutions fails, we are left with the more abstract theological ideas of the book – its concepts of God, of sin, of ethics, *etc*. It has been inferred from the allegedly 'advanced' stage of its thought that the book is late. In particular, it has been claimed that the specific way in which the book grapples with the problem of suffering (see section x, below) was only possible after Israelite thinkers had to cope with a monumental national calamity of the scope of the Exile. Hence the book was written during or after that period.

But we have already observed that there is nothing explicit in the book to link the sufferings of Job with those of Israel as a nation. There is no hint of allegory. The questions raised in Job did not enter people's heads first with the collapse of the Judaean state. As we have seen in section IV, even outside Israel sensitive and reflective souls had been searching for an explanation of human misery from the dawn of literature, and the plight of the righteous, destitute person is an ancient and persistent theme in Israel's historical writings.

From another angle many scholars (*e.g.* Gray, *ICC*, p. lxix) date Job after the rise of individualism (seventh century BC) but before Israel accepted belief in life after death (second century BC). Although we cannot argue the case fully here, we believe that the use of such signposts is quite untenable. Belief in personal responsibility before God and in the continuation of personal existence after death were both part of Israel's ancient faith, and fully in vogue by the early monarchy. Moses (or Abraham), not Jeremiah, first made religion personal. And, at the heart of the whole matter, the uncompromising moral monotheism of Job is identical with that revelation of one gracious and stern God, Creator, Owner and Protector of all men, which attained its maturity in the age of Moses and underwent very little further development from that time onwards. Once the idea of progressive evolution is removed from the history of Israel's religion, and the Old Testament's own account of Moses as the consummator, and not merely the inaugurator, of Israel's faith is accepted, it follows that Job's idea of God could have been current at any time during the monarchical period (tenth to seventh century BC).

More concrete attempts to date Job have been based on its suspected quotations from other biblical books, such as Deuteronomy or Isaiah. Job obviously must have been written after them. Numerous parallels to passages in other parts of the Old Testament are found in Job. But, quite apart from such debatable questions as the dates of the books which Job is said to quote, the similar material in other texts could be quotations from Job, making it earlier than these works. Or both could be drawing on a common tradition. Hence such arguments are inconclusive.

All we can say is that Job could have been written at any time between Moses and Ezra. Our own opinion, which we admit we cannot substantiate, is that the substance of the book took shape during the reign of Solomon and that its normative form was settled by the time of Josiah. An Israelite, rather than Judaean, setting for its most definitive stage, together with its location in northern Gilead, suggests a date around

750 BC, before this community was decimated by the Assyrian conquests.

X. THE PROBLEMS OF SUFFERING IN THE BOOK OF JOB

In the story of Job the problem of evil in the world is not dealt with abstractly, but in terms of one man's agony. The three friends and Elihu do their best to apply general principles to Job's case; but they do not help him, and what they say is finally declared invalid by God Himself. This is a surprise, for their arguments have the familiar ring of sound doctrine.

Strictly speaking, human misery, or the larger sum of evil in all its forms, is a problem only for the person who believes in one God who is all-powerful and all-loving. Outside such faith there are many explanations of evil which involve a denial, or a limitation, of either God's sovereignty or of His goodness. The argument has been expressed with philosophical clarity as follows: If God were perfectly good, He could not tolerate the existence of violence, disease, *etc.*; therefore there must be some limit to His ability to control such events, that is, He is not almighty. Alternatively, if God does have complete power over everything that happens, His failure to curb the wrongs that occur must be due to the fact that He does not see anything wrong in them, that is, He is not good.

Many thoughtful people, horrified by the helplessness of humanity in the face of natural disasters or outraged by the ruthless exploitation of 'the downtrodden and the injured' by the unscrupulous masters of political or economic power, have lost faith in the goodness of God. 'If I had the power of God,' they protest, 'I could do more about these things than He seems to be doing!'

A reasoned theodicy – the justification of the ways of God to men – is a legitimate task for Christian apologetics. The book of Job is not such a treatise, but the story of one man, his loss, his search and his discovery. This search takes place entirely within the household of faith. All the characters, the three friends and Elihu as much as Job himself, are fully committed to belief in one supreme God who is unquestionably just in all His acts. Solutions which lie outside such biblical revelation are not even considered in the book of Job. Polytheism, in which each god has his own limited domain, survives in a simpler form in various kinds of dualism, in which evil (perhaps in the person of the Devil) exists over against good. Naturalistic belief in a closed universe where God does nothing has found expression in 'God is dead' theology. It is another kind of dualism; even if the world is said to be God's creation, His effective removal from the scene is a rag of deism, pitiful beside the robust biblical belief that God owns the world and is always at work in it. The book of Job similarly accepts no suggestion of limitation in either the power or the goodness of God.

Like the rest of the Bible, the book of Job also takes the world seriously. It is God's making, and God's property, and it is good. While God is delighted with all His creatures, human beings are His special friends, for only men share with God the wisdom which is His image in them. A man is able to talk to God, and God answers him. Human existence in this created world, as God's creature, is the place where the goodness of God is supremely displayed and experienced. Hence Job's insistence on a meaningful life, here and now, even though a man's life must be comprehended in the completeness that embraces birth and time and death.

But this joyful acceptance of creaturehood, this insistence on seeing the goodness of the Lord in the land of the living, accounts for the reluctance of Job to postpone satisfaction until after death, even though he confidently expects to go on living with God after that event. The moral question central to Job arises from the biblical teaching that a man reaps what he sows – in this life. Rewards for virtue and punishments for vice cannot all be postponed to heaven and hell. But troubles and benefits are not distributed to mankind by an even-handed justice, it would seem. The wicked prosper, the righteous suffer. Evil is not always – not often! – punished in proportion to guilt; good is not always – not often! – rewarded in proportion to merit. The case of Job precipitates the test of faith in its severest form – the supremely righteous man who sustains the most extreme calamities. How can he, or anyone, continue to believe that God is right and fair in what He sometimes does to people? There can be no doubt that it is God, only God, who is responsible for all that happens to Job. It cannot be blamed on 'Nature' or the Devil, for these are but His creatures.

It is worth observing that a solution that eastern religions have found attractive, viz. the reversal of the inequalities of one existence by compensation in some future reincarnation, never finds an entrance to biblical thought, with its vivid awareness of the once-for-all-ness of each man's individual existence in history.

We should notice also that the book of Job does not resort to a line of thought that has been paramount in western Christianity since the triumph of Augustine over Pelagius. The dogma of the original and inherited depravity and guilt of all mankind, if permitted to deny any possibility of goodness in human conduct, must contradict the premise of the book of Job that its hero was a 'blameless and upright' man (1:1). Job's friends are the ones who infer, as they must infer in order to safeguard the doctrine that each person reaps what he sows, that Job is paying for his sins. On this basis there is no such thing as a righteous man, no-one ever receives as much punishment as he deserves, and most receive far less. Job's insistence on his integrity can, then, be only hypocrisy, adding to his sin. So speak Job's friends, with the sound of orthodoxy. It is no wonder that commentators whose exposition is controlled by the traditional doctrines of the fall and corruption of every member of the human race, have joined the friends in condemning Job, and seen the purpose of God as a discipline to bring Job to repentance. But such interpretations crumble at the word of God Himself that Job is 'blameless and upright' and that he, and not the friends, was correct in what he said in the discussion. That is, Job was right, but not self-righteous, to insist on his own integrity, to complain that his suffering was undeserved, and to demand from God Himself an explanation of how His justice was to be found in such unprovoked torture. The book of Job loses its point if the righteousness of Job is not taken as genuine.

God's final endorsement of Job's speeches is also surprising for another reason. It silences the cant of those who remind us of the inscrutability of God, and smugly say, 'It is not for us to question the ways of the Almighty!' For that is precisely what Job does, and God says that he was fully justified in doing so. The Lord welcomes this exercise of moral judgment from man's side, even when it is directed in judgment on God Himself!

The apparent injustice of God is seen in the disproportionate share of ills that come to many good people. Experience contradicts the teaching that each person reaps what he sows. Within the accepted framework of common belief that God is sovereign and God is just, Job and the other speakers gather together most of the solutions to this problem which are presented in the Bible. When the wicked prosper and the righteous suffer, something more than a simple doctrine of rewards and punishments is needed.

The Bible, including Job, has several distinct ways of reconciling human suffering with the justice of God. Most of them are heard on the lips of Job's friends, and Job finds them unsatisfactory. But if they are not completely satisfying, and if, in particular, they do not apply in Job's case, this does not mean that they are wrong. What makes this collision of minds so dramatic is the soundness of their views and the cogency of their arguments. The author has not set up men of straw against Job. To that extent the argument ends in a stalemate, as Elihu recognizes.

The covenant of Yahweh with Israel set two ways before the people – life, through obedience, or death, through disloyalty. A simple correlation of these causes and their effects is expressed in the cursings and blessings recited with the covenant (Lv. 26; Dt. 27–30). Put simply, you reap what you sow (Gal. 6:7; Ps. 34:11–22; 1 Pet. 3:10). This is the starting-point of much biblical teaching. These are not just threats and bribes; God's moral administration of the world requires that the rightness of right should lead to well-being, and the wrongness of wrong should lead to disaster. But the connection is not often obvious, and life is much more complex than this simple formula. Human suffering is more than a system of rewards and punishments.

Holy men, brooding on this mystery, and anxious to protect the character of God from slander, saw that outward appearances might not give a true picture of what was happening between a man and God. The material prosperity of the wicked is not an index of his happiness, and its permission is not an oversight on the part of God. The rich are really miserable, because wealth is insecure and transient. If it is ill-gotten, their conscience is always in dread of a day of reckoning. By contrast, the inward joy of the righteous cannot be destroyed by outward misfortune, for his communion with God is safe from any change due to circumstances (Ps. 73).

By such a test, Job is condemned, and his agitation is inexcusable. But God did not suspend each individual in isolation, to find fulfilment solely in communion with Himself. God put each man with family and friends and things, with property and work. Only a false piety, a disdain for things as evil (the Manichean heresy), a contempt for emotions as weak (the Stoic error), would expect in Job an unflinching fortitude in the midst of such loss and pain. Job rightly grieves his bereavement; he is authentically depressed by his illness. He is human. The untrammelled serenity which some prescribe as the goal of 'victorious living' is a negation of whole areas of our experience as God has made us. Job lives fully. The calm attained by the psalmist (Ps. 73:23-28), and by Job also at the end, was reached only through, and as the fruit of, terrible suffering.

Men seek an explanation of suffering in cause and effect. They look backwards for a connection between prior sin and present suffering. The Bible looks forwards in hope and seeks explanations, not so much in origins as in goals. The purpose of suffering is seen, not in its cause, but in its result. The man was born blind so that the works of God could be displayed in him (Jn. 9:3). But sometimes good never seems to come out of evil. Men wait in vain. They find God's slowness irksome. They lose heart, and often lose faith. The Bible commends God's self-restraint. The outworkings of His justice through the long processes of history, which sometimes require spans of many centuries, are part of our existence in time. It is easier to see the hand of God in spectacular and immediate acts, and the sinner who is not instantly corrected is likely to despise God's delay in executing justice as a sign that He is indifferent or even absent. We have to be as patient as God Himself to see the end result, or to go on living in faith without seeing it. In due season we shall reap, if we do not faint.

So there are passages in the Bible which postpone the resolution of the incongruities in God's moral administration to the last eschatological moment, or even to an occasion beyond history itself. The book of Job is moving in this direction, but its attention is mainly on this life. Given time, the wicked will receive his just deserts and the righteous will find deliverance and compensation. This teaching, expressed by Zophar in Job 20, puts a strain on Job's faith. He cannot wait indefinitely to see justice done. He contradicts Zophar vigorously (chapter 21). And, even if everything is set right later on, can this ever neutralize the wrong treatment that people have received before that later settlement? The biblical answer is that God (but only God!) can actually transform evil into good, so that in retrospect (but only in retrospect!) it is seen to have actually been good, without diminishing in the least the awful actuality of the evil it was at the time.

If the book of Job cannot take on this full eschatological dimension, it is largely because it does not yet have the achievement of Jesus Christ to include in the picture. For in Him the greatest evils, the betrayal and crucifixion of the Son of God, become, and now are, the greatest good for all mankind. Job does see part of the answer by teaching that, when the experience is over, the sufferer will appreciate it in a new way because of what he has learnt. Suffering is not always punitive or even corrective. It can be instructive. It is a discipline and a warning. This is a common Wisdom theme (Pr. 3:11; Heb. 12:12f.). This is affirmed by Eliphaz (Jb. 5:17) and especially by Elihu. Suffering is morally therapeutic and prophylactic.[1]

Such answers to any man's question, 'Why am I suffering?' are confined to the individual. They are valuable and valid, because they take the human person seriously in his moral connections with God. But no individual exists in isolation. The Bible views man as both a singular and a social being. Individual responsibility was emphasized by Jeremiah and Ezekiel, not as the only truth, not even as the highest truth, but to correct the error of those who quoted a proverb about social solidarity ('The fathers have eaten sour grapes, and the children's teeth are set on edge') in order to evade blame.

Neither side gives the whole picture. Each man stands directly before God; but no man stands alone. One man sins, and the consequences reverberate through the entire race. Others are more likely to profit from a man's goodness than himself. Each is linked to others, ultimately to all in one vast web of inter-personal humanity. No-one's suffering is ever completely private in either its causes or its results. The

[1] For detailed discussion see J. A. Sanders, 'Suffering as Divine Discipline in the Old Testament and Post-Biblical Judaism' (*Colgate Rochester Divinity School Bulletin*, XXVIII, 1955).

Bible recognizes as a fact that consequences of evil are inherited from our ancestors, shared with our contemporaries, bequeathed to posterity. This emphasis escapes from one problem only to fall into another. If a disaster is punishment for sin, why should Job suffer for anyone's faults but his own? Job knows that his troubles are caused by criminals, by the forces of nature, by disease – things that could happen to anyone. We know that behind these events lay the malice of the Satan. But behind all that it is harder to see the fairness of God, let alone His good intentions.

Yet, in spite of these disturbing thoughts, it is part of the answer that a person can willingly accept suffering as the tribute he pays to other people's freedom. He may be sobered by the remembrance of occasions when he has caused hurt to others, deliberately or carelessly. And, when tempted to complain, 'Why didn't God stop them from doing that to me?' he might ask himself what his life would be like if God paralysed his arm each time he lifted it to strike an angry blow, or to steal.

It is part of the answer that it is possible for one person to share the burdens of others. The price paid for this can be suffering. But, when done in love, such suffering becomes a person's noblest task. This aspect of the matter is barely glimpsed in Job. That suffering can be voluntary and vicarious is one of the most amazing and liberating of all the truths revealed in Scripture. The patient endurance of wrong can conquer evil by love. The sufferer can fortify others by his example. The ills of life can sweeten a man or turn him sour. The metal has no strength that has not been tempered in the fire.

In the extreme of self-giving, suffering can be redemptive. It must be admitted that this part of the Old Testament revelation, which finds its clearest expression in Isaiah 52:11 – 53:12, scarcely enters into the discussion between Job and his friends.

The Bible tries to affirm two contrary truths which collide in the book of Job. Suffering is the common burden of all men and the lonely burden of each man. It explains it as punitive, corrective, exemplary, vicarious. From one angle, suffering is inflicted by God in justice; from another angle, it can be accepted by persons in love.

These truths have to be stated with great pastoral sensitivity to become true for any sufferer. It is amazing how trite, stale or sanctimonious they can become on the lips of Job's friends. Their ineptitude does not invalidate what they say. The truths in their speeches cannot be given up without leaving the universe a moral chaos. They are quite right, as far as they go. The teaching of the Bible is clear: 'God is no respecter of persons.' 'He pays back every man according to his deeds.' This is where justice begins; but it is not where love ends. These truths do not cover all the facts. They certainly do not apply to Job, as he knows, and God knows, and as we, the readers, also know. But Job's friends cannot perceive the innocence of his heart as God does; they cannot detect the good-will of God – nor can Job. They must do the best with what theology they have, as we all must.

Job's friends were well-meaning, but presumptuous. Job's case was 'special' and escapes the generalized doctrines. Nothing but the Voice from the tempest can meet his case, and when that happens, Job keeps his secret. Beyond the frontier reached by the best human understanding of God's revelation – for we must remember that the theology of Job's friends is excellent – lies the abyss of undeserved suffering into which Job is plunged. The case of Job opens up a whole new dimension. There is a vast area of human misery which is neither penal, nor remedial, nor redemptive. It is just meaningless. The answer to the question, 'Who sinned, this man or his parents, that he was born blind?' is 'Nobody sinned' (Jn. 9:2f.). *Job did not sin* (Jb. 1:22).

To condemn the miserable wretch as one already rejected by God is the final human cruelty. Job's friends, trying to apply their best insights to help him to spiritual recovery, unintentionally add to his pain. What he needs is compassion, not advice. The helplessness of Job is pathetic. If he had sinned, he could repent. But he cannot dishonestly invent imaginary sins to repent of. There is nothing he can do, except to cry out to God from the depths (Ps. 130:1). In this gulf of anger he is alone, until he discovers that God has not deserted him permanently. But, like Jesus, he does not at first – not for a long time! – receive any answer to his desolate cry, 'My God, my God, why hast thou forsaken me?' Yet the *via dolorosa* becomes the road to God. Mary paid a price for bearing the Son of God; a sword was thrust through her own heart (Lk. 2:35). She could not escape her agony, which was also her holy privilege and her joy. Of all human beings, the innocent sufferer stands nearest to God. One might ask if there is any pathway into the light, except through dereliction. Job's final contentment is inexplicable unless he found in the valley of the shadow of death a place of spiritual growth.

The Bible, especially the New Testament, sees two sides to this opportunity. From the agony of abandonment by God comes a ministry of compassion that extends to all companions on this dreadful journey (2 Cor. 1:3-7). What is an unendurable indignity at the time becomes a holy honour in memory. Moses in Midian, David in his hide-out, Jeremiah and Joseph in the pit, Daniel in the lions' den, Paul in more than one prison. Like Job on the city dump, their life would seem to have reached its end. The long wait, sometimes for years. The silence of God. But deliverance came, and with it a gratitude never felt by those who never knew despair.

The heroes of faith in Hebrews 11 were all sufferers, and many died without deliverance. Now no suffering seems pleasant at the time, but *afterwards* 'it yields the peaceful fruit of righteousness to those who have been trained by it' (Heb. 12:11). This is not a thing for anyone to arrange for himself in order to gain spiritual benefits. God alone may send it. No-one who has felt His rod would wish to go that way again; but no-one who has come with Job to 'what the Lord is aiming at' (see Jas. 5:11) would ever wish not to have trodden his path. The body of Jesus for ever bears the scars of crucifixion, and they are its chief glory. If the passion of Job was an early sketch of the greatest Sufferer, it remains for His later followers to enter into 'the fellowship of his sufferings' (Phil. 3:10, AV) and joyfully to supply what is still needed to complete the sufferings of Christ (Col. 1:24). For He is the chief Pilgrim and Pioneer of this way, 'a man of sorrows, and acquainted with grief' (Is. 53:3). His Gethsemane was a human experience, but it exceeds all others in its intensity and in its healing power. The full burden of our anxieties crushed Him. What Job longed for blindly has actually happened. God Himself has joined us in our hell of loneliness, and acquired a new completeness through what He endured (Heb. 5:7-9). All the 'meanings' of suffering converge on Christ. He entered a domain of suffering reserved for Him alone. No man can bear the sin of another, but Jesus carried the sins of all. As the Substitute for all sinners, His sufferings were penal, a bearing of the death penalty for sin. They were also a full and authentic sharing of our human condition with a love that gave itself completely into the furnace of affliction. That the Lord Himself has embraced and absorbed the undeserved consequences of all evil is the final answer to Job and to all the Jobs of humanity. As an innocent sufferer, Job is the companion of God.

ANALYSIS

I. THE TESTING OF JOB (1:1 – 2:13)
  a. The integrity of Job (1:1–5)
  b. The first test (1:6–22)
     i. The first assembly (1:6–12)
     ii. The first disasters (1:13–19)
     iii. Job's first reaction (1:20–22)
  c. The second test (2:1–10)
     i. The second assembly (2:1–7a)
     ii. Job's illness (2:7b, 8)
     iii. Job's second reaction (2:9, 10)
  d. The arrival of Job's friends (2:11–13)

II. DISCUSSION BETWEEN JOB AND HIS FRIENDS (3:1 – 27:23)
  a. Job's lamentation (3:1–26)
  b. First round of speeches (4:1 – 14:22)
     i. Eliphaz (4:1 — 5:27)
     ii. Job (6:1 – 7:21)
     iii. Bildad (8:1–22)
     iv. Job (9:1 – 10:22)
     v. Zophar (11:1–20)
     vi. Job (12:1 – 14:22)
  c. Second round of speeches (15:1 – 21:34)
     i. Eliphaz (15:1–35)
     ii. Job (16:1 – 17:16)
     iii. Bildad (18:1–21)
     iv. Job (19:1–29)
     v. Zophar (20:1–29)
     vi. Job (21:1–34)
  d. Third round of speeches (22:1 - 26:14)
     i. Eliphaz (22:1–30)
     ii. Job (23:1 – 24:25)
     iii. Bildad (25:1–6)
     iv. Job (26:1–14)
  e. Job's conclusion (27:1–23)

III. INTERLUDE (28:1–28)

IV. JOB AND ELIHU (29:1 – 37:24)
- a. Job (29:1 – 31:40)
  - i. Job's former estate (29:1–25)
  - ii. Job's present humiliation (30:1–31)
  - iii. Job's ultimate challenge (31:1–40)
- b. Elihu (32:1 – 37:24)
  - i. Introduction (32:1–5)
  - ii. Elihu's first speech (32:6 – 33:33)
  - iii. Elihu's second speech (34:1–37)
  - iv. Elihu's third speech (35:1–16)
  - v. Elihu's fourth speech (36:1 – 37:24)

V. YAHWEH AND JOB (38:1 – 42:6)
- a. First round (38:1 – 40:5)
  - i. Yahweh (38:1 – 40:2)
  - ii. Job (40:3–5)
- b. Second round (40:6 – 42:6)
  - i. Yahweh (40:6 – 41:34)
  - ii. Job (42:1–6)

VI. THE OUTCOME (42:7–17)
- a. Yahweh's verdict (42:7–9)
- b. Job's restoration (42:10–17)

COMMENTARY

I. THE TESTING OF JOB (1:1 – 2:13)

a. The integrity of Job (1:1–5)

1. For an Israelite living west of the great rift valley of the Jordan, everything across the river was *Qedem, the east* (verse 3), ranging all the way from Midian in the south (Jdg. 6:3) to Aram-naharaim in the north (Gn. 29:1). This is where a political refugee such as the Egyptian Sinuhe went into exile;[1] here a second-class son would seek his fortune (Gn. 25:6). It was the edge of civilization, surrounded by an atmosphere of romance. It was wild in parts, and from it came brigands to maraud and pillage more settled folk (Jdg. 6:3, 33; 7:12; 8:10). In its turn it was exposed to raids from bandits even further out, such as the Sabeans and Chaldeans (Jb. 1:15, 17). It was not desert, for in fertile places there could be tillage and towns, at least in good times. Here could be seen both nomadic shepherd and settled farmer; and sometimes the same person could be both. Here lived *a man . . . , whose name was Job.*

Qedem cannot be identified with any state, for it covers the entire eastern fringe of Israel. Here lay the mysterious lands of Amaw (Nu. 22:5), *Uz* (Jb. 1:1), Tob (Jdg. 11:3) and Retenu,[2] the peoples of Midian, Amalek and Edom to the south, Moab and Ammon more directly east, and the Aramaeans to the north (Is. 11:14; Nu. 23:7). Besides the reputation that Balaam gave it for sorcery (Nu. 23:7), it was renowned for wisdom (1 Ki. 4:30). We do not know where in this vast tract of territory along Israel's landward frontier Job's home was located. Some biblical passages connect Uz with Edom (Je. 25:20; La. 4:21); others associate it with Aram (Gn. 10:23; 22:21). Since Job is given no tribal identification, we do not even know if he was an Israelite of Transjordan. He was certainly a believer in Israel's God. A location to the north-east of the Sea of Galilee would suit his manner of life quite well and would account for much of the general background of the book. It is supported by early tradition from Josephus onwards.

[1] *ANET*, pp. 19–21. [2] *ANET*, p. 329.

The story begins simply: *There was a man.* Since a parable (2 Sa. 12:1) and a history (1 Sa. 25:2) begin with the same grammatical construction, the style does not indicate whether Job was meant to be fact or fiction. *Job* is mentioned in Ezekiel 14:14, 20 as an ancient hero of faith. The name is attested several times throughout the second millennium BC as an old Canaanite name sometimes borne by royal personages. It occurs in an Egyptian execration text of the nineteenth century BC.[1] It is represented at Mari[2] and Alalakh.[3] Later the Ugaritic *ayab*[4] agrees with the South Canaanite name *A-ya-ab* in Amarna Letters numbers 237 and 256 (fourteenth century BC)[5] and supports the explanation that the name originally meant, 'Where is Father?' It is not altogether clear how the later pronunciation could have been derived from this earlier form; but it would seem to rule out any connection with the root *'yb*, 'to display enmity', as suggested by many commentators. It can be admitted, nevertheless, that to later Israelite readers, who would have long forgotten its ancient form, the name might have suggested someone 'alienated' or 'discovenanted' rather than an 'adversary' or 'hater' of God. But Job's character and experience do not suggest that the name was intended to have any such meanings. His association with such ancient worthies as Noah (of the Flood) and Danel (the hero of a very old Canaanite epic) in Ezekiel 14:14, 20 probably goes back to the story of a real man *whose name was Job*, and no further meaning should be sought in the supposed derivation of the name.

Job *was blameless and upright.* The personality of Job is most attractive, and pleasing to God Himself (Jb. 1:8; 2:3). The phrase, literally 'complete and straight', affirms his thorough rectitude. He was completely honest. The following words expand and explain this wholeness. Job's goodness had two

[1] *ANET*, p. 329.
[2] Herbert B. Huffmon, *Amorite Personal Names in the Mari Texts* (1965), pp. 103, 161.
[3] *JCS*, VIII, 1954, p. 60, n. 126. For a doubtful instance of the same name for a female from Chagar Bazar, see *Iraq*, VII, 1940, p. 36.
[4] *Mission de Ras Shamra VII: Le Palais Royal d'Ugarit II* (1957), No. 35 rev. line 10; Frauke Gröndahl, *Die Personennamen der Texte aus Ugarit* (1967), p. 93.
[5] *ANET*, p. 486. W. F. Albright, *BASOR*, No. 83, 1941, p. 36; No. 89, 1943, p. 11.

aspects, like wisdom in Job 28:28. He was devout; he *feared God*, like Abraham (Gn. 22:12). And he was moral; negatively stated, he *turned away from evil*. He rejected what was wrong; he did not merely shun it. The scope of Job's fine conduct is unfolded as the story advances. It reaches its climax in his final testimony (chapters 29–31), where he insists that his achievements are public knowledge (29) and denies any serious failure (31). He was beyond reproach by men (4:3–6) or God (42:8).

The fact of Job's genuine righteousness is essential to the book. It begins with a clash of opinion between Yahweh and the Satan on this point. The slanderer denies it; Yahweh sets out to prove it. This insistence on Job's uprightness should not be weakened in the interests of a dogma of universal human depravity. Job is not considered to be perfect or sinless. All the speakers in the book, including Job himself, are convinced that all men are sinful. Job's first recorded act is to offer sacrifices for sin. This is not the point. It is possible for sinful men to be genuinely good. It may be rare, but it is possible for a man who loves and obeys God. It requires effort, but Job had made that effort.

The Satan is cynical about the sincerity of Job's religious character; but the Lord is delighted with him. The Satan jibes that Job's piety is motivated by self-interest, and has not been tested by misfortune. The Lord is confident that a man of Job's character cannot easily be broken. And the Lord was right, answering all pessimists who see only the incurable badness of the human race. Job was as faultless as a man can be. He is not Everyman; he is unique. God boasts that 'there is none like him on the earth' (1:8, 2:3). As such he presents the case of the innocent sufferer in what is almost its acutest form. In one Life only is Job excelled, in both innocence and grief: in Jesus, who sinned not at all, but who endured the greatest agony of any man. In His perfection of obedience and of suffering the questions of Job and of all of us have their final answer.[1]

2. Job had an ideal family of *seven sons and three daughters*, both numbers and their sum being symbols of completeness, a clear token of divine favour.

3. He was *the greatest* of the Qedemites. Affluence is in

---

[1] G. Campbell Morgan, *The Answers of Jesus to Job* (1950).

mind, and 'richest' would be a better translation. His wealth was measured in livestock, and once more the numerals indicate the ideal. Similar property-lists in Genesis (*e.g.* Gn. 24:35) describe the wealth of the patriarchs, suggesting that Job's way of life was like theirs. But the number of draught bullocks shows that Job was not a nomad, like the bedouin, but an agriculturalist with extensive farmlands (*cf.* Jb. 1:14) as well as a pastoralist. This agrees with the fuller portrait of Job the townsman in chapters 29–31. The inventories in Genesis often list male and female slaves along with the animals, and the abstract noun '*abuddāh*, found only here and in Genesis 26:14, could be another way of referring to such possessions. Hence RSV *servants*. But the verb with this root can mean more specifically 'cultivate (the soil)', hence 'tillage' is a possibility. The rendition 'work animals' (NAB) has less to commend it, since these have already been explicitly listed.

4. Job's children were able to enjoy the best of everything. The general picture of their happy life is clear, but the details are hard to secure in translation. In spite of the intimacy of the extended family, rich or royal children might each have their own residence, without necessarily being married (Gn. 25:5, 6; Jdg. 10:4; 2 Sa. 13:7; 14:24, 31). Compare Job 1:18. Presumably the sisters were still living with their parents.

5. *The days of the feast* could imply a weekly cycle. Zöckler's suggestion that the feasts were birthday parties (*cf.* 'his day' in Jb. 3:1, AV, RV) is plausible, but hard to prove.

No disapproval of this pleasant life is expressed. We need not suppose that they spent all their time in roistering and did no work. There is no hint of drunkenness or licence or laziness. Job expresses no anxiety on this score, although he is aware of the danger that they might slip into profanity. These delightful family gatherings are part of the atmosphere of well-being that begins the story. They are a mark of good fortune, or rather of God's blessing. They also explain how all the family, but not the parents, could be killed by a storm striking one house.

The finishing touch to this happy scene is the godly parent making doubly sure that all is well. As head of the family Job was a priest with God. The sin which he fears that they might commit, cursing God in their hearts, is the very one the Satan hopes Job will fall into (1:11; 2:5) and to which his wife will tempt him (2:9). The word translated *cursed*, here and in 1:11; 2:5, 9 (*cf.* 1 Ki. 21:10, 13), is literally 'blessed'. It could be a euphemism, introduced by the scribes, to avoid even reading such a horrid expression. Driver and Gray (pp. 4ff.) have a full note on the use of such an antiphrasis. It could be, however, that out of such a practice the word actually acquires the opposite meaning when the context determines. Job's religion was inward and spiritual; but it recognized the need for ceremonies and sacrifices. His own act of intercession, in offering *burnt offerings* to restore the holiness (*sanctify*) of his children, shows a belief in the power of a mediator that will lead to his desire later on that someone should do the same for him.

The phrase *rise early in the morning* is a common Hebrew idiom for conscientious activity, not necessarily the time of the sacrifice. *Thus did Job continually*, literally 'all his days'; it was a lifelong habit.

b. The first test (1:6–22)

i. The first assembly (1:6–12). 6. Throughout the Old Testament the Lord is represented as the Creator and Ruler of the universe, which is inhabited by a numerous community of beings, its 'hosts' (Heb. *ṣᵉḇāʾôṯ*). The population of His realm on earth is all mankind, but Israel is His 'host' in a special sense, with *ṣāḇāʾ* commonly used to describe the muster of the people as the Lord's army. The 'host of heaven' (*e.g.* 1 Ki. 22:19) consists of all superhuman beings, including stars (Jb. 38:7). As God's attendants these creatures are called 'messengers' or 'angels' (*e.g.* Gn. 32:2; *cf.* Ps. 103:20) or 'slaves' (*e.g.* Jb. 4:18). As associates of God they are 'holy ones' (Jb. 5:1). As supervisors of God's realm, such agents were later called 'watchers' (Dn. 4:13, 17, 23), active in the affairs of men, patrolling the earth (Zc. 1:10f.; 6:5f.) to observe and to protect. One of the great names of God – The Lord of hosts – probably means that He is the sole Creator of them all, leaving no room whatever for polytheism. Another name for these beings is *the sons of God* or, simply, 'gods' (Ps. 97:7) or 'spirits' (Zc. 6:5). When gathered in assembly they constitute 'the divine council' (Ps. 82:1) or 'the assembly of the holy ones' (Ps. 89:5) or 'the council of the holy ones' (Ps. 89:7). Since in Israel only the Lord received divine honours, His supremacy is never in doubt. He presided over the meeting like a king on his throne. The angel courtiers are seen surrounding Him when a man is granted a glimpse of His splendour (1 Ki. 22:19; Is. 6:1; Gn. 28:12).[1] The incomparable Lord has no colleagues; His attendants are shadows, scarcely persons. Even the pre-eminent 'angel of the Lord' remains a nameless functionary. Only later do Michael and Gabriel emerge with something like individuality. So minor is their role, so completely dominated by the incontestable sovereignty of the Lord, that no ideas of polytheism are present, even when they are called '(children of) god(s)'. Nor is there any hint in the Old Testament of an alien order of spirits or demons with a rival realm outside the Lord's dominion. Even the bright morning star (Is. 14:12, NEB) and the 'towering cherub' (Ezk. 28:14, NEB), despite their frightful power and the great disasters they have wreaked in the world by proud rebellion against God, are dismissed with contempt and disgust. And the terrible *Satan* is only another of *the sons of God*.

Most commentators assume that the Lord's court assembles in heaven.[2] There is nothing in Job about the location of the levy; for all we are told, it might have occurred on some mountain where the Lord has His headquarters (Dt. 33:2; Jdg. 5:4f.; Is. 14:13), an idea that is historicized at Sinai and Zion and eschatologized in other places (*e.g.* Is. 2:2–4). Isaiah saw 'the Lord of hosts' in the temple, and His glory filled the earth, not heaven (Is. 6:1–3).

The phrase *among them* has been interpreted as showing that the Satan was a regular member of the court. Indeed Driver and Gray (p. 11) argue that he is not only one of *the sons of God* but 'peculiar or preeminent in the class'. This is going too far. In many places the preposition *among* is used to refer to an intruder. It is because the Satan has no right to be there that he alone is asked his business.

It is hard to examine the role and character of the Satan in Job without thinking of the Devil that he became in later literature – the accuser in Zechariah, the Spirit of Perversity in the Dead Sea Scrolls, the tempter of the New Testament,

---

[1] Study of the wide recent literature on the divine council may begin with C. H. W. Brekelmans, 'The Saints of the Most High and Their Kingdom' (*OTS*, XIV, 1965, pp. 305–329).

[2] Jones, p. 24.

to say nothing of the fancies that gathered around him in later tradition. If he is still only the provoker of men, and not the opponent of God, we should not follow the commentators who see him here as simply another of God's loyal servants. His insolence shows a mind already twisted away from God, but his hostility is not on the scale of a rival power. There is evil here, but not dualism. The Satan may be the chief mischief-maker of the universe, but he is a mere creature, puny compared with the Lord. He can do only what God permits him to do. In the assembly he is more like a nuisance than an official. To compare him with the roving secret police of the Persian administration, who spied on the dis-affected and reported disloyalty to the king,[1] is conceding too much to him. He is not God's minister of prosecution; it is the Lord, not the Satan, who brings up the case of Job.

The contribution of the Satan to the action of the book is minor. His place in its theology is even less. In the subsequent discussions the misfortunes of men are never traced to a diabolical foe, and it is impossible to believe that the purpose of this tremendous book is to teach us an explanation of evil that Job and his friends never think of, namely that human suffering is caused by the Devil. The Satan does not appear again after Job 2:7.

7. The conversation is informal, in keeping with a popular tale. The Lord's first greeting is the same as Jacob's to the men of Haran (Gn. 29:4), and means little more than the commencement of conversation. On the lips of God the question does not betray a need for knowledge, but an invitation to state his business. The Satan's reply is non-committal. It attains the form of a poetic bicolon:

> 'From going to and fro on the earth,
> and from walking up and down on it.'

The evasive answer involves play on the verb *šûṭ*, 'rove'. This does not settle the derivation of 'Satan' but it nicely describes a restless, ubiquitous being, a vagabond among the angels (Mt. 13:25). Pope's translation is 'strolling', which is a bit too casual. We have rejected the idea that the Satan is one of the Lord's civil servants, sent out to bring back information about the world. Yet his journeyings are not

---

[1] Tur Sinai, pp. 38–45.

aimless; he 'prowls around like a roaring lion, seeking some one to devour' (1 Pet. 5:8).

8. The Lord's next question is in the form of a four-line poem. He speaks about Job with affection and pride. Although the word translated *servant* can mean 'slave', it is often used in the Old Testament as a title of honour, and only a favoured few have been called 'the Lord's Servant'.[1] In praising Job, the Lord repeats what has been said in verse 1. Righteous men are rare. It may be hard to find a few (Gn. 18:22–33) or even one (Je. 5:1) in a city. But it is possible; and when the Lord observes a good man, He is delighted (Is. 42:1).

9, 10. Cynicism is the essence of the satanic. The Satan believes nothing to be genuinely good – neither Job in his disinterested piety nor God in His disinterested generosity. Faith in God's goodness is the heart of love and hope and joy and all other radiant things: cynicism is studied disbelief; and a mind turned in upon its own malice is the final horror of the diabolical. The Satan asks his sneering question: *Does Job fear God for nought?* He knows enough about religious people to be persuaded that they are in it for what they can get out of it. Doubtless this is sometimes true. But 'worldly cares and the false glamour of wealth and all kinds of evil desire' (Mk. 4:19, NEB) soon deflect such people from God. The Satan knows how hurtful a taunt it is to remind God of such disappointments. His argument is clever. Job's godliness is artificial. It has never been proved by testing. And God is no better. He has made it easy for Job to be good. He has secured Job's devotion by bribery, and shielded him from harm. The repeated *thou* of verse 10 is an accusation. The *hedge* is a protective fence (*cf.* Ho. 2:6), but it could imply also that Job has been hemmed into a very limited experience of life. *His possessions have increased* uses a verb that pictures the livestock 'breaking out' in all directions. It is possible that God is the subject of all the verbs, as in LXX. Just as *miqneh*, *possessions*, refers to animals, so *the work of his hands* refers to farming (*cf.* Gn. 5:29). Job prospered in both agriculture and animal husbandry.

11. So the basic questions of the book are raised. God's character and Job's are both slighted. Is God so good that He can be loved for Himself, not just for His gifts? Can a man hold

[1] See C. Lindhagen, *The Servant Motif in the Old Testament* (1950) for its covenant associations.

on to God when there are no benefits attached? The Satan suggests a test to prove his point.[1] His language is abrupt; he commands God with imperative verbs: literally, 'But now, you just extend your hand and damage all his property.' The next clause begins with *'im*, 'if'; literally, 'if to your face (*i.e.*, openly, defiantly) he will bless (*i.e.*, curse – see commentary on 1:5) you.' It is the consequence, not the condition. Hence the conjunction is probably interrogative, and so assertative because the question is rhetorical: 'Won't he curse you?' That is, 'He is sure to curse you.' This conjunction is also used to state the condition of a vow with an oath, which becomes an auto-imprecation: 'I'll be damned if he doesn't curse you to your face!' The vernacular Hebrew, rendered literally in the AV, gives a flavour of mocking familiarity to the Satan's insolent speech. Like Goethe's Mephistopheles, he despises everything decent. With vulgar manners he refuses to use the conventional courtesies of court etiquette which avoided the personal pronouns by addressing a superior as 'my lord' instead of 'you' and using the deferential 'your slave' instead of 'I'. The Satan's 'thou' is thus insulting. Incidentally, this is further evidence that the Satan does not belong to the circle of God's respectful servants.

12. The Lord accepts the challenge. The Satan is given permission to do what he likes with all Job's property. But he must not touch Job's person. The Satan goes out, eager to get on with the mischief.

ii. The first disasters (1:13–19). 13. The scene changes to Job again. In swift succession four messengers come with news that his happy world has fallen in ruins. Since his children were feasting *in their eldest brother's house*, this was probably the beginning of the weekly cycle. Delitzsch aptly remarks (I, p. 60) that this would be the day when Job had offered sacrifices to ensure the favour of God. Nothing could have stunned him more than the arrival of such news just as he had made fresh peace with his Lord.

14. The same formula is used to describe each of the four calamities, as in a folk-story. The supreme disaster is when there is no survivor (Ex. 14:28). In the epic tradition one

---

[1] Many commentators speak of the arrangement as a wager (*e.g.* Hölscher, p. 2; Jones, p. 28). This goes beyond the text. There were no stakes, such as the soul of Job, as in later trivial imitations.

refugee, called '*the* fugitive' (Gn. 14:13; Ezk. 24:26), is needed to convey the tidings. Each fresh report falls like a weight into Job's mind. The farm animals (verses 13–15), the flocks (16), the camels (17), finally his children (18, 19) are lost.

As already noted in the Introduction, the actual speeches are in verse. Each has four lines, except that the last, the climax, has eight.[1] The identical last line of each is particularly impressive. There is artistic symmetry in the agencies; the violence of men alternates with the violence of nature. There is progression to the climax: Job's dearest are destroyed last. The effect is tremendous. It is more effective because everything is so natural. The hand of God is concealed; the hand of the Satan unsuspected.[2] Desert brigands, lightning and cyclone are all part of man's life in the East. Things like this happen to everyone, if not always on the same scale. The intense faith of Job immediately sees the hand of God in every 'natural' event. There are no 'accidents' in a universe ruled by the one sovereign Lord. Hence Job's problem. Such mishaps are not a problem for the polytheist, the dualist, the atheist, the naturalist, the fatalist, the materialist, the agnostic. An annoyance, a tragedy even, but not a problem. Suffering caused by human wickedness or by the forces of nature is ultimately a problem only for a believer in the one Creator who is both good and almighty; so this problem can arise only within the Bible with its distinctive moral monotheism.

15. *Sabeans* are located in two or three places in the Bible. Best known is the kingdom of Sheba in South Arabia, made famous by the queen who visited Solomon.[3] These people are known as traders, never as bandits, at least so far from home. In some texts Sheba is associated with Dedan, much nearer Israel; but this could be because their caravans came that way. If Job's home was in northern Transjordan (see commentary on 1:1) this would be even further away from the usual haunts of Sabeans. Captured bulls and donkeys could not be taken far into the desert.

---

[1] Pope (pp. 2f.) and Gordis (p. 235) recognize the poetry, but find five lines in the first, three in the second. By any method of scansion the lines are uneven in length.

[2] Needless to say, Job knows nothing of what has just transpired in the divine council.

[3] For extensive bibliography on what is now known about this country see A. G. Lundin, *Gosudarstvo mukarribov Saba'* (1971).

16. *The fire of God* is usually lightning (1 Ki. 18:38; 2 Ki. 1:10-14; Jb. 20:26), unless it is volcanic fall-out (Gn. 19:24). Something unusual would be needed to consume 7,000 sheep.

17. *Chaldeans* are known to have lived near the Tigris in the ninth century BC. They are of Aramean stock, and it is as hard to explain their marauding in southern Trans-jordan as it is to explain Sabeans in northern Transjordan. Job could have been within reach of both if he lived east of Galilee.

Three companies. Although the stratagem of a three-pronged attack is used several times in Scripture, the circumstances vary considerably. If Gideon's tactics were similar (Jdg. 7:16), the aim would be to drive the animals in a desired direction.

18. The repetitions used in the four reports support the reading of *'ôd, yet*, not MT *'ad* in this verse.

19. The *great wind* must have been a whirlwind of some kind, especially since only one residence was demolished. The home was clearly not a tent, but since a messenger had to bring the news, it is more likely that we have a house in the farmlands than in the town. This arrangement reminds us of Jair's apportionment of his estate to his thirty sons who resided in thirty settlements called 'towns' (Jdg. 10:4, NEB). The victims are called *the young people*, literally 'boys', the same term used to refer to 'the servants' killed in the preceding disasters. Perhaps here it includes Job's children, but more likely their death is implied by the circumstance that only the messenger survived.

iii. Job's first reaction (1:20-22). 20. Job's response was magnificent. His actions were deliberate and dignified, like David's (2 Sa. 12:20) and Hezekiah's (2 Ki. 19:1). Men of standing wore a *robe* over their tunic. It was ripped as a gesture of grief immediately on receiving bad news. Shaving the head was part of the mourning rituals in Mesopotamia and Canaan, often described in ancient texts. Because of its heathen associations it was actually forbidden by the Law, but it is often mentioned in the Old Testament. Since nothing wrong is seen in his action here, it is worth noting that Job does not resort to gashing his body in the way Israel's neighbours often did in bereavement. ... *and worshipped*. The language of Job is often laconic, *i.e.*, abbreviated idiomatic expressions are often used when the full meaning is clear. The object of this verb is clearly God.

21. Job's exclamation is the noblest expression to be found anywhere of a man's joyful acceptance of the will of God as his only good. A man may stand before God stripped of everything that life has given him, and still lack nothing. His essential being came into life naked from his mother's body, and in that second birth into another world which is death, he will pass in similar nakedness. The literal meaning of 'I shall return there' need not be pressed. The suggestion of some commentators that it refers to Mother Earth as man's origin and goal finds no support in Scripture. The thought is as general as Ecclesiastes 5:15 or 1 Timothy 6:7. A man comes from his mother and returns to dust. But *šāmmāh*, 'thither', could be a euphemism for Sheol, 'that place', as in Job 3:17, 19.

Job sees only the hand of God in these events. It never occurs to him to curse the desert brigands, to curse the frontier guards, to curse his own stupid servants, now lying dead for their watchlessness. All secondary causes vanish. It was the Lord who gave; it was the Lord who removed; and in the Lord alone must the explanation of these strange happenings be sought.

22. Job passed the first test. He did not *charge God with wrong*. The meaning of the Hebrew word *tiplāh* (which Job did not ascribe to God) has been often discussed, with no firm result. It probably does not refer to Job's manner of speech as 'foolish' (*cf.* AV). Moffatt says he did not 'give offence to God', but the text clearly means that he did not find the fault of *tiplāh* in God, as might have been expected. The nearest we can come to the root meaning is 'tastelessness' as in Job 6:6. But there is no proof that it has to do with spitting as a gesture of moral abhorrence.[1]

However this problem is solved, Job's attitude is clear. 'He did not sin in all this; he did not accuse God of anything monstrous.' Satan's jibe proved false. Job did not worship God for the side-effects of prosperity. He knew that 'a man's life does not consist in the abundance of his possessions' (Lk. 12:15). He knew what it meant to be simply a man with God. As naked as a baby or a corpse, he was himself – no

[1] See Driver–Gray (pp. 10f.) for an ample note.

more. He began life with nothing but himself; he will go out from life stripped of everything but what he has become. God has given him a rehearsal for death. All things belong to God, absolutely, to be given as gift, not claim, to be taken back without wrong. There is no talk of human 'rights'. The Lord is the sovereign owner of all, and Job rejoices in this wonderful fact.

Job's faith does not relieve his agony; it causes it. Job loved the Lord, his Father and Friend, as no Greek could ever love even the best of his gods, as no Babylonian, Canaanite or Egyptian could love any of their numerous gods.[1] Contrary to the Satan's forecast, Job has the same good opinion of God's blessedness, even when things go wrong. But this faith cannot survive without a terrible struggle. Because Job sees nothing but the Lord's hand in everything, how can he escape the horrible thought that God has done something bad? He knows no cause for such a wilful act. It is harder to say 'Praise the Lord' when He takes away than when He gives. Job is hurled into a cauldron of doubt concerning the justice and equity of God's ways with him. He must suffer and grow before he can see why this has happened. So far he has begun superbly. His confidence in God's blessedness goes beyond Eli's submissive resignation (1 Sa. 3:18), beyond David's (2 Sa. 16:11), for these are receiving the just deserts of their wrong actions. Job does not have the satisfaction of knowing that he is paying for his sins, for he has none. None, at least, deserving of punishments of such magnitude. What, then, is God doing to him that he can perceive to be good (Rom. 8:28)? The answer to this question will be found only when we reach the end of the story.

c. The second test (2:1-10)

The action moves into a second round. The same verbal formulae are used, with minor variations. Compare 1:6-12 with 2:1-4. The atmosphere becomes more tense.

i. The second assembly (2:1-7a). 3. This time, after repeating what He said about Job in the first meeting, the

---

[1] It is a fact easily verified by reading their religious literature that none of Israel's neighbours had 'Love God!' as their first law. We search in vain for expressions of grateful delight and joy in God; but in the Old Testament, especially the Psalms, such sentiments are abundant.

Lord adds that Job *still holds fast his integrity, although you moved me against him, to destroy him without cause.* Job's 'loyalty' (Moffatt) held. The Satan's efforts to discredit Job had failed. The translation of *waw*-consecutive by 'although' or the like secures a good sense, but it lacks grammatical support.[1] The second clause in verse 3b can be made the parallel (or consequence) of the first by translating, 'and so (you see) you have incited me against him to ruin him – all for nothing!' The last word, Hebrew *ḥinnām*, means 'unjustly' in Job 22:6; hence *without cause.* But there was a cause. The Lord did have a good reason for hurting Job, namely to disprove the Satan's slander. The word is translated 'for nought' in Job 1:9, where it means more literally 'gratuitously', with no motive of personal gain. But in Proverbs 1:17 the word means 'in vain', 'futile'. This suits here. The Satan's experiment was all for nothing.

4. *Skin for skin!* The slanderer is not dismayed. His cynical reply is ready: 'Skin for skin!' There is a riddle here. No-one knows the meaning of this cryptic proverb; commentators have made their guesses. The best clue is the remark which immediately follows, since this is doubtless an exposition or application of the byword. It suggests that Job's skin is being referred to. But the preposition translated *for* also causes trouble, and it should be given the same meaning in the two parallel statements. If a man will give all his possessions in exchange for his life, then the allusion is to trade by barter. Is 'A pelt in exchange for a pelt' a saying from the market-place where hides were sold? *Skin* then means 'leather'. But the exchange of one skin for another is not a likely commercial transaction. And Job has not been asked to relinquish his property in order to secure his life in return. Another suggestion is that there is a second skin beneath the outer skin. The Satan has accused the Lord of keeping a protective hedge around Job. Here he suggests that Job's wealth was like a shield or garment of leather over his human skin. He implies that Job was not hurt by these dreadful calamities because all he cared about was himself.

5. The first round was not a true test, because the adversary had not been permitted to hurt Job himself (1:12). Now the Satan dares the Lord to injure the inner skin, for the outer skin was only scratched by the loss of wealth and family. If

[1] NEB reverses the sequence of the two clauses.

Job's body, *his bone and his flesh*, feels the touch of God, he will show his real character by open vituperation of God Himself. The Satan has changed his ground. He had not asked for so much the first time. Then he had said it would be enough to lay waste Job's property to make him curse God (1:11). The Satan is unabashed by this first discomfiture, but Job's faith had proved tougher than he expected.

It is worth noting that, although the agents of Job's first misfortunes were natural forces and evil men, and the instigator was the Satan, from God's point of view it was He who had destroyed Job (verse 3). Next time also it will be necessary for God to *put forth* His *hand* (verse 5) to do Job further harm.

6. Once more it is the Satan who is the agent. He is given authority (lit. *hand*) to do what he pleases, short of killing Job, which, of course, would give Job no chance to prove his mettle.

ii. Job's illness (2:7b, 8). 7b. The continuity in the narrative at this point, in contrast to the break between 1:12 and 1:13, which suggests a lapse of time, shows the alacrity with which the Satan set about his gruesome experiment. Job is smitten with a horrible disease that covers his entire body. There has been much inconclusive speculation as to the identity of his complaint. The word *s̆eḥîn* is general. Tradition favours either leprosy (Lv. 13) or elephantiasis, for these exotic diseases had a fascination for Europeans who had never seen them. The simple story does not indulge in the exaggerated fantasies loved by tales and legends. The lack of detail prevents clinical diagnosis. In assessing the symptoms described by Job in the dialogue, we must remember the poetic medium. The brief data point to boils, ulcers, or one of the numerous diseases of the skin. Compare the allusion to skin in verse 4, and note that 'his bone and his flesh' refers simply to the physical body, so that the statement that his bones are aching or rotting(lit. 'pierced'; Jb. 30:17) may be no more than a description of acute and deep-seated pain. The Hebrew was more conscious of the bones as vital organs than we are. Some kind of acute dermatitis spreading everywhere and developing infections with darkened (Jb. 30:28) and peeling (30:30) skin and constantly erupting pustules (7:5b) would manifest the pruritus and purulence highlighted in 2:7. Other symptoms may be the results of complications in the wake of such a severe malady: anorexia, emaciation (19:20), fever (30:30b), fits of depression (7:16; 30:15f.), weeping (16:16a), sleeplessness (7:4), nightmares (7:14). These and other general sufferings, such as putrid breath (19:17; *cf.* 17:1), failing vision (16:16b), rotting teeth (19:20) and haggard looks (2:12) are less direct clues. They add up to a hideous picture of a man tortured by degrading disfigurement (Is. 52:14) and unendurable pain, a bleak reminder that a man is flesh, made out of soil from the ground.[1]

8. The miserable wretch *sat among the ashes* (*cf.* 2 Sa. 12:16). The reference is probably to the rubbish-dump outside the city, and could indicate that he was now an outcast, like a leper in the quarantine imposed by the taboos of Israel's public health regulations. But in that case his friends might not have had access to him. This self-abnegation was more likely his own sorrowful way of accepting his new status as a piece of human trash to be thrown out with other refuse 'in this place of discarded things'.[2] *To scrape himself.* He scratched himself with a bit of broken pottery. It is more likely that this was because of the itch, rather than lacerating himself in grief in the manner of El in the Ugaritic legend, who slashed himself with sticks and stones at the death of Baal. LXX adds the explanation that Job used the *potsherd* to scrape away the pus.

iii. Job's second reaction (2:9, 10). 9. At this point
the pattern of the first round is not followed. There Job immediately uttered his noble words of blessing. Here his *wife* enters the drama for the first time. No details of her character are given, so commentators have had to guess what kind of woman she was. The silence of MT has been made up for by traditions which have given her either a longer speech,[3] or spoken of her activity on his behalf. Christians have generally been much harder on her than Jews and Muslims. She was the Satan's ally. Augustine called her *diaboli adjutrix*, Chrysostom 'the Devil's best scourge', Calvin *organum Satani*. In this view she tempted her

---

[1] Jb. 7:5; see the commentary on Gn. 2:7 in E. A. Speiser *Genesis* (*AB*, 1964), p. 16.

[2] *NBCR*, p. 424a.

[3] The LXX expansion, a translation of which can be found in Pope (p. 22), represents her not unfavourably as sharing Job's misery, so that her motive in wishing him dead was to end his unendurable sufferings speedily.

husband to self-damnation by urging him to do exactly what
the Satan had predicted he would do. But this coincidence of
language is probably an irony of the author. The Satan's
temptation did not reach Job openly, so that its evil source
would be recognized; it came more subtly, through the solici-
tude of a loving wife. She pays tribute to his tenacious faith,
using the same words as God (2:3b). Her question could be
a taunt. 'Do you still insist on maintaining your integrity?
What good has it done you?' If so, she has already lost faith,
and wants Job to join her. At best her suggestion expresses a
sincere desire to see Job out of his misery, and the sooner the
better. She does not seem to see the possibility of the recovery
of health and restoration of wealth. The friends do, and
recommend repentance as the way to reverse Job's fortune.
She sees death as the only good remaining for Job. He should
pray to God (lit. 'bless') to be allowed to die, or even *curse
God* in order to die, an indirect way of committing suicide.[1]

10. Whatever lay behind her words, Job rejects them with
fury. But he does not call her 'wicked', merely *foolish*, that is,
lacking in discernment. She thinks God has treated Job badly,
and deserves a curse; Job finds nothing wrong with what has
happened to him. At this point Job's trial enters a new phase,
the most trying of all. Instead of helping, the words of his
wife and of his friends cause him more pain and put him
under more pressure than all the other things that have
happened to him so far. He never curses God, but all his
human relationships are broken. His attitude is the same as
before (1:21). It is equally right for God to give gifts and to
retrieve them (round one); it is equally right for God to send
good or *evil*[2] (round two). *Receive* is a good active word, implying co-operation with Providence, not mere submission.
Such positive faith is the magic stone that transmutes all to
gold; for when the bad as well as the good is received *at the
hand of God*, every experience of life becomes an occasion of

[1] It must be admitted that we cannot tell just what she is proposing, and
even less what her motive was. If the distraught woman could no longer
endure the sight of her patient, tormented husband, and for love's sake
would rather death end his misery, then her desperate remedy may be
pardoned. The simple sequence, *Curse God, and die*, could mean 'Curse God
before you die', that is, while there is still time. She wants God cursed
more than she wants (even if it means) her husband's death.

[2] The Hebrew word refers to anything 'bad', and does not imply any
wickedness in God who sends such calamities (*cf.* Is. 45:7; Am. 3:6).

blessing. But the cost is high. It is easier to lower your view of God than to raise your faith to such a height. We shall watch the struggle as Job's faith is strained every way by temptations to see the cause of his misfortune in something less than God.

Job did not sin. Again the Satan's predictions do not come true. Some rabbis, splitting verbal hairs, inferred that, because he *did not sin with his lips,* only his speech was blameless; his thoughts had already begun to waver. Rashi, following the Talmud,[1] said, 'But in his heart he sinned.' This is a specious distinction, and takes sides with Job's friends in condemning him for insincerity; and it contradicts the text. For God says twice, 'My servant Job has spoken correctly about me' (see 42:7, 8). The Lord would hardly have said that if Job's heart were wrong. If Job felt differently from the way he spoke, he did sin with his lips. Job's religion was more than outward propriety. He knew that to curse God in one's mind was a grievous sin (1:5). If Job's fine words were not honest and from the heart, the Satan had already corrupted him. Nor can we concede that later on Job weakened, and fell into sinful speech. However impious and shocking some of the statements he makes during the dialogue may seem to us, his transgression of the conventional bounds of decorous religious talk might incur the disapprobation of cautiously reverent men, but the only censure they receive from God is that Job obscured the divine purpose by talking in ignorance (38:2).

d. The arrival of Job's friends (2:11–13)

11. The previous basis of the friendship is not explained. Job, as the leading person in his own country, was evidently an international figure, and his friends came from three different countries. But this does not justify the tradition that they were kings. Teman is a place associated with Edom (Je. 49:7, 20; Ezk. 25:13; Am. 1:12; Ob. 8, 9); and *Eliphaz* is an Edomite name (Gn. 36:11, 15), and that Eliphaz had a 'son' (eponym?) Teman (Gn. 36:11; *cf.* Gn. 36:42). Teman has, however, been linked also with the Tema in Arabia.[2] The linguistic affinities of the name *Bildad,* let alone its meaning, have not been settled, although such a name is known from

---

[1] *Baba Bathra,* 17b.

[2] W. F. Albright, 'The Name of Bildad the Shuhite', *AJSL,* XLIV, 1927–28, pp. 31–36.

Nuzi.[1] But there is a plausible identification of his home with a place on the Middle Euphrates, mentioned in cuneiform texts, and connected in Genesis 25:2 with a son of Abraham. The name *Zophar* is not known outside Job.[2] A land or tribe of Naamah is not known; the Judean town mentioned in Joshua 15:41 hardly qualifies.

Including Job, the homes of the four speakers cannot be identified with certainty. But this does not mean that they are imaginary places. The same applies to Elihu (Jb. 32:2). Nor is there any point in looking for clues to their characters or theological positions in the symbolism of their names. They evidently lived in neighbouring regions. The fact that they met by *appointment* shows that they were already acquaintances who felt it would be better to come *together*. There is no reason to doubt that they were genuine friends, and that their motives for coming *to condole with him and comfort him* were sincere. Their subsequent behaviour shows sympathy for Job's plight, and we must suppose that the words they utter later, however undiscerning and at times tactless, had the same intention.

12. *They did not recognize him.* Since they were still some distance off, this does not mean that they thought he was someone else; they could already see how different he now looked from the person they had last met. *Cf.* Isaiah 52:14; 53:3. The conventional gestures of grief, ripping the outer garment and flinging dust into the air so that it fell on the head,[3] accompanied by wailing, need be no less heartfelt because they followed etiquette.

13. The same applies to their joining him *on the ground*. This would not have been possible if Job had been an outcast in the technical sense. If Job were a leper, such an act of identification would be matched only by the compassion of Jesus (Mk. 1:41). *Seven days* was the statutory period of mourning for the dead; but it would be too literal to infer

[1] Although both elements are attested in Amorite personal names, the name itself is not, and the first syllable is most likely a loan from Akkadian.

[2] In view of the frequent archaic spellings in the Balaam story (Nu. 22–24), the name of Balak's father might have been Zophar, with 'Bird' as a later misunderstanding.

[3] Some commentators find a contradiction between throwing dust *upon their heads* and *toward heaven*, and accept the reading of LXX by omitting the latter as an addition. Pope (p. 25) suggests that it expresses frenzied disdain, but such a sentiment would be quite out of place at this stage.

that the three considered Job as good as dead. Ezekiel sat down stunned for seven days when he met the exiles (Ezk. 3:15). Here there is a similar reason: *they saw that his suffering was very great.*

Attention is focused, not on the abstract mystery of evil, not on the moral question of undeserved suffering, but on one man's physical existence in bodily pain. There was nothing to be said. These wise men are horrified and speechless. They were true friends, bringing to Job's lonely ash-heap the compassion of a silent presence.

II. DISCUSSION BETWEEN JOB AND HIS FRIENDS (3:1 – 27:23)

In the present arrangement of the MT there are at least seventeen speeches in this section, nine by Job, three by Eliphaz, three by Bildad and two by Zophar. The number could be increased by recovering a supposedly lost speech by Zophar from the material in the third round (see Stage 6 in section VII of the Introduction). We have not included chapters 28 or 29–31 in Job's tally, but chapter 27 is introduced as a distinct speech, concluding the discussion with the friends and making ten in all.

It is hard to know what to call this section. 'Discussion' makes it sound as if some scholars are talking about a problem, and some commentators (*e.g.* Jones) speak of each person's 'contribution' as if the main interest of the book lay in ideas or possible solutions to the academic question of suffering. To call it a 'debate' suggests something more argumentative, but this also conveys the wrong impression of an intellectual exercise. The talk reported here is not a philosophical symposium; Job's dunghill is not an improvised Wisdom school. The speeches are too long to be called conversation, or even dialogue. There is not enough connection between them to enable the argument to be traced through logically. In this, and in the poetic form, the artificial arrangement is most obvious. Each speech is a complete piece, whose inner completeness enables a whole lot of ideas to be thrown forward. This is typical of the technique of 'contest' literature, a form of debate in which the prize is awarded to the person who develops the best case by making the best speech. The speeches are judged by their inherent quality and cleverness, not by their effectiveness in refuting an opponent.

An audience is implied. The speakers are not trying to convince one another, even when they address each other. This is why it is often hard to find the connection between one speech and the next. This is why it is hard to trace progress in the discovery of the truth as the argument advances. This is why it is hard to ascribe a consistent and well-defined 'position' to each of the four speakers, although broad characterizations have been attempted.[1] There is no use of formal logic to test the validity of the assertions made. The seemingly undirected discussion is truer to life, in spite of the formal artistry pointed out above, than the studious pursuit of a theme by characters who are merely the author's puppets. The speeches are often emotional, and sometimes resort to personalities. We cannot often find in one speech a direct reply to the one immediately before, making one a clue to the other. Commentators are not agreed as to how the argument moves – whether Job speaks first and his friends reply in turn,[2] or whether each of Job's speeches is a response to what the friend has just said.[3] The texture of the discourse does not lend itself to such fine analysis, although it is always worth while looking for connections between succeeding speeches, as if each person is responding in some way, if only partially or indirectly, to what has just been said.[4]

There is one important respect in which Job's speeches differ from those of his friends. It strengthens the impression that there is not much meeting of minds in this clash of words. They talk to Job about God. Job too talks about God, and sometimes he addresses them. Here it is in order to look for something like a debate. But much of Job's utterance is in an entirely different direction. Job is not arguing a point; he is trying to understand his experience. Hence he often talks to

[1] Attempts to find in each of the friends a distinct religious 'type', even to the point of caricature, have not yielded consistent results. Their outlooks overlap in various ways. They are too human to be stereotypes.

[2] Elihu's assessment (32:2–5) implies that the friends had tried to refute Job. *Cf.* W. E. Hulme, *Dialogue in Despair* (1968).

[3] Jones, pp. 74–96.

[4] It would be going too far to divide each speech into two, the first part a response to what has just been said, the second a development of new material to which the next person replies. The speeches of Job, however, which are longer as well as more numerous than the others, occasionally lend themselves to such an analysis.

himself, struggling in his own mind. He is also trying to retain (or recover) his lost friendship with God. Hence he appeals to God again and again. His prayers may shock his religious friends, but at least he keeps on talking to the heedless God. His friends talk about God. Job talks to God. And this makes him the only authentic theologian in the book.

Attention to this feature of the Job speeches is essential for an understanding of the book as a whole. God's eventual endorsement of Job's stand does not mean that every theological statement he makes is correct, or that what his friends say is wrong. The matter is not as simple as that. It is hard to find any proposition in the book which is not to some extent correct, taken in isolation. The book is not a polemic against any 'theory'. Some of Job's prayers are wild, and must have seemed dangerous to his dignified friends. His audacious attempts to reach the mind of God leave us breathless, and must have worried his cautious friends. He is passionate; they are cold. Job is dreadfully in earnest, and transparently honest. He tells God exactly how he feels and just what he thinks. There could hardly be better prayers than that.

Another general feature of Job's speeches cannot be emphasized too strongly. Scholars who find his volcanic outbursts in the dialogue utterly different from his tranquillity in the prologue[1] overlook the fact that nowhere does Job bewail the losses of chapter 1 nor the illness of chapter 2. In this he is utterly consistent. His concern from beginning to end is God; not his wealth or health, but his life with God. It is because he seems to have lost God that he is in such torment. This vivid consciousness does not remove the particulars of his human life – his work and his family and his body – from the scene as having nothing to do with God. Nothing could be more alien to his thought, and to Israelite religion in general, than to isolate the relationship with God as the only thing of value for a man, rendering him indifferent to poverty, callous in bereavement, heedless of pain. On the contrary, the relationship with God is known in and by means of these ordinary things. Without them Job does not only lose his humanity; he loses God. Already we are prepared for an answer that comes, not when God (alone) confronts Job (alone), but when God is found in His world (the Yahweh

[1] See the Introduction (pp. 42ff.) for the use of this alleged contrast to assign the prose and the poetry to two different sources.

speeches) and when Job finds himself once more surrounded by animals and friends and family.

a. Job's lamentation (3:1–26)

In the first speech the spectacle of human misery is presented with a poignancy that is quite overwhelming. Job is stunned because he cannot deny that it is the Lord who has done all this to him. Even more piteous than his question 'Why?', which the best answers of his friends cannot satisfy, is his desperate need to find again his lost Friend. Under these conditions, the friends can hardly be blamed, even though their well-meaning efforts aggravate Job's troubles more than they calm him (16:2). For only the Lord Himself, in the end, can heal Job's innermost mind. It is not that He answers the questions better than the friends; He does not seem to answer them at all. But after He has spoken, Job has altogether left behind the questions.

1. It is Job who breaks the long silence (*cf.* 2:13). He has had time to brood over his heart-break. He is horrified, crushed by the unbearable weight of sorrow. His grief is intensified because life had promised, given, so much. He is not philosophizing about man's universal condition, although the extension is easy to make, and what he says any sufferer can apply to himself. His present state threatens to cancel his belief in the goodness of God in making him a man. God's best handiwork, capable of so much; Job himself, the best of all and God's own pride (Job does not know this), industrious, noble, devout, the paragon of the world, now sitting in the dirt, his past lost, his future empty, his present pain. Or, if he thinks of the future, all it offers is death, welcomed as the release from present despair, but abhorred as the final mockery of a futile life. In such a mind, a woman or a child may weep. It is fitting for a man to curse. *Job opened his mouth and cursed.*[1] It is important to note that Job did not curse God. In the beginning the Lord had cursed the miserable conditions that followed on the sin of our first parents. God did not curse man, and Job does not curse himself. He *cursed the day of his birth* (lit. 'his day'), echoing God's own execration. He does not yet question God, let alone reproach Him. That will

---

[1] That Job's first speech is already passionate shows that his exasperation cannot be blamed solely on the provocation of his friends, as Hölscher maintains (p. 4).

come later. He does not ask why the Lord sends storm and crime to lay waste a man's achievement. He is not curious to find out why the undeserving suffer, that is, to find a convincing explanation in God. Even if his friends can bring irrefutable answers to such questions, the facts that appal him would still remain. How wretched human existence can be! So wretched that it would be better to end life quickly, and best never to have existed at all. So Job complains. He curses his birth (verses 3–10), he longs for death (11–19), he deplores life (20–23) and ends with a moan (24–26).

It cannot be emphasized too strongly that the startling sentiments expressed in this speech do not mean that Job has cracked under the strain. There is no hint that the Satan has finally made his point. The bourgeois etiquette that has dominated the *mores* of western Christendom, especially in the Puritan tradition, is no guide to the rightness of Job's speech. Self-control is something quite different from not showing one's emotions. Job is no Stoic, striving to be pure mind with no feeling. The Bible knows nothing of such dehumanizing philosophy; but we stand in a long tradition of a pallid piety that has confused the Christian way[1] with the noble but heathen ethic of the Stoa. Further perversions were fostered by various kinds of gnosticism and manicheism, until Christian perfection is defined as the triumph of reason over passion,[2] sometimes masquerading under the Pauline terms 'spirit' and 'flesh'. Its prescription for the afflicted is torpid resignation to the unquestionable will of God, a strict curb on all feelings, or at least on the outward expression of them, with disapproval of the weakling majority who cannot walk calmly in the furnace with 'tranquillity undisturbed

[1] The history of interpretation of that fruit of the Spirit generally translated 'self-control' (Gal. 5:23) is very instructive in this regard. From that self-mastery that releases the energies of an athlete into a superb performance (1 Cor. 9:25) it withers to a purely negative suppression of desire, especially condemning the gratification of bodily needs so that sexual continence, for instance, becomes in itself a great virtue.

[2] One need only refer to the reiterated theme of William Law's *Serious Call to a Devout and Holy Life*. Here is a typical passage: 'The Religion of the Gospel is only the refinement, and exaltation of our best faculties, as it only requires a life of the highest Reason, as it only requires us to use this world as in reason it ought to be used, to live in such *tempers* as are the glory of intelligent beings . . .' (*Editio princeps*, 1729, p. 75). Commentators trained in such piety could only conclude that Job was a great sinner for being so emotional.

by the fierce fires of passion'.[1] It is little wonder that this tradition has not taken Job as its patron saint and has found James's reference to his 'patience'[2] incredible, and his over-mastering sorrow,[3] his outburst of anger, unspiritual. But Job is a man bereaved, humiliated, and in pain. His skin is festering and his nerves are on fire. A man of stone or bronze (Jb. 6:12) might remain unmoved, but a real man is all turbulence. The Lord's testing is not to find out if Job can sit unmoved like a piece of wood.

2. Job's lamentation belongs with other biblical psalms of grief, including Jeremiah 20:14–18 and Lamentations 3:1–18; and all are gathered up into that horrifying dereliction of Jesus (Mt. 27:46) as the true cries of lost humanity, trying to find its lost God. There can therefore be no question of disapproving what Job says. Form-criticism also helps us to understand the conventional purpose of this kind of speech. Though in the form of a lurid curse, elaborate and exaggerated, it is intended to bewail a man's misery and so to evoke human and divine pity.[4] The poetry catches the wild cries. The ejaculations are taut and the grammar is difficult, almost to the point of incoherence. Translators spoil the art by making it smooth. These features, which present themselves as difficulties to the purist, probably preserve the intentional effects of the author, and are not to be blamed on later deterioration in the text.

3. In the first lines of the poem we are already in the thick of such difficulties. Items in poetic parallelism do not match. The indefinite *day* (translators have supplied the article) corresponds to definite *the night*. The verbs change

---

[1] Froude in a letter to Carlyle.

[2] Jas. 5:11, AV. The word really refers to the active virtue of endurance, of steadfast persistence. *Cf.* NEB.

[3] The example of Jesus (Mk. 14:34) should for ever silence all criticisms of Job, for His tears (the Logos took a human body in order to weep with it) make it true – *res est sacra miser*. The deep hold that the virtue of the 'stiff upper lip' has taken in Anglo-Saxon standards of propriety (especially for men) can be traced to the impact of Cicero and others on Renaissance man. See, for example, de Montaigne's essay *On Sadness*. In our day the press continues to applaud public figures who are stoical in bereavement. Job's friends show a limited capacity to 'weep with those who weep' (Rom. 12:15), and our embarrassment in the presence of mourners betrays a similar failure all too often.

[4] For a similar motive in Babylonian intercessions see J. Nougayrol, 'Une version ancienne du "Juste Souffrant" ', *RB*, LIX, 1952, pp. 239–250.

their forms: *I was born* (imperfect) and *is conceived* (perfect) both refer to past time.[1] Most problems of this kind can be solved without emending the text, but the technical discussions needed to vindicate the result would be out of place in a commentary of this kind. The word *said* is the greatest difficulty in the verse. It is not likely that *the night* is personified to speak and 'to bear witness to what happened in it',[2] or 'to report of it to the High One'.[3] *Cf.* RV, RSV, *AB*. It is not easy to take the verb as impersonal (AV). Harsher remedies, such as changing *said* to 'when', have no textual support. Poetic balance would be improved by omitting this troublesome word altogether. Then 'the day (when) I was born' and 'the night (when) I was conceived (as) a male' would match more closely, and the lines would be more nearly equal in length. But it would be a mistake in critical method to allow prejudice about poetic synonyms in parallel to make the two lines as similar as possible. We still have to reckon with the illogical sequence of birth before conception. Since the sex of the child is known only at birth, the word 'male', which makes the second line that much longer than the first, probably goes equally with both. Comparison with Jeremiah 20:15 suggests that *said* refers to the announcement of the birth to the father, the climax of the delivery. Jeremiah curses the man who did this. It is not likely that the conception was independently announced. It was precisely the birth of a boy that made Jeremiah's father's heart glad. But Job views his own birthday as a disaster.

4. The parallelism of *day* and *night* is continued, with more expansion at each stage. *That day* is cursed in verses 4 and 5; *that night* is cursed in verses 6 to 10. One should not be too pedantic in separating the night of conception from the day of birth. Night and day together constitute the twenty-four-hour period, for which Hebrew has no special word. Job is talking about the beginning of his life in general terms. The curse of the day consists of two tricolons, and nothing is gained by trimming them to simpler two-line units, as many commentators have done. The six lines, in fact, form a well-

---

[1] The Hebrew tense system is not so loose that such variations can be put down merely to 'style' (Hölscher, p. 14). Job's *'iuwālēd* is a genuine archaism, in contrast to Jeremiah's classical (and apparently more 'correct') *yullaḏtî* (Je. 20:14).

[2] Driver–Gray, p. 31.

[3] Delitzsch, I, p. 77.

wrought pattern, since the first line introduces the whole, and the last line rounds it off.[1] The general idea is clear. Since divine interest gives existence to times and seasons, Job wishes that God had not thought of that particular day, or that somehow it had remained in darkness.

5. That day properly belongs to darkness, so *let . . . darkness claim it*, by redemption from alien hands, retrieving it for its own (RV) because they are akin. The Hebrew root *g'l*, found also in Job 19:25, means 'redeem'. AV 'stain it' is based on a late meaning 'defile', and this interpretation has been revived in NEB 'sully'. The choice is a matter for continued debate among commentators. Aubrey R. Johnson has made another suggestion, translating 'cover', with the possible meaning of 'protect' rather than 'defile'.[2] A more serious problem is presented by the last line of verse 5, because it is not known whether the word *kmryry* means 'bitter' or 'black'.

6. Job expresses similar wishes concerning the night. It, too, is to be smothered by darkness and, indeed, obliterated from the calendar. NEB has spoilt the flow of the poem by translating the jussives as imperatives. The more literal RSV is much to be preferred (it is still favoured by Rowley[3]), although its *rejoice* as well as AV 'joined' should both be given up. Dahood has frequently drawn attention to the use of the same parallelism in Genesis 49:6 and has adduced comparative evidence for the meaning 'be seen'.[4]

7. The meaning of the Hebrew word *galmûd*, translated *barren* (RSV), seems to be 'stony', and it is used quite literally in Job 15:34. A stone uterus would be a good picture of a sterile woman, who does not receive seed the way good soil does.[5] If so, Job is repeating the thought of verse 3. But

---

[1] The verbal tapestry is clearer in the Hebrew. The repeated 'not' in the second and third lines of verse 4 binds them together as an exposition of the first line. The first two lines of verse 5 are closely parallel, leaving the last line as the climax. All six lines are unified by verbal signals. Note the repeated *upon it*. The first and sixth lines match to some extent, and the strophe opens and closes with the word *day*. The integrity of the text is abundantly attested by rhetorical devices of this kind, but space precludes all but a few illustrations.

[2] 'The Primary Meaning of *g'l*', *SVT*, I, 1953, pp. 67-77.

[3] Rowley, p. 44.

[4] The bibliography is conveniently assembled in Anton C. M. Blommerde, *Northwest Semitic Grammar and Job*, p. 38.

[5] At verse 10 below we shall raise the question of whether the uterus is shut against sperm, or closed to stop the baby from coming out.

it is the night that is said to be stony, and the next line contrasts this with the *joyful cry*, suggesting that the unproductivity of the night is the silence of inactivity. But it should be remembered that it is not the night as such that is damned, but the birth events that transpired in it.

8. Since Gunkel first proposed in 1895 that *ym*, 'sea', be read for *day*,[1] the steady accumulation of supportive evidence has gradually won over more scholars, so that now NEB translates 'those whose magic binds even the monster of the deep'. This is probably going too far in remythologizing old Canaanite ideas which in Israelite literature have become merely decorative imagery. There can be no doubt that *Leviathan* is the chaos dragon of the ancient myths, and the parallelism is strongly in favour of the new reading.[2] The difficulty of verse 8b remains, however. Parallelism helps to some extent, suggesting the use of dark powers to manipulate celestial phenomena, so that the old chaos dragon will bring on an eclipse.[3] The meaning of the word translated *skilled* ('ready', NEB) is not clear. The same applies to *rouse* ('tame', NEB). Somewhere in this language there is a connection between the destructive forces held in check by God's power in creation and Job's desire that his birthday at least be claimed once more by chaos. We do not need to go beyond this to uncover resort to magicians or conjuration by prayer.

9. Just as Job wishes that the sun had never risen on the day of his birth and never set on the night of his conception, now he says, *Let the stars of its dawn be dark*. The full verse describes the three phases of daybreak, carefully distinguished in Hebrew vocabulary. It begins with the failing of the last stars of night (verse 9a). The word *light* (verse 9b) refers here specifically to the sun, whose rising (which makes morning) is to be forestalled by prohibiting even the pre-dawn twilight (verse 9c), called vividly 'the eyelashes of Shahar',[4] the

---

[1] H. Gunkel, *Schöpfung und Chaos in Urzeit und Endzeit* (1895), p. 59.

[2] Rowley (p. 44) lists authorities on both sides. Dhorme (p. 29) and Driver–Gray (p. 34) argue well for 'day'. The orthographic studies of D. N. Freedman (*EI*, IX, pp. 35–44) supply an additional (and methodologically independent) support for *ym*; for, influenced by the frequency of the word *ywm* in the passage, *ywm* would be an innocent modernization, made all the more acceptable by the general obscurity of the verse.

[3] So earlier commentators, especially Delitzsch. *Cf*. Jb. 26:13.

[4] The use of this name of the Canaanite god of dawn is purely poetic, without taint of polytheism.

corona of the still-hidden sun. This evocative image matches Homer's celebrated love for the hues of the new day; but for Job the soft beauty of the sunrise mocks the ugliness it makes visible.

10. This verse completes the damning of Job's birthday. The provision of *it* could mean that the night did not shut out the fertilizing seed, or that the day did not close in the foetus. But in the Old Testament it is God (only God) who shuts or opens a woman's womb, and 'God' is best identified as the implied subject here. The use of the dual *doors* (as again in 38:8) points picturesquely to the labia rather than the uterus, without settling the question of whether they are to be opened for impregnation or delivery. The translation *of my mother's womb* (RSV), or the paraphrase 'of the womb that bore me' (NEB), loses the brevity which in Hebrew is simply 'my belly'. The suffix, apparently 'my', could be an old genitive ending, and by referring to 'the double doors of the abdomen' Job could be expressing the wish that his mother had remained a virgin (*cf.* Ct. 4:12). The resolution of this question probably lies in verse 10b which, in current translations, does not have much parallelism with verse 10a. *Nor hide trouble from my eyes* is a completely different idea, as if Job is now talking about the wearisomeness of life in general. But trouble that is seen by the eyes is too external to describe Job's complaint about his own burdensome lot. The word describes toil and the suffering it occasions, so a reference to the agonizing exertions of childbirth would fit the context here quite well. Instead of reading *mē-'ēynāy*, some form of *mē'ayim* can be recognized. We now have parallelism, for this word means the paunch or outer belly, matching *beṭen*, the inner belly.[1]

Everything now falls into place. That the negative refers to both lines of the verse has long been acknowledged. Job wishes he had remained safely behind the locked doors of the body by the prevention of labour.[2] If the primary reference is to birth rather than conception, verse 10 rounds off the talk about *that day*, completing verses 4 and 5, while

[1] The word is a synonym of 'womb' in Ru. 1:11, and has the same kind of poetic parallelism with *beṭen* in Gn. 25:23.

[2] *Cf.* Moffatt: 'close the womb on me'; Dhorme: 'seal the doors of the womb in which I lay'. These don't quite catch the nuance of not letting the womb open. The idiom used in Gn. 20:18 for closing the womb to prevent conception is used in Is. 66:9 for preventing childbirth. We suggest that a careful study of the LXX will support our result.

verses 6 to 9 deal with *that night*. But, by whatever means of expression, Job wishes that he had never been born.

11. At this point Job's speech changes from cursing to questioning. There is a progression of thought. He wishes he had not been conceived; or, if conceived, that he had died in the womb; or, if not that, that he had not been born; or, if born, that he had died at once; or, since he has grown to maturity, that he might die soon.[1] The literal AV and RV 'from the womb' have been replaced in RSV by *at birth*. It is possible that the preposition *min* is locative meaning 'in', and many translations, including LXX, support this. We have, then, the thought of death either before or after birth.[2] But the synonymous parallelism achieved in RSV is demanded by the matching pairs 'from the uterus' . . . 'from the belly' and 'die' . . . 'expire'. The wholeness of the verse is seen once it is recognized that 'why' and 'not', found in the first line, belong to both lines, and that 'I came out', found in the second line, also belongs to both lines. Great brevity is achieved as a result of this poetic trick, and a full translation becomes rather overweighted in English:

'Why did I not (come out) from the womb (and) die;
(Why did I not) come out from the belly and expire?'

12. Genesis 50:23 suggests that verse 12a is the father's acceptance of the newborn; but a reference to 'my mother's knees' (NEB), as in Isaiah 66:12, makes all of verse 12 describe the first acts of nursing.

13. If Job had died, by whatever means, he would have been better off; not because death offers compensations or joys; simply because it ends life's miseries.

Death is an important theme in the book of Job. As we have already seen in section x of the Introduction, the doctrine of rewards and punishments in the next world is not found in Job as an answer to the moral problem of the unequal fortunes of the present life. Job does not hope that death will rectify the injustice of his undeserved sufferings. It will be enough that it ends them. In the theology of this book, judgment is not postponed to the afterlife. It is only

---

[1] The same thought recurs in Jb. 10:18ff.
[2] Dahood's ingenious reading of a passive participle leads to the translation 'enwombed', with the same general result. See *Biblica*, XLIV, 1963, pp. 204f.

in a negative sense that the turbulence of life abates (verse 13) and the inequalities of life become irrelevant (14–19). In spite of the vagueness with which the living conditions of Sheol are described, the continuation of conscious personal existence and identity after death is clearly believed. The book knows nothing about the heaven of bliss or the hell of torment in later eschatology, but there is never a thought that death means extinction. In fact, Job provides a long list of the denizens of Sheol, ranging from those who had achieved the highest eminence (kings and others, verse 14) to those who had achieved nothing (the stillborn, verse 16).[1] He envies them all, for nothing happens in the grave.

14. The social inequalities are evened up in the grave. This is summed up in verse 19, which says that the small and the great, the slave and his master are now all alike. Two lists of representatives of the two ends of the scale are given, with nice symmetry. There seem to be four categories in each list: *kings, counsellors*, builders, *princes* (or rich) in verses 14 and 15; the wicked, the over-worked, criminals, the exploited in verses 17 and 18. This grouping makes it clear that verse 16 is in its proper place in the middle, while verse 19 sums up the whole by bringing both classes together.

The meaning of verse 14b has never been clarified, in spite of numerous attempts. Kings do not build *ruins for themselves*, and, although *bnh* sometimes means *rebuild* as 'build', such works are not as memorable as original constructions. *Ruins* does not just mean something old, like a pyramid, so a reference to tombs, although it fits the general context of death, is unlikely. Just as the *princes* (verse 15) cannot take their wealth to Sheol, so the buildings of kings, now in ruins, mock their worldly splendour, since in death they are no different from slaves.[2]

15. Similar considerations suggest that the *houses* of *princes* stored with *gold* and *silver* are not their tombs, in which treasures are buried, but their opulent homes which are of no value to them in Sheol.

---

[1] This is only one of several good reasons for leaving verse 16 in its present position, instead of moving it around as has become fashionable in modern translations (JB, NEB, NAB).

[2] It is worth pointing out how utterly different this Israelite view of death as the same for all men is from the Egyptian belief that only the Pharaoh, or at most the nobles, had any prospect in the next world. It carries the reflex that already in this life all men are equal.

17. Sheol is the place of rest and relief (verse 13). Even *the wicked*, far from receiving their long overdue punishment, find repose. It is less likely that he means that they are now prevented *from troubling* others. The same word is used at the end of verse 26 to describe Job's present 'agitation'. It implies that *the wicked* live in a state of emotional disturbance which happily ends for them in death. We are already near the bitter thought that being good or bad makes no difference in the end.

18. Since it is *ease*, not liberty, that the *prisoners* find in Sheol, they are not people in gaol, but captives brutalized by forced labour. So probably only one class, not two, is referred to in this verse.

19. As we have already said, this verse rounds off the list. The adjectives 'little' and 'big' can refer to size, age, status or wealth. See the commentary on 1:3, where 'great' means 'rich'. NEB 'high and low' contrasts social level; RSV *the small and the great* is less specific, but retains the chiastic pattern that unifies verses 14-19:

A   Privileged (verses 14-15)
B   Underprivileged (verses 17-18)
B' 'small'/'slave'
A' 'great'/'master'

The usual translation of verse 19b, illustrated by RSV *and the slave is free from his master*, is not altogether satisfactory, since the trend of the entire passage is that all social distinctions disappear in Sheol, not that *the slave* becomes a freedman there. The exact technical meaning of *ḥopšî* is a distinct problem, discussed at length in larger commentaries. It would seem that *slave, free* and *master* (not necessarily a slave-owner, but a land-owning citizen) represent three strata in society, all of which disappear after death.[1]

20. So far Job has found life intolerable (verses 3-10) and death desirable (verses 11-19). Now he strikes deeper into the problem by asking *why* any of this should happen at

[1] For grammatical arguments pointing in a similar direction, see A. C. M. Blommerde, *Northwest Semitic Grammar and Job*, p. 39. But many loose ends remain. The singular 'he' is a worry, when plural is expected. Waw-explicativum, which marks apposition, is harder to believe than simple co-ordination of the second colon. Why should only one noun in the list have enclitic *mem*? And the singular pronoun *his* does not fit if *master* (=*great*) contrasts with *slave* and *free* (=*small*).

all. *Light* and *life* are similar, since the realm of death is a dark place. Why should the result of God's good gift of life be that those who have it wish to be rid of it?[1]

21. They *long for death*. Yet suicide as a means for attaining it is never contemplated. Death also must be God's gift, and for Job now, this has become the only possible evidence of His goodness.

22. The words used here to describe the exultation of the dead, *when they find the grave*, are very vigorous. *Gîl* describes the abandoned joyfulness of the dance, but some scholars have used the parallelism to find another word for tomb, assisted by Arabic cognates.[2]

23. This verse repeats the thought of verse 20, completing the strophe. The incompleteness of the Hebrew is smoothed over by RSV, which repeats *Why is light given* from verse 20. But the connection is correctly perceived. The words are even more bitter, for there is an ironical echo of what the Satan had said in 1:10. The Satan saw God's *hedge* as a protection; Job finds it a restriction. He feels trapped.

24. The last three verses of Job's speech are so unintelligible in the Hebrew original that translators have had to take various liberties to secure reasonable English. The words *sighing* and *groanings* are not strong enough. The latter describes the roaring of lions, and reading *km-ym* instead of *k-mym*, which requires no change in the text, yields a more powerful simile: 'my bellowings cascade like the sea.' The apparent reference to *my bread* in the preceding line has defeated all commentators, unless 'my flesh'[3] affords a clue. *Sighing* is too feeble a sound to express Job's tragic sorrow. The impression is given that groans come from his whole body.

25. Job had not been complacent in his prosperity; he

---

[1] Although translations agree in making *him that is in misery* and its parallel *the bitter in soul* the indirect objects of the verb *given*, this makes sense only if it means, 'Why does God keep on giving light and life to such persons, instead of letting them die, as they would prefer?' But the enquiry is more fundamental. Why is life given at all, since it results only in exhaustion (see comment on *trouble* – the same word – at verse 10) and disillusionment (the bitterness describes someone who has nothing to live for, especially a desolate widow). The preposition thus points to the outcome of the gift, not the recipient.

[2] Rowley, p. 48.

[3] *Cf.* Pope, p. 51 (on Jb. 6:7).

took precautions against forfeiting God's favour (1:5). Yet calamity struck just the same. Comparison of RSV (*fear*) and NEB ('haunted') illustrates the difficulty of the verb tenses. The AV is preferable. The very thing he had dreaded, namely the loss of God's favour, has happened to him, and he has no idea why.

26. The last verse has four sharp clauses, each of which stabs like a knife:

> 'I cannot relax!
> And I cannot settle!
> And I cannot rest!
> And agitation keeps coming back!'

b. First round of speeches (4:1 – 14:22)

i. Eliphaz (4:1 – 5:27).[1] **1.** The sympathetic silence of the friends is now broken by sympathetic speech. Job's desperate words, although not addressed to the friends, demand some comment. Eliphaz ventures a reply that is tactful in its manner and unobjectionable in its matter. He does not yet charge Job openly with any fault, but already there is a note of gentle disapproval, if not reproof, in his words.

2. He begins politely. Without entering too far into the thorny grammatical questions which divide the commentators, we can accept RSV as near enough to the general idea.[2]

We should call attention immediately to a feature in the construction of Eliphaz's speech which will be met several times in other parts of the book. In the over-all structure of his discourse, which is a single piece, we should not look for the introduction of a theme at the beginning, its development along a straight line of thought with the proof at the end, followed, if necessary, by the practical application to Job's need. Such logical neatness is not found. Instead there is a

---

[1] See K. Fullerton, 'Double Entendre in the First Speech of Eliphaz', *JBL*, XLVIII, 1929, pp. 320–374.

[2] The problem lies in the introduction of conditional *if*, not found in the Hebrew. The question *will you be offended?* supposes that the interrogator is separated from the verb by three words, a strain on grammar even beyond the elasticity of poetry. The parallelism suggests that Eliphaz is dubious about speaking at all, not about Job's reaction, even though he cannot refrain himself. This is in keeping with his courteous, almost decorous manner. We suggest: 'Should one venture to speak to you while you are so upset? But no-one could withhold words (under the circumstances).'

symmetrical introverted structure with the basis of the argument in the centre, and with theoretical development before and after it. The advice that emerges from this doctrine is embodied in two balancing blocks, which, although separated in space, constitute the sum of Eliphaz's exhortation.

A   Opening remark (4:2)
    B   Exhortation (4:3–6)
        C   God's dealings with men (4:7–11)
            D   The revelation of truth (4:12–21)
        C'   God's dealings with men (5:1–16)
    B'   Exhortation (5:17–26)
A'   Closing remark (5:27)

The portions arranged in this way are not all of equal size, not even the matching pairs. Nor is all the material uniform in literary character. The author has assembled smaller poems of familiar types. Thus 5:9–16 is a celebration of the greatness of God which lists His characteristic acts in a credal hymn that could be used in a liturgical setting and of which the Old Testament affords several other examples. It is fruitless to ask whether the author borrowed, adapted or imitated such a composition. It is enough to observe both its distinctiveness and also its harmonious incorporation into the larger speech.

3, 4. Eliphaz begins with a pleasing tribute to Job's reputation, especially his ability to help others in their difficulties.[1] *Instructed* is the technical term for 'education' used in Wisdom circles for training for life through discipline.

5. Already there is the insinuation that Job is unable to apply to himself what he preached to others. The words *impatient* and *dismayed* have been given a physical interpretation by Moffatt ('you droop', 'you collapse'), but emotional distress would be less excusable. Pope translates 'aghast' to describe Job's state of shock. Since the author has not told us what tone Eliphaz used in making these remarks, commentators have found them smug, sarcastic, hypocritical. I would prefer to give Eliphaz the benefit of the doubt, and find his words, not a taunt, but a kindly reminder that Job's past life of godliness has given him resources for the present crisis.

6. *Fear of God*, the standard term for wholesome piety ('religion' is Moffatt's translation), is Job's hallmark (1:1,

[1] See Job's own account of this in chapter 29.

8, 9, *etc.*).[1] Its necessary consequence, *integrity* of conduct,[2] based on the same root as the word that describes Job in 1:1; 2:9, completes the character of the godly man. It should provide Job with a basis for *confidence* and *hope*. Eliphaz is far from accusing Job of sin. He endorses his faith, and tries to revive his spirit with the reminder that Job's whole life had been built on the belief that God helps the good and hinders the bad.

This is the teaching that all the friends will affirm in one way or another. It is also Job's belief. They cannot say anything else without suggesting that moral effort is not worth while or that God is somehow unfair. But a terrible pitfall is not far away from all of them. The friends must infer from Job's suffering that he has sinned; Job must infer from his innocence that God is unjust.

7. Eliphaz's question, which implies a universal rule, precipitates the issue. By using the extreme words *perished* and *cut off*, he implies that Job, as a righteous man, can count on speedy relief. He is not so naïve as to pretend that the righteous never have trouble. As he will say at the end of his speech (5:17–26), the Lord delivers the righteous from their troubles.

8. But Eliphaz goes too far. It is one thing to appeal to an abstract principle which seems self-evident to the mind of a man with moral sense. It is quite another to apply it to Job's particular case. Eliphaz claims that he has never observed an exception to the rule: 'You reap what you sow.' Like the psalmist who could say so complacently, 'I have been young, and now am old; yet I have not seen the righteous forsaken or his children begging bread' (Ps. 37:25), Eliphaz deserves the retort, 'You haven't seen much!'[3] The doctrine

---

[1] The Hebrew is literally 'your fear'; but 'your fear of God' is meant. While this reflects the grammatical difficulty of attaching two possessives to one noun, it is worth emphasizing that the abundant use of such laconic expressions in Job gives its language a high concentration of meaning, but also frequently leaves translators baffled.

[2] The Old Testament often uses the word 'paths' (*ways*) to describe ethical habits.

[3] Since Ps. 34, which is a joyful expression of the same confidence, is quoted with approval in 1 Pet. 3:10–12, this teaching holds its place as a promise of the gospel. This commonplace of the Old Testament (Pr. 22:8; Is. 3:10f.; Ho. 8:7; 10:13) is repeated bluntly by Jesus: 'The measure you give will be the measure you get' (Mk. 4:24; *cf.* Gal. 6:7). Paul is equally emphatic: 'There will be tribulation and distress for every human

is not based on observed events. Job's case does not fit it. His faith must now sail through a storm of contradicting fact.[1]

9–11. What Eliphaz's argument lacks in substance he makes up for with rhetoric. He illustrates his point with an elaborate figure.[2] Beasts of prey may terrify the world unchecked for a time; but the angry *breath of God* easily destroys them.

12. How does Eliphaz know this? He has appealed to experience. But, as if suspecting that his position is vulnerable, he falls back on a claim to more immediate knowledge of divine mysteries. He came to understand the fate of the wicked as the result of a dream revelation. Unlike the classical prophets, who heard the Word of the Lord with all their faculties alert, Eliphaz's experience is more like that of Balaam (Nu. 24:15f.). The author has succeeded in creating a very spooky atmosphere.

13, 14. There is no need to call Eliphaz a mystic; nor is there any need to question his sincerity by saying that his claims are spurious. The *deep sleep* is the same as that of Adam (Gn. 2:21), Abraham (Gn. 15:12) and Saul (1 Sa. 26:12) – all induced by God – and the words are heard, not in an artificial trance, but during a dream. The word translated *thoughts* occurs only here and in Job 20:2, and suggests the agitation in the presence of the supernatural which is described in a rather conventional way in verse 14.

15. The description of the dream vision is evocative rather than photographic. There was a definite *form* (verse 16), but it was indescribable. The *spirit* is a distinct being who talks; yet with the ambiguity of Hebrew, in which the

being who does evil, . . . but glory and honour and peace for every one who does good. . . . For God shows no partiality' (Rom. 2:9–11).
[1] Paul makes clear what Job gropes after. This faith will be broken by life, unless it is held eschatologically, in hope; for 'the harvest is the close of the age' (Mt. 13:39), and Eliphaz's truth will be seen only 'on that day when . . . God judges the secrets of men by Christ Jesus' (Rom. 2:16).
[2] If the metaphor in which the wicked are wild animals destroyed by God seems overdone (there are no fewer than five different words for 'lion' used here – for their specific meanings, see the larger commentaries and also M. Dahood, *Psalms II*, *AB* 17, p. 61), and mixed with the metaphor of sowing and reaping, this is no reason to reject it as an inferior later addition. On the contrary it gives Eliphaz's words that touch of pomposity that betrays his limits as a counsellor.

word means also 'wind', it is not clear whether this is just 'a cold breath of air' (Rowley, p. 34), which ruffled *the hair of my flesh*, or whether an intelligent phantasm, the Spirit of God Himself, made his hair bristle with fright.[1]

16. The eerie effect is continued by describing a visible shape which cannot be discerned, and an audible *voice* which was *silence*. It is better to preserve this dream atmosphere, which gives the report a ring of authenticity, rather than make it clearer, but more prosaic, by speaking of a dimly-perceived shape, and silence followed by speech. (Dreamers can be aware of hearing speech which they know is not sound.)

17. After such a build-up, we expect to hear a revelation, not a truism. The literal translation of the Hebrew, used by AV and RV, is the question:

'Shall mortal man be more just than God?
Shall a man be more pure than his Maker?'

The thing is so obviously impossible, that the banality makes Eliphaz sound pretentious. And quite unfair; for Job has not questioned the ways of God, let alone claimed to be better than God. All he has done so far is to say how miserable he feels, how he wishes he were dead. Eliphaz is reading a lot into this to find implied criticism of God. The only fault he has seen in Job is weakness (4:5). Hence RSV has softened the question into a more general theological problem: 'Can a man be pure before his Maker?'[2] It is a question of fact. The implied answer is, 'No!' The question of 'how' a man can be right with God is not raised.

18. It is not clear how far the text of the dream oracle extends. It could be restricted to the bicolon in verse 17, so that verses 18–21 are Eliphaz's exposition. Translators generally continue the quotation to the end of the chapter. Eliphaz is following a path of truth that will lead him into a great error. This is why it is impossible for Job to refute him; he must admit the premise, but contradict the conclusion. The difference between God and all His creatures is immense,

---

[1] It is one of several grammatical difficulties in the Hebrew of this verse that the word for *wind*, which is commonly feminine, has apparently a masculine verb. By using *it* and *its* in verse 16, RSV has obscured the important fact that the Hebrew '*he* stood' and '*his* appearance' continue the masculine gender. To my mind this proves that it is the Spirit of God, and not the wind.

[2] NEB has reverted to 'more righteous . . . purer'.

infinite. The author's monotheistic belief has moved radically from the polytheism whose vocabulary he still uses. Far above men are God's *servants* (lit. 'slaves'), *angels* (lit. 'messengers'), 'saints' (5:1, AV; lit. 'holy ones'). In contrast to fragile humans, who dwell in houses of clay (verse 19),[1] these superior spirits seem so close to God, yet they are so inferior to Him that He does not entrust His secrets to them. The fact that the verb in verse 18a means 'believe' does not mean that the angels are 'fallen' and so are liars. It is rather that these majestic beings cannot be relied on; God Himself performs His own essential tasks. The meaning of the word translated *error* in verse 18b, which occurs only here, is quite unknown, and has occasioned much guess-work and emendation.

19–21. The same applies to the apparent reference to *the moth*,[2] which has evoked some fantastic suggestions. Not a few scholars have deleted the line altogether. The recent attempt to penetrate the secret of verse 19b by Blommerde[3] arrives at the result 'would then they . . . be pure before their Maker', with Job 15:15f. and 25:5f. as supporting passages. Since this proposal involves many technicalities, we must leave it to the test of time.

The general idea, however, is clear. Eliphaz could be using a string of disparate similes, loved by Wisdom teachers, to drive home man's frailty. The reference to *the moth* might then remain, since there is evidence that the preposition translated *before* can sometimes mean 'like', and the following remark about a person being *destroyed between morning and evening* would apply aptly to an ephemeral insect.

Eliphaz's final image of man's precarious existence is that he is like a tent held up by a single rope. The effect is dismal in the extreme. *They perish for ever without any regarding it* (20b),[4] *they . . . die . . . without wisdom* (21b).

The last recorded statement of Job's friends is that man is a

---

[1] If this refers to the human body, made from soil (Gn. 2:7, *etc.*), it is an image without parallel in the Old Testament, which never speaks of the body as a person's residence (contrast 2 Cor. 5:1). The parallel 'foundation . . . in the dust' points to humble dwellings made of mud.

[2] The unintelligible RSV *crushed before the moth* has at least the virtue of being literal.

[3] A. C. M. Blommerde, *Northwest Semitic Grammar and Job*, p. 42.

[4] Eliphaz's well-meant exaltation of God has led to a horrible result. If He cannot be bothered even with angels, how much less would He care about men.

maggot (Jb. 25:6). Job is prepared to agree. 'God is not a man, like I am,' he says (9:32). But how different the inferences! The gulf between Job and his friends is already opening up. Job's position is more audacious, more believing, than Eliphaz's insipid insinuations. It is precisely God's enormous advantage over men, in their fragility, that makes His treatment of them seem so unfair. God is so great that it is not necessary to put man down in order to protect God from competition. God does not have to preserve the mystery of His being by concealing His secrets from men. The friends are right to appeal to the incomprehensibility of God. But they take a perilous step which Job refuses to follow. From the irresistibility of His omnipotence they infer that His justice is equally remote from man's ideas.[1] Job knows only too well that he is merely a creature. But a creature of such a God cannot be a 'mere' creature. He will not be silenced by reminders that it is not for puny man to question the ways of the Almighty. His questions may be unanswerable, but he will ask them, insist on his right to ask them. His questions arise from what he knows about God. His response to the question in 4:17 will be: 'It is essential for a man to be right with God; it is essential for a man to be in agreement with God about what is right; it is essential for a man to receive from God an assurance that what God does is right, right by human standards; it is essential for a man to receive from God an affirmation that the man is in the right, right by God's standards.' See Job 27:2–6.

5:1, 2. Viewed in this light, Eliphaz's next word is a terrible blow to Job. He says that it is futile to *call* out in prayer, for no-one will answer. This is not a general statement, for Eliphaz himself has just claimed to be the receiver of a private revelation. It is Job himself who is disqualified. Eliphaz seems have concluded that by his *vexation* and *jealousy* (verse 2) Job has become a fool. He has despised 'the chastening of the Almighty' (5:17). Later Eliphaz will prescribe the frame of mind in which Job might hopefully pray. Job is equally ineligible for the mediatorial services of *holy ones*.

The idea of a go-between who might help a man to make contact with God or conduct negotiations between them is

---

[1] As Jones puts it (p. 70) in reference to Elihu: 'God cannot be a criminal because he cannot be caught.'

an important one in Job. Job himself sees the need for a Mediator with increasing clarity. The idea is not new. Near-eastern lamentations of the kind discussed in section IV of the Introduction were customarily addressed to the sufferer's personal god, a minor deity, who would then present his case in the divine council.[1] Eliphaz's rejection of this route to God in verse 1b sounds like good Israelite polemic against such polytheism. But a barren result of this trend was to isolate God from all possible contact with His creatures, and a new mythology had to be invented later on to fill the vast empty space with the angels of later Jewish thought. Since their creaturehood was not in doubt, they were no threat to monotheism.[2]

Job can only grope after the need he recognizes, and could hardly have guessed the incredible solution that would, in due time, be supplied; namely, the incarnation of God Himself in the man Jesus, the 'one mediator between God and men' (1 Tim. 2:5).[3]

3. There is a balance between the sketch of the misfortunes of *the fool* (the technical term shows that we have here a typical piece of 'Wisdom' teaching) in verses 3–7 and the benefits of 'the chastening of the Almighty' (5:17) received by his opposite number, the wise man, as described in verses 17–26.[4] *The fool* may seem to flourish for a while, but suddenly his fortune will be reversed. Verse 3b suggests that the curse of a good man, like Eliphaz,[5] can secure the downfall of the

---

[1] *Cf.* Wolfram von Soden, *ZDMG*, LXXXIX, 1935, pp. 143–169.

[2] It is an interesting question in the history of ideas how much the recognition of angels as distinct individuals represents the emergence from the underground of popular superstition of the old discredited gods. The archaic names of the archangels are particularly suspicious in this regard.

[3] It is not in a spirit of criticism, but simply as an acknowledgment of the great difference between Jewish and Christian faith at this point, that we quote the following: 'Between God and man stands no one – not God-man, not angel, not advocate. Nor is intercession or intervention required' (Milton Steinberg, *Basic Judaism* (1947), p. 57). 'In sum, there is and can be no vicarious salvation. Each man must redeem his own soul' (*ibid.*, p. 58). These are extraordinary statements in view of the teaching of the Old Testament that the Lord is Israel's Redeemer, or even that the great prophets were effective intercessors.

[4] This important counterpoise, contrasting the two opposite ways of life open to every man, has not been shown in the broader scheme on page 111, above.

[5] Here his vanity, his self-complacency, to say nothing of a certain lack of pity, spoils his otherwise kindly pastoral word. To insist too strongly on the

unworthy. The action of cursing *his dwelling* has caused commentators much perplexity.[1] It complicates the picture if the judgment of God or the natural growth of trouble out of sin has to be activated by a prayer. But the same combination of God's will, natural processes and human intercession is found everywhere in the Bible.

Special interest attaches to the word translated *dwelling*. It is a pastoral term, describing grazing-lands. Some Arabic usage suggests the goal of the nomad's trek, for grazing or camping.[2] That the word already meant 'encampment' in the Middle Bronze Age is attested at Mari,[3] but, through its collective meaning, it embraces the entire region to which the shepherd has grazing rights, and hence comes to mean his domain.[4] This more comprehensive meaning suits the wide coverage of the disasters described in verses 4–7. Furthermore, the man who illustrates Eliphaz's point is not a shepherd, but a farmer.

4. Later, Job will object to the doctrine that a man's sins are visited upon his children (21:19f.). Instead of *gate*, we should probably read 'tempest', and see in this verse a rather cruel reference to Job 1:19.[5] *There is no one to deliver them* is a frequent indication that an event was an act of God which no-one could prevent.

justice of God's rewards for the godly will make it harder to find room for mercy towards the wicked. Here again the Old Testament is heading into a problem (a problem for God!) which only the imputed righteousness of Jesus will solve.

[1] Rowley (p. 58) has a long list of attempts to dispose of it.

[2] In view of Hebraists' long reliance on this cognate, the proposal of Guillaume (p. 81) to use *nawhun* to yield the translation 'his shoots rotted' should be treated with great reserve. It requires overwhelming arguments to introduce a completely new root into Hebrew when a well-attested word yields good sense.

[3] D. O. Edzard, 'Altbabylonisch *nawûm*', *ZA*, XIX, 1959, pp. 168–173.

[4] This semantic shift has occurred in Hebrew by the Late Bronze Age, for this is the meaning of the word in Ex. 15:13, where the parallel in verse 17 shows that it describes the covenant land as the Lord's estate. It is only under the influence of a later Zion theology that the Lord's 'mountain (collective)-heritage' contracts to the single holy mountain of Jerusalem, and *nāweh* acquires the specialized meaning of 'shrine'. In later Hebrew it is secularized to mean 'habitation'. NEB 'home' should therefore be replaced by 'estate' in the most general sense.

[5] Instead of *šaʿar* read *śaʿar*, which needs a change in only one dot. The word for 'storm' has both masculine and feminine forms, although the former is usually spelt with *s* not *š*, while the latter is spelt with either.

5. The meaning of this verse is less clear. While it could mean that the rich man's family are reduced to beggary (*cf.* Ps. 37:25), most translations give an impression of the ruination of his crops by pilferers.

6, 7. These verses imply that man's troubles are innate and inevitable. In Genesis 3:17–19, man's worries, by divine decree, come from his struggle with a hostile or intractable environment. Eliphaz seems to deny this, hinting at another source. In the following poem (verses 9–16) he ascribes such experiences to God, so, although a divine agent is not named in verses 3–7, he is probably insinuating that the Lord is the hidden cause of the fool's troubles, even though they are so universal that they might appear to be natural (verse 7).

The apparent fatalism of verse 7 has disturbed commentators, and some who have been unable to rewrite it to fit the context better have simply expunged it. If the familiar simile *as the sparks* (the Hebrew is literally 'the sons of Resheph') *fly upward* simply describes something that happens unavoidably all the time, then Eliphaz has given up the attempt at a moral explanation, and offers dismal comfort to any sufferer. We cannot hope for further progress until we can find out who 'the sons of Resheph' are. Since Resheph is a Canaanite god about whom we now know a great deal,[1] the possibility must now be faced that we have here another scrap of imagery from the old myths, rather than the more prosaic 'sparks' or 'birds'. In weighing this question, more attention needs to be given to the fact that the verb describes height as tallness, not as distance above the ground. Hence man's arrogance could be in mind, even though the last word suggests the flight of birds.[2]

8. So far Eliphaz's teaching has been rather gloomy. Now he tries to strike a more cheerful note. Faith in God delivers from pessimism. English translations such as RSV and NEB ('For my part') do not bring out the contrast in the Hebrew *'ûlām*, 'but', which gives to Eliphaz's words a distant, judgmental tone. The invitation to pray is couched in legal terms. To *seek God* is a deliberate act, not just leaving his

[1] The search for information on this deity can conveniently begin with the frequent references in W. F. Albright, *Yahweh and the Gods of Canaan* (1968).
[2] C. F. Fensham, 'Winged Gods and Goddesses in the Ugaritic Tablets', *Oriens Antiquus*, V, 1966, pp. 157–164.

cause to God, but submitting (lit. 'I present') his case. The advice is a little fatuous, for there is nothing that Job desires more than this.

9–16. This credal hymn is one of the most beautiful examples of this genre in the Bible and also one of the clearest passages in the book of Job, so that no comment is needed. Many individual lines have parallels in other parts of the Old Testament. The poem recites the attributes of God by describing His activities in participle phrases. The present tense implies that these are His characteristic and continual deeds. No distinction is made between creation and redemption. God has absolute power over nature (verses 9f.); He is supreme in the affairs of men (verses 11–15). The rain (verse 10) is an apt example of the innumerable and incomprehensible activities of God; for it can be used to destroy or to sustain man. Already in the Flood this element killed and saved. Its ambivalent use will be expounded with terrific power in the Yahweh speeches.[1] It is thus a fitting illustration of the destructive and beneficial acts of God, all of which inspire confidence in His justice. The strophe in verses 11–15 arranges the three bicolons, which say how God thwarts the clever and unscrupulous (12–14), inside the two which describe the encouragement of the disheartened (11) and the rescue of the destitute (15).[2]

15. RSV *fatherless*, NEB 'destitute', *etc.*, are based on emendations which have no textual support. MT is literally 'and he saves from a sword from their mouth' (*cf.* RV and RVmg.). Most scholars have tried to make this more intelligible. An obvious lack is a parallel to *needy* in the next colon; hence 'orphan' has won wide acceptance. But the many alternatives proposed[3] show that the problem is far from resolved. We suggest that the best clue is afforded by the phrase translated

---

[1] For the background ideas see Philippe Reymond, 'L'eau, sa vie et sa signification dans l'Ancien Testament', *SVT*, VI, 1958; Otto Kaiser, 'Die Mythische Bedeutung des Meeres in Ägypten, Ugarit und Israel', *BZAW*, LXXVIII, 1962; Jill L. Manton, *A Study of the Significance of Water in Biblical Literature* (unpublished M.A. dissertation, Melbourne, 1972).

[2] The pattern is a little more complicated than that. Each aspect receives three verses. Verse 14 sums up verses 12 and 13; verse 16 sums up verses 11 and 15.

[3] The combined inventories of Dhorme (p. 66), Fohrer (p. 133) and Rowley (p. 63) offer a dozen different solutions to choose from.

the hand of the mighty. In spite of the apparently masculine form of the adjective,[1] a reference to God's powerful hand (not the wicked) fits the emphasis on salvation. Scholars have been misled by the search for neat bicolons. The missing parallel to *needy* (15b) is supplied by *poor* (16a), while verses 15a and 16b are brought into parallel by the common word *mouth.* In any case, the affirmation is nicely rounded off: wrongs are redressed, *injustice* is silenced.

17–26. The fifth[2] poem in Eliphaz's miscellany sings of the happiness of the man who takes the troubles of life in the right spirit.

17. When disaster hits the godly man, he recognizes this as part of God's training, and so can rejoice in adversity. This is a new idea to cover the case that was not included in the simplistic classification of verses 11–16, where the wicked are confounded and the good are helped. Neither applies to Job. He is a good man confounded, not helped. The teaching that such experiences are *chastening* (*mûsār*) was the staple curriculum of the Wisdom schools.[3] Eliphaz began his speech by addressing Job personally. In the middle part he lectures. Now, by switching back to the second person, he comes nearer to preaching. His words are good, and doubtless Job had said the same thing to depressed souls many times (4:3, 4). Troubles are tests; the person who realizes this responds creatively. The rebellious only make more trouble for themselves by resentment (*cf.* 5:2).

For the book of Job, this poem is remarkably well preserved. It is a beautiful tribute to the fatherly care of God, strict but kind. His apparent severity in sending sickness (verse 18), setbacks (19), famine and war (20), fire and flood (21), plagues and wild beasts (22) – there is not the slightest doubt that all these natural things come immediately from His sovereign hand – is more than outweighed by His goodness in sending remedies for all these disasters. At least that is

---

[1] This is easily explained if we read either of the nouns *ḥōzeq* or *ḥēzeq* to make a phrase equivalent to *ḥōzeq yād* of the Exodus.

[2] According to the scheme on p. 111. But see footnote 4 on p. 117 which recognizes Jb. 5:3–7 as a matching strophe.

[3] *Cf.* Ps. 94:12; Pr. 3:11, AV, RV; Heb. 12:5. It is also the best suggestion that Elihu can make (Jb. 36:10) and the nearest that any of them can come to a 'solution' to Job's problem. That it is not the solution is shown by its complete absence from the Yahweh speeches.

how it will work out for the trustful man who is not impatient[1] of *the chastening of the Almighty*.

23-26. The pleasing sketch of a wise man's life, not free from troubles, but, much better, transforming difficulties into nurture in blessedness,[2] lists in verses 23-26 the acts of God which counteract the problems in verses 18-22, but in inverse sequence (introversion).

23. God will control the wild animals of verse 22. Parallelism suggests that *the stones of the field* are untamed beasts.[3] Pope has a fascinating note on his interpretation of the phrase as 'field sprites'.[4]

24. His home and stock will be preserved from the fire and flood of verse 21. The literal translation *tent* gives the wrong impression that Job is a simple shepherd, not a sophisticated townsman, as in chapter 29. This old word, like its parallel *fold* (the same word *nāweh* as used in Jb. 5:3; see the comment there), has acquired new connotations with urbanization.[5] Comparison with Ezekiel 14:21 suggests that the evil threatened in our verse 21, described literally as 'tongue' and 'devastation', is pestilence. The point is, then,

---

[1] The verb translated *despise* means 'refuse', because the value of the outcome is not appreciated, through lack of wisdom rather than from contempt for God.

[2] The word *happy* (17) – an exclamation: 'Oh, the happinesses of the man . . .' – is another technical term of the Wisdom schools, corresponding to the beatitudes of Jesus.

[3] There is no need to touch the text, for, as Blommerde (p. 45) has suggested, *'abnê* is *bᵉne* with prosthetic aleph. The analogies he quotes include instances long known, as well as new examples. But other Old Testament instances of *'eben/'abnê* as a biform of *ben/bᵉnê* make his 'perhaps' a certainty, in my opinion. Thus in Gn. 49:24 the inexplicable 'stone' becomes 'the shepherd of *the sons of* Israel'; in Is. 14:19 'the sons (not *stones*) of the Pit' are the denizens of Sheol; in Ezk. 28:14, 16 'the sons (not *stones*) of fire' are the effulgent residents of God's holy cosmic mountain land.

[4] Pope, p. 46.

[5] The cognate in Akkadian becomes the common word for 'city' (*CAD*, Vol. 1, A Part I, pp. 379-390). The whole of this entry repays careful study, especially section 3, for the historical semantics show remarkable analogies with *nāweh* as already discussed. Associations with 'community' and hence 'estate' in either the pastoral or agricultural sense persist, and in some texts, especially legal ones, are used very precisely to mean 'property'. The detailed study of E. A. Menabde (*Khettskoye obshchestvo*, 1965) has shown that similar usage developed in Hittite society. The collocation of the same root with *qhl* in Sabaean, where 'tent' means 'tribe', gives support to our point from another quarter.

that neither his family (*tent*) nor his estate as a whole[1] will show any diminution when it comes to the annual stock-taking.[2] In view of what has already happened to Job's family and property, Eliphaz's bumbling cant infuriates Job, and understandably so. It is only a wooden criticism that misses this bitter twist in the speech, and sees only the formal contradiction between this sketch and the information in chapter 1, to be resolved by assigning the passages to two different sources. It is precisely the reader's knowledge of the situation that makes Eliphaz's recital of homely wisdom truths, which everyone has heard before, sound so horrible.

25. In the same way, the promise of numerous *descendants* can hardly comfort a person who has just been rendered childless. (The cause in Jb. 1:19 is not the same as that in 5:20-22.)

26. Finally Job himself is promised life in good health to a ripe old age, a fitting end for one who loved and feared God. This is what God Himself has promised to those who obey Him in the covenant blessings proclaimed by Moses (Lv. 26:3-13; Dt. 28:1-14). Eliphaz's comparison of an old man's contented death with the harvesting of grain in full ripeness adds beauty to the truth of his teaching.

27. He speaks for all Wisdom scholars; hence his use of *we*. He is quite confident that what he says *is true*. Now it is for Job to give heed and to experience it for himself (27b).[3]

It is hard to find anything wrong with Eliphaz's theology. Delitzsch rightly says: 'The skill of the poet is proved by the difficulty which the expositor has in detecting that which is false in the speech of Eliphaz.'[4] Where is the defect? Why does the Lord say to Eliphaz in the end (42:7) – He singles him out from the others – 'my anger flares up against you . . . because what you say about me isn't correct'?

Eliphaz's fault is not that his doctrine is unsound; it is his ineptness as a counsellor. True words may be thin medicine

---

[1] Job was both a crop-farmer and a grazier, as chapter 1 shows. Hence *tent* and *fold* cover all aspects of his domestic and economic life.

[2] The word *inspect* implies something formal and official by way of accounting. NEB 'you will look round your home' implies something altogether too casual.

[3] Rhetorically the emphatic 'and thou', which is lost by the translations, balances and contrasts with 'but I' in verse 8. This *inclusio* brackets 5:8-27 as a unit.

[4] Delitzsch, I, p. 109.

for a man in the depths. It is not that Job is at present rationally inaccessible, to be treated as a neurotic. His depression is legitimate and wholesome. The reality that God has given him is poverty and sickness. It is not a return to truth to deflect his mind to a promise of health, while he is scratching himself on his ash-heap; to promise him wealth, while the brigands make off with his animals; to give him dreams of numerous descendants, while his children lie crushed by the fallen stones. Eliphaz has done his best, with the best of the old theology. But the author of Job is about to take giant new strides into a vaster, but more mysterious, understanding of God. By binding God to certain rules, Eliphaz safeguards His morality. But to bring God under obligation to a morality beyond His will is a threat to His sovereignty, especially when it is a man who thinks he knows what that morality should be.[1]

Job believes that God, as Sovereign, may give or retrieve His gifts at His pleasure (1:21b); He may send good or bad (2:10b). He is not accountable to any man for such actions. Eliphaz thinks he knows how to get along with a predictable (and that means, to some extent, manageable) God. Job, who has no such pretensions, faces the agony of getting along with a God over whom he has absolutely no control or even influence. Eliphaz's speech, with which Job has no quarrel as a general statement of the power and justice of God, is beside the mark, because it simply does not fit Job's case. Job had long since learnt to view his good life as a gift, not a reward, so he has no complaint when it is removed. He has submitted no petition for its restoration. Even in the end that will not come as an answer to prayer. Hence he does not want from Eliphaz the soothing word that if he would only do this or that, everything could be restored to 'normal'. As if Job 1:1–5 defined the norm! The affirmations which Job has so magnificently made in 1:21 and 2:10 lead him into a new task. He must normalize, find the rightness of, his relationship with God as it is 'now' (6:3). His lament in chapter 3 marks his entry upon that assignment. To find consolation in the thought that his afflictions will be brief, that soon all will be as it used to be (5:17–26), would deflect

---

[1] For a penetrating analysis of this problem see Lev Shestov, *Potestas Clavium* (English translation by Bernard Martin, 1968).

him from this necessary and immediate task. Unless we see this, we shall not appreciate the vehemence of the outburst that instantly follows in Job's next speech.

The reader knows, and Job believes, that what has happened is not punishment for some past sin. If there is a grain of truth in Eliphaz's teaching about 'the chastening of the Almighty' (5:17), it is not in the negative sense of training so that a person is restrained from potential sin. Job had long since attained perfection in this stage of character development (1:1, 8; 2:3). The reader knows what Job does not know, namely that Job's highest wisdom is to love God for Himself alone. Hence Eliphaz's words, far from being a comfort, are a trap. The violence with which Job rejects them shows his recognition of the danger.

Job is being tested.[1] It is essential that he does not know why. He must ask why. He must test and reject all the answers attempted by men. In the end he will find satisfaction in what God Himself tells him.[2] The final restoration of Job to the happy circumstances described by Eliphaz in 5:17–26, including the peaceful death in grand old age, surrounded by descendants to the fourth generation (42:11–17), is not in conflict with the conclusion reached at this point that Eliphaz is wrong. For one thing, all that restoration comes well after Job has settled everything with God, and it is not the means by which God renews their friendship. Furthermore, Job's way back to this happy state is completely different from the route prescribed by Eliphaz in his first speech.

Eliphaz has appealed to experience as well as to revelation. But history, certainly Job's history, does not support his theory that you reap what you sow (4:8). Goodness does not pay. The book of Daniel may supply an inspiring pattern of loyalty to God; it does not always supply the pattern of deliverance, for God does not often deal with the lions as Eliphaz says (Jb. 4:9–11). Either time and chance happen to all indiscriminately – the gloomy but realistic theme of

---

[1] Gn. 22 is a miniature book of Job. Abraham was driven into an ordeal as cruel as Job's, and he could never again be as he was before. He had enlarged his life with God through suffering. The theology is the same. Abraham's agony, like Job's, was neither punitive (for the sinner) nor corrective (for the saint).

[2] Many critics do not share Job's satisfaction with the Yahweh speeches, precisely because they are not what they expect God to say!

Ecclesiastes – or, worse, the righteous are always at a disadvantage.[1]

The speeches of Job will face these realities more courageously than those of his friends. Job's search will find its ultimate statement in the life of Jesus – the best of men, the most cruelly treated by men, the most deserted by God. The fate of Jesus is the final proof that it is futile to be good. Unless . . . It is the 'unless' of the gospel which Job has not found in Eliphaz's message. Unless it is the reality of God Himself that we see in the suffering love of Jesus. Unless it is God's own human likeness that we see being formed in His other suffering children; in Job, God's servant, in whom He is well pleased. Unless also the vindication of goodness, God's or man's, lies beyond its ultimate testing in death, when the victory of resurrection proves the indestructibility of the good life. At the cross the darkest mystery of our human agony is embraced by God Himself, and transformed from moral outrage to 'glory'. When the Victim is the willing sin-bearer, His suffering becomes the conquest of evil and the display and proof that God is love. But of this gospel Job's friends know nothing, and he himself is still groping for it in his own darkness.

Meanwhile Eliphaz's stale aphorisms about sowing and reaping do not apply to Job. It seemed, from the opening scenes, that Job was to be tested; but now the matter has become much more serious. The Lord and the Satan discuss Job's character. Job and his friends discuss the Lord's character. Eliphaz's speech presents to Job's mind the horrible thought that God is not merely indifferent, but perverse, even demonic. Eliphaz's analysis forces Job to face this squarely, and it drives his torment to a higher pitch. His loss of certainty about God's goodness is a poverty and a pain more desolating than all his other troubles. Everything else may go without loss, if God remains. It is the threat to his faith, not his running sores, that becomes the upper hurt in his mind. 'The friendship of God' (29:4) is all that matters now.

ii. Job (6:1 – 7:21). The discussion between Job and his friends, in spite of its artificial poetic form, has the loose structure of living dialogue. There are few patterns of formal

[1] There is a moving description of the defencelessness of the godly in *The Wisdom of Solomon*, chapters 1–3.

debate, and little direct reply to what has just been said. This incoherence not only injects realism into the artistic composition of the verse; it also serves a dramatic purpose. The emotional impact of the speeches is more important than their rational cogency. The gulf between Job and his colleagues is more than it appears, because their formal theological agreements are extensive.[1] They concur completely in the supreme truth that God is sovereign. Nowhere in the entire book is this questioned. Yet Job's thought is on a different level from theirs, even if it has the same formal expression when it comes to the character of God in His dealings with men, or, more exactly, in His dealings with Job.

To be generous with Eliphaz, let us assume that his chiding was gentle, not mocking. Yet Job is stung by it. His response is a tremendous emotional outburst. He defends himself mightily, protesting against his friend's insinuation that somewhere in his life there must be some fault which needs correction. Job insists that his wild words are fully justified (6:2–7). He still wishes to die (6:8–10); his hope that his friends would refresh him has been disappointed, leaving him even more desperate (6:11–23). He challenges them to be straightforward in their accusations (6:24–30). Then he returns to the theme of man's miserable lot. Hope for relief requires more strength than any man has to hold on. The only way out is death, the sooner the better (7:1–10). Since this remedy lies solely in God's hands, Job turns to Him with greater passion (7:11–21). In his closing words he looks into the abyss of doubt which is the worst torture for the person who loves God – he must have some measure of understanding of God's ways to guard his mind against the thought that God is not fair.

2, 3. Job is not in the least sobered by Eliphaz's reproof. He has warned Job against the fatal consequences of bad temper (*ka'aś, vexation,* 5:2). Job not only admits, '*My words have been rash*'; he insists that his behaviour is justified by the infinite weight of his *vexation*. He uses the familiar figure of *the sand of the sea* for what is immeasurable.[2]

---

[1] This consideration alone would restrain us from assigning parts of Job's speeches in the third round to Bildad or Zophar, just because they seem inconsistent with his 'position' and sound more like what the others would say. See Stage 6 in section vii of the Introduction.

[2] This means that the parallel words in verse 2 – *vexation* and *calamity* –

4. Job is terrified. The word used in verse 4c, which is not the same as the verb in 7:14, describes the armament of God set in battle-array against him. This image of God as a (chariot-riding) archer probably goes back to Middle Bronze Age warfare. Here it is a literary figure. It is the apparent enmity of his God that poisons his spirit, like a terrible rain of arrows.[1] Dhorme (p. 77) argued for the poisoning of arrow-points from classical evidence, but Tur Sinai (p. 116) rejected the idea as unknown in the biblical world, so that no more than comparison of arrow-heads with serpent-fangs may be involved. Pope (p. 50) accepted the reference to poisoned arrows as authentic, but unique. Since then Dahood has adduced more biblical examples.[2]

5, 6. The questions are rhetorical. This is often done in Wisdom discourse to point out something absurd. There is often a hidden meaning, as in the string of enigmatic questions in Amos 3:3-8. Comparison of human conduct with the behaviour of animals is often made in such proverbs. The husbandman knows how to interpret the cries of animals; he doesn't just get annoyed. Job also has a right to *bray* like a hungry *wild ass* and to bellow like a starving bull.

The questions in verse 6 deride Eliphaz's speech as insipid, like tasteless food which can be nauseating if not seasoned. Like many ancient bywords, the purport was remembered after the reference was forgotten. Even in antiquity the scholars did not know what foods Job was referring to. The familiar 'white of an egg' (AV) comes from the rabbis, and still has many supporters. Its nearest competitor, *the slime of the purslane*, goes back to ancient versions, but the precise vegetable whose juice (or exudation) is in mind has not been identified.[3] Because the word *slime* in its only other occurrence, in 1 Samuel 21:13, seems to refer to the mucus from the mouth or nose of a madman, Tur Sinai (*ad loc.*) has suggested 'the

---

combine in the single idea of the distress caused by his tragedy. He is not, as Delitzsch suggests (*ad loc.*), weighing his outburst against its provocation to show that they are commensurate.

[1] The difference between RSV and NEB 'their poison soaks into my spirit' arises from grammatical uncertainty as to what is the subject of the verb.

[2] *Psalms II* (*AB*), pp. xxiv, 104.

[3] Since most modern readers have never heard of purslane, let alone tasted its juice, it is a pity that the reading has an amusing effect which ruins the shock that Job's exasperated words should have on us.

saliva of dreams'. This is not very meaningful, except in anticipation of the nightmare motif that becomes prominent in the latter part of this speech. The present context demands something that is eaten, presumably familiar, in spite of the poor attestation of the name. Pope (p. 51) argues for some kind of soft cheese. A. R. Millard has equated Hebrew *ḥlmwt* with *ḥilimitu* of the Alalakh Tablets,[1] which supports the case for an edible vegetable, but does not yet identify the species.

7. This sums up the point. Once more the details cause difficulty, especially in the second line. NEB's use of 'throat' instead of *appetite* (AV 'soul') is an improvement, but its proposal of 'and my bowels rumble with an echoing sound' for verse 7b shows that we are still far from agreement on the meaning. The general effect of verses 5–7 is, however, clear, even though its connection with verses 2–4 is hard to find. Since Job is concerned with God rather than with Eliphaz, it is not certain that these remarks are an attack on his friend's recent speech, as it is commonly assumed, even though this is the burden of verses 14–30, and the theme of 'taste' reappears at the end.

8, 9. At this point Job more obviously prays. He has been encouraged to entrust his problems to God (5:8). Job has only one *desire*, already expressed in chapter 3. It is to die. If God were really compassionate, He would *crush* him at once (verse 9a). He could do this as effortlessly as a weaver snips off a thread. So completely is God's sole power over life and death recognized that the thought of suicide as a remedy for life's ills never enters the book of Job, in contrast to the ancient pessimist[2] and later Stoic.[3]

The fact that Job speaks about God in the third person should not be permitted to give the wrong impression. He is actually praying, not talking to Eliphaz. Such a convention is common in the respectful address to a superior.

10. The text is difficult, and no solution is in sight. RSV has done well to retain a fairly literal translation. Job has not been accused of denying *the words of the Holy One*, unless he has sensed in Eliphaz's lecture the hint that Job must somehow

[1] 'What has no taste? (Job 6:6)', *UF*, I, 1969, p. 210.
[2] *ANET*, pp. 405ff. See Introduction, above, p. 30.
[3] 'The open door for quitting the game' (Epictetus *Discourses*, Book I Chapter XXIV).

be at fault. If so, he is already insisting, as he will to the end, that he is not aware of any failure, and the line is a preparation for the challenge in verse 24. Under these conditions, God owes it to Job to release him from his agony as a tribute to his faithfulness. Unfortunately the meaning of the root *sld* (*exult*) is unknown.

11. Any suggestion of insolence in Job's defiant words, 'I would revel in the racking pain',[1] is removed by the hopelessness of his next words. He simply hasn't the strength to hold out for the renewal Eliphaz promised in 5:17–27.

12, 13. Job has no false fortitude. He is a man of *flesh* and nerves, not *stone* or *bronze*. All his resources are spent; he has no endurance left.

14. Rowley (p. 71) says, 'The Hebrew of this verse is very difficult.' Pope (p. 52) claims that the difficulties commentators have found in the passage are imaginary. If, up to this point, Job has been praying, or at least soliloquizing, now he makes a more direct attack on the friends (the 'you' in verse 21 is plural). By complaining that their failure to supply *a friend* with *kindness* (this is the familiar Hebrew word for covenanted loyalty) has forfeited their claim to be religious men, Job seems to be very harsh with kindly Eliphaz, who, after all, seems to have done his best. His words strike deep, for Job's own religion, as described in chapter 29, consisted almost entirely of ministering to the needs of his fellow men. His disappointment at Eliphaz's failure is greater because Eliphaz's confident manner promised so much. He makes his point with a simile developed to Homeric proportions.

15. His friends (he calls them *my brothers*) have proved false like a wadi stream. In the Holy Land a sudden rain can fill a dry gulch with rushing flood-waters, but they vanish just as quickly into the porous rock. Jeremiah uses the same bold image for the fickleness of God (Je. 15:18).

16. This could be a further development of the previous image, or another very similar example. The references to the black lumps of ice and the snow on the surface[2] suggest the seasonal torrents caused by melting of winter snows, a different matter from the flash floods of the rainy season.

---

[1] Pope's translation of verse 10b.
[2] The root *'ly*, 'to be upon', plus a suffix, yields better sense than the traditional *'lm*, 'hidden'. In any case the idea of the snow hiding itself, although a literal translation, seems too fanciful to be correct.

Incidentally this touch supports our suspicion that Job's homeland was to the east of the Lebanon complex, rather than near Edom, where snow waters would not be seen.

17. Most likely this verse means that the streams, not just the ice and snow, disappear as soon as it gets warm. The fact that the water was so cold makes its disappearance all the more remarkable.

18. Travellers who are counting on supplies of drinking-water at their camping-sites make their stages hopefully from point to point of permanent springs. But if they trust in the wadis, the highway *caravans*[1] turn aside, go up into the uninhabited *waste, and perish*. The earlier interpretation of the 'tracks' as watercourses running off to lose themselves in the desert sands should now be given up.[2] Streams do not *go up*, unless evaporation is meant.

19. The desert merchants from *Tema* and *Sheba* gaze everywhere, hoping to find water as desperately as Job hoped for consolation from his friends.

20. Like Job, they were all the more *disappointed* because their hopes had been built up (by a mirage?).[3]

21. This is evidently the punch-line, since verse 22 makes a new beginning. Because of its importance as the final stab in Job's bitter recrimination, it is regrettable that the Hebrew of verse 21 presents so many difficulties. To accuse them of being *afraid* seems to introduce a completely new and irrelevant idea. So far the friends have not displayed fear. To complete his image, he should compare his own disappointment with that of the thirsty caravaneers, and not switch to the response of the friends to the sight of his suffering. To get the translation *to me* the Hebrew word *not* has to be changed. LXX has already done this. The translation *such* similarly arises from the tenor of the passage, riding roughly over the

---

[1] Read a construct phrase, with enclitic *mem*.

[2] RSV has completed the moderate trend of RV, and other versions (*AB*, JB). Gordis keeps the reference to streams. The further improvement proposed here recognizes *their course* as part of a phrase (note 1) and not the object of the verb.

[3] The verb translated *were confident* is singular in Hebrew. Several solutions suggest themselves, without changing the text. An infinitive absolute or an adverb would serve. In any case the chiastic arrangement of *disappointed* and *confounded* leaves the middle section together meaning 'even though (NEB has finally recognized the concessive meaning of *kî*) they came to it confidently'.

Hebrew. The magnitude of the textual difficulties can be gauged from Dhorme's detailed discussion (p. 89). The best we can do until these problems are solved is to take the general sense.

Job is disappointed because the response of the friends (he addresses them in the plural, even though so far only Eliphaz has spoken) has been insipid (verses 5–7) and dry (verses 15–20). Rowley, disagreeing with commentators who dispose of the inexplicable complaint that the friends are *afraid* by removing verse 21b altogether, makes the suggestion that Job is rightly charging them with cowardice. Their cautious and conventional response betrays an unwillingness to get too involved with a former friend who, they suspect, is now under the displeasure of God. There is a profound pastoral insight here; it is often fear that prevents a would-be counsellor from attaining much empathy with his client. On the face of it, Job is unreasonably severe. Eliphaz has just started, and is doing his best. Let us give him the benefit of the doubt. There is no act of pastoral care more unnerving than trying to say the right thing to someone hysterical with grief. It is early in the day for Job to lose patience with them. But the point is not whether Job is unfair: this is how he feels. The truth is already in sight that only God can speak the right word. And Job's wits are sharp enough to forecast where Eliphaz's trend of thought will end – in open accusation of sin. Hence he gets in first with a pre-emptive strike, anticipating in the following denials his great speech of exculpation in chapter 31.

22, 23. His counter-accusation does not follow our logic. He lists some specific charges before inviting more general accusation. First he denies that he is guilty of saying the four dishonourable things. The sayings come in two similar pairs. He has asked for neither *gift* nor *bribe*. He has not relied on any rescuer. But Eliphaz has not alleged such things. Why the need for a disclaimer? This is one of many instances where the successive speeches do not dove-tail very well. And it is not as if these would be crimes; the choice of the word *bribe* implies this, but a gift from someone's *wealth* (the word means 'produce') could be genuine charity, and the only dishonour would be the humiliation of a formerly rich man begging. To redeem captives from *oppressors* was a social obligation to which Job had a right; so what was the virtue of never having made such a legitimate request? Is Job saying that, since he is not indebted to them for anything, he can speak his mind freely? Do we have here the pride of a man who has always paid his own way, and even now, in dire need, will not even take advantage of friendship, with a request on which a shade of a question might fall? By starting with this very marginal fault, Job defends his integrity long before open failures are alleged.

24, 25. The inference that Job must have sinned was latent in Eliphaz's first speech, and will soon come out into the open. Verse 25a should be translated: 'How effective is straight talk!' In verse 24 Job protests that he is not even aware of any sin of inadvertence (*how I have erred*).[1] In verse 25b he demands, not only a specific indictment, but proof. This thought will be completed in verses 28–30.

26. Here Job seems to be saying that his words, *the speech of a despairing man*, which he has indignantly justified in verse 3, have been treated by them as something to be blown away (lit. 'for the wind').

27, 28. If it comes to gratuitous accusations, Job can give as good as he gets. Now he seems to retaliate with charges of his own: You would even gamble over an orphan[2] *and bargain over your friend*. This is pretty rough stuff. There is no more indication that the friends gambled for orphans than there is that Job asked for bribes. Perhaps this is what Job is getting at. But their relationship has certainly deteriorated if they are already swopping insults like this.[3]

28–30. This begins a new speech, as shown by the intro-

---

[1] Jacob Milgrom (*JQR*, LVIII, 1967, pp. 115–125) points out convincingly that here we already reach the crux of Job's argument, and are provided with a key to the whole book. A man is accountable for conscious faults.

[2] Because the preposition is usually ʿ*ly*, perhaps *tôm*, an echo of Jb. 1:1, should be read. The usual parallel to *fatherless* is widow, not friend. Dhorme's objection (p. 93) that 'Job is not arguing on the basis of his innocence (v. 26), but is excusing his language by pleading the extremity of his sufferings' does not get to the heart of the matter. His sufferings are exacerbated precisely because he thinks they are unfair. If God's justice were more obvious, Job 'would even exult in pain unsparing' (6:10). No change in text is required, for, although ʿ*l ytwm* could be a false normalization of ʿ*ly tm*, *twm* can be read as a part of the *tôm/tām* isogloss (see *Psalms II* (*AB*), p. 369). On the other hand, ʿ*ly ytwm* can be read by the well-known orthographic principle of writing only once a consonant which comes twice.

[3] The plural verbs prove that he is addressing all the friends, not just Eliphaz, and that he is not quoting an accusation that they might be hurling at him.

ductory words *But now* . . . He urges them to change their minds.[1] Using a solemn legal oath,[2] he insists that he can distinguish the validity of his position from the invalidity of theirs. This assumes that the reference to *my tongue* and *my taste* (lit. 'palate') is a figure for discernment. NEB, however, takes these words more literally as a reference to the rectitude of Job's speech.

7:1. The rest of Job's speech is more like a soliloquy which turns into a remonstration against God Himself. His theme is once more the *hard service* that men have *upon earth*. The word can mean obligatory military service (RV 'warfare'), so the *hireling* could be a mercenary. A more general meaning is possible. The 'host' (= *hard service*) is also the work-force in corvée. A man's life-time (lit. *days*; *cf.* 1:5) is a period of harsh employment. In either context the burdensome thing is that the toil is not of one's own choosing nor for one's own benefit. Chapter 1 shows that Job did not mind hard work. It is the indignity of his present plight that he resents.

2, 3. The Israelite, forced by poverty to become a *hireling*, lost his self-respect as if he had become *a slave*. But Job does not even have the satisfaction of rest or *wages* at the end of his work-day. The ideas in verse 3 are in chiasmus with those in verse 2. Instead of pay there is *emptiness*; instead of rest, *nights of misery*. Job is like Koheleth, the Preacher (Ec. 1:1), in his tough-minded assessment of human existence as unrelieved futility. But he is saved from the Preacher's sourness by the tenacity with which he questions his way through to an answer.

4. There is no point in quibbling that Job complains one minute about the endless 'months . . . and nights of misery' (verse 3) and the next about the 'swiftness' of life (verse 6). Such conflicting thoughts are bound to rage in the mind of one who says *I am full of tossing*. Once more the general meaning of the verse is clear, even though the details confront the scholar with insoluble problems. Job hopes to find relief in sleep, but the night is the worst time for the depression that comes with the shock of sudden deprivation.[3] On the one hand, there is insomnia; but sleep is worse (verses 13-15).

[1] NEB 'Think again' (verse 29) is much better than RSV 'Turn'.
[2] Translations have not caught the significant use of '*im* for asseverative denial in verses 28 and 30.
[3] On the clinical aspects of Job's depression, which we have already

5. The mental anguish is inseparable from the physical pain and reinforced by a repulsive description of his degrading illness: 'My flesh wears maggots as clothes; my skin is caked with dirt; it's scabby and festering.'[1]

6. For another image of the brevity of life, see 14:1f. Here the comparison with the *weaver's shuttle* has been questioned, because the meaning of the rare word is not clear. Various alternatives have been proposed. Parallelism lends support to interpreting the words *without hope* in verse 6b as another part of the illustration taken from weaving. Hence NEB, 'My days . . . come to an end as the thread runs out', a suggestion as old as Ibn Ezra.

7. Job's long lament, which began with a protest to the friends, has prepared the way for more direct address to God. Job asks no gift; and he is far from adopting the approach recommended by the friends. Actually Job doesn't know what to ask. That is a major part of his torment. In one respect, all he wants is for God to take notice of him. Otherwise he will come into life and go into death all for nothing (verses 7–10); so completely does God fill Job's desire. Hence his pathetic appeal: *Remember that my life is a breath.* But, in another respect, as verses 11–19 show, all he wants is for God to leave him alone; so terrifying has God become to Job. His uppermost longing is still for death, since *my eye will never again see good.* His life's thread has run out (verse 6b), and it is time God snipped it off (6:9).

8–10. The problems in verse 8, which is lacking in LXX and has been discarded by many modern commentators, can be partly solved. The desire to see God is central to Job's need. He expresses it clearly in 19:27 and it is finally satisfied in 42:5. But God must first look on Job. Similarly, reversing the sequence of 5:1, God must call first before Job can answer (*cf.* 14:15 – the importance of this verse for the

described as normal, see Peter Stone, 'The Many Faces of Depression', *Australian Family Physician*, II, 1973, pp. 578–581. On grief see Lorraine D. Siggins, 'Mourning: A Critical Survey of the Literature', *International Journal of Psycho-Analysis*, XLVII, 1966, pp. 14–25. I am particularly grateful to Dr Siggins for valuable comments on the psychiatric aspects of Job's response to bereavement.
[1] This translation uses punctuation different from that usually followed. Without going into the technical difficulties, for which larger commentaries should be consulted, this result seems better than discarding difficult words, the way NEB does. For the pathology, see the commentary on 2:7b.

whole book of Job cannot possibly be exaggerated). Since verses 9 and 10 emphasize the finality of death, from which there is no return, verse 8 seems to imply that God Himself, as well as Job's human acquaintances, might soon find that it is too late.[1]

11, 12. For some persons it is philosophical to accept the sad fact that death is the end of all and then to make the best of one's transitory and futile life. Not so Job. He has already experienced richly that life can be meaningful in a right relationship with God, a relationship which is not a hidden and altogether spiritual link between the soul and God but which is precisely existence in creaturehood in the concrete particulars of family and work and bodily health. Only God can maintain, as only God can give, that relationship. Eliphaz is wrong to suggest (5:8) that a man can secure it, either by his righteousness or by his faith. But why did God – it can only be He – throw Job's relationship into ruins? Job's existence has turned into a nightmare in which God, like Death in the old myths, is trying to strangle him. He protests: 'Why?' He asks God: 'Why?' The very asking of the question sustains his access to God. Job does not now 'adorn' 'the hidden person of the heart with the imperishable jewel of a gentle and quiet spirit, which in God's sight is very precious' (1 Pet. 3:4). But this does not mean that his opposite mood disqualifies his claim to godliness. 'A calm and heavenly frame' for 'a closer walk with God' is not the uniform standard for biblical religion. Hannah prayed with the incoherence of a drunken woman (1 Sa. 1:13). 'Jesus offered up prayers and supplications, with loud cries and tears . . . and he was heard' (Heb. 5:7). So Job makes his way to God with prayers that are sobs. Narrow and inhuman is the religion that bans weeping from the vocabulary of prayer. So Job, in his anguish, does not curb his speech, but breaks out into even greater vehemence.

> 'I won't shut up!
> I'll shout from the torment of my spirit!
> I'll protest from the bitterness of my soul!

[1] Repunctuation in verse 8 is justified by the length of the first colon and the incompleteness of the second. Without supplying detailed arguments, we suggest the following outcome: '(Your) eye(s) will (assertative *l*' is strongly indicated) gaze for me: your eyes will look for me; but I won't be there.'

Do you think I'm Yam or Tannin,
That you're trying to muzzle me?'[1]

Yam, *the sea* as a god, and the associated *sea monster* were the
worst enemies of God in the old stories.[2] The names point to
a Canaanite rather than a Mesopotamian background. Job
has no idea what he might have done to incur such extreme
hostility from God. It is ludicrous to suggest that Job is in any
way a threat to God, like the primeval chaos.

13, 14. Even sleep gives him no relief from terrors. For then
God – it can only be He – comes in horrible nightmares.

15. The *strangling* referred to here is more likely to be a
dream sensation rather than a feeling of choking connected
with Job's physical disease. The RSV translation, although
literal, is incoherent. It assumes that Job is already saying
(as he will in verse 16) that he would prefer to die than to go
on suffering, and NEB, by taking considerable liberties, brings
this thought out more clearly. What is needed is a translation
that sticks to the original text, fits the context, and makes
sense in English. This can be done once it is recognized that
'my soul' (AV), which RSV has taken simply as *I*, should be
kept with its more literal meaning of 'throat'. *Strangling*
should also be taken concretely to refer to a 'strangler'. This
is *death* or Mot, another great Canaanite god, like the ones in
verse 12. *My bones* can also be taken literally, without changing
it to 'my sufferings' (NEB). The background of the image is
easily found, for the theme of Mot, as a lion, mauling Baal,
as a bull, is prominent in Canaanite myth and profusely
illustrated in Near-Eastern iconography – ivories, seals,
coins.[3] In Israelite theology Yahweh embraces all the functions
of all the old gods, including lordship of the underworld.

---

[1] For a discussion of Dahood's suggestion see Pope, p. 61. The mythological background of the imagery is important for the point we shall make
at verse 15.

[2] See references, above, p. 120, n. 1.

[3] The association of the storm god, under whatever name, with the bull
calf is certain, and persists in the syncretistic cults of Hellenistic times.
Whether Baal takes over the epithet 'Bull' from El as he usurps his leader-
ship role is more debatable, and even less certain is whether he actually
assumes the form of a bull in any of the stories. But our recovery of the
imagery of Job's poetry does not depend on such identifications, however
much we might suspect that this is their origin. In any case, the use by an
Israelite of an illustration from a theology which, from his point of view,
had been dead for a thousand years, was as innocuous as Milton's references
to the gods of Greece and Rome.

So it is no surprise that He is often described as dealing out death like a lion ripping its victim (Ho. 5:14). A literal translation of verse 15 thus gives a clear picture:

> 'And selected   Strangler   my neck
>   Death   my bones.'

That is, Death the strangler has chosen the bones of my neck. Such was Job's dream.

16. Each part of this verse is too long to be a single poetic colon, especially as each has two verbs. The four short staccato lines represent an abrupt change in rhythm. The words *my life* are not in the Hebrew. Verse 16a is a statement of fact, not a wish, as in the translations. Since his life is so fragile and brief (*a breath*), and since God is terrorizing him (verses 13–15), his only wish is for God to leave him alone (16b) long enough to swallow his spit (19).

17–19. The language of verse 17 is too similar to that of Psalm 8 to be a coincidence. Scholars are divided as to which came first. Many think that Job is twisting the hymn into a parody. Far from rejoicing in man's dignity as God's best work in the world, he finds that the attention devoted to men by God is the real cause of their misery. He wishes only that God would give him a moment's privacy (verse 19). Far from feeling separated from God, Job is vividly aware of being under His constant scrutiny. In other places in the Old Testament, the trustful man finds security in the thought that God is his supervisor (Ps. 121:4). But for Job, God's unceasing inspection[1] has the sinister result that he is being treated as a nuisance and an obstacle (verse 20).

20, 21. At the end of his speech, Job returns to the repeated question, *Why . . . ?* What he is questioning is not altogether clear, although verse 21b is obviously the counterpart of verse 8, unifying the entire passage. Similarly the questions of verses 12, 17 and 19 are summed up in 'What have I done to you?' (20a). The addition of the word *If* before *I sin* has no support from the Hebrew text. It has been influenced by an interpretation that makes Job's speech rather insolent, implying that human sin makes no difference to God.[2] Such

---

[1] In 13:27 and 14:16 he returns to the idea that God is watching his every step.

[2] The difficulty is solved another way by Pope, who drops the words 'I have sinned' altogether.

a thought would have been impossible to a person like Job. He does not know why God has treated him as something to be smitten (*mark*, RSV; 'target', NEB). He has already requested his friends to detect his hitherto unsuspected sin (see commentary on 6:24); now he appeals to God to help him in the same way. Job knows that he is a sinner. The first word of verse 20a states that quite candidly.[1] He also knows that God's remedy for sin is forgiveness. But he cannot understand why he has not been forgiven, since he has already shown his penitence and offered the sacrifice (see commentary on 1:13). He is unaware of any further sin requiring repentance, certainly none of a magnitude to warrant the extreme assault God is making on him now. The reader knows that this stand of Job is entirely correct. His sufferings are so beyond the proportion of any sin he knows of that there must be some explanation beyond the categories of guilt and punishment.

Job's thoughts are as violent as the sieve of testing in which God has permitted the Satan to shake him.[2] He appeals to God to make his agony endurable by making it meaningful. Otherwise let Him show pity by bringing Job to death. Job's pain has the authenticity of all who have been injured in their wrestling with God, even though they limp for the rest of their life (Gn. 32:31). If he seems defiant, it is the daring of faith. All Job has known about God he still believes. But God's inexplicable ways have his mind perplexed to breaking-point. Job is in the right; but he does not know that God is watching with silent compassion and admiration until the test is fully done and it is time to state His approval publicly (Jb. 42:8).

iii. Bildad (8:1–22). 1–3. The disagreement between Job and his friends becomes wider in this first speech of Bildad. He does not begin as courteously as Eliphaz, but accuses Job bluntly of being a windbag, vehement but empty (verse 2b). Moffatt's translation – 'wild and whirling words' – is very effective.

---

[1] In verse 21a he speaks with equal frankness of *my transgression* and *my iniquity*. The fact of his sin is not disputed. It gives Job a quite undeserved attitude of self-righteousness to make this hypothetical by adding the word *if*, which is not in the original.

[2] *Cf.* Lk. 22:31. Jesus may have had a combination of Job and Am. 9:9 in mind.

Bildad is objective and analytical in his speech about God and man. As a result he is a neat but superficial thinker. He is a moralist, and in his simple theology everything can be explained in terms of two kinds of men – the blameless (*tām*, verse 20a; used of Job in 1:1) and the secretly wicked (*ḥānēp*, verse 13b). Outwardly the same, God distinguishes them by prospering the one and destroying the other. To suggest that it ever happens otherwise is to throw doubt on God's justice. And this, according to Bildad, is what Job is doing. So he asks:

'Does El twist justice,
Or does Shadday twist right?'

This bicolon illustrates the poetic device of spreading over two parallel lines words which make up a single phrase. This is not synonymous parallelism, since God's name is 'El Shadday' and what He does is 'genuine justice' (*mišpaṭ ṣedeq*). The verb is identical in both lines, so the whole amounts to a single sentence: 'Does El Shadday twist true judgment?'

4–7. Job had not said this. He believes in God's justice, but he cannot see it. The Shuhite sees the dangerous implications of Job's unanswerable questions. Because God's actions match a man's behaviour, he can reason backwards. Job's *children* must have sinned. This is getting near the bone; for Job had been concerned about this very point and, by sacrifice, had provided against even their hidden sins (1:5). Bildad does not recognize the possibility of forgiveness. Nothing can come between sin and its consequences. The only alternative is to be *pure and upright* (verse 6a; the second word is the one used for Job in the Prologue). On this basis Job might *seek God* and be rewarded. God will enrich (an alternative possibility to RSV *rouse*) Job, restoring his legitimate estate.[1]

His life will thus be transformed from small beginnings to a splendid end (verse 7). Some commentators have found an inconsistency in the advice to *make supplication* (5b), literally 'implore favour'. We should not see here a subscription to the

[1] Conventional translations of the last phrase of verse 6, such as RSV *rightful habitation* or Gordis' 'righteous dwelling' miss not only the wider meaning of *nāweh* which we have pointed out in the commentary on 5:3, but also the legal connotations of *ṣedeq*, translated *right* in verse 3. Furthermore, the verb *šillēm* as used here probably means literally 'make whole' and not 'pay back'. The latter meaning, however, does fit Bildad's strict legalism. *Cf.* verse 20.

doctrine of grace on Bildad's part. The favour of God is a reward for righteousness, not a pardon for penitence. In this respect he is more severe than Eliphaz.

8–10. As often happens, the weaker the case, the more confidently it is stated. Bildad appeals to the wisdom of the ancients, as if what he is saying is common knowledge. There is a delightful touch of satire in this paragraph. Here the author of Job seems to hint at one of the purposes of his work: to question such tradition and to upset the people who hold it unthinkingly. Bildad and Job start from the same point: *Our days on earth are a shadow* (verse 9b; *cf.* 7:7, 16). But they go in opposite directions. We *know nothing*, both admit. One man's brief experience needs to be augmented by the accumulated experiences of the past, or, better, by the purer wisdom of the golden age of beginnings.[1] The research[2] of *the fathers*[3] is the source of sound knowledge.

11–19. It is part of the author's artistry that he does not make Bildad a man of straw. His case is well stated and the best poetry is used. The ensuing sketch of the destruction of the wicked is brilliant. It is a companion piece for Eliphaz's lovely painting of the good man in 5:17–26.

It opens with the rhetorical question: *Can papyrus grow where there is no marsh?*[4] As soon as the precious moisture is cut off, they *wither before any other plant* (12b), even though they were luxuriant with foliage. Once more related materials are scattered through the poem, and it would be a violation of the writer's art to bring them together. Thus verse 16 continues the description of the outward thriving of *the*

---

[1] The exact meaning of the phrase *bygone ages* (lit. 'first generation') has been much discussed.

[2] *Ḥēqer* means 'investigation', either the enquiry already conducted by the patriarchs (RSV) or a present study of their findings. In either case there is a hint, in view of verse 9, that the longevity of the ancients permitted them insights which we can no longer gain.

[3] The literal Hebrew 'their fathers' has evoked much discussion and many solutions. J. A. Fitzmyer (according to W. F. Albright in *Yahweh and the Gods of Canaan*, 1968, p. 142 [p. 124 in the London edition]) suggests 'their ghosts'. But, apart from the unlikelihood that Bildad is recommending necromancy as a technique for gaining knowledge from the past, the parallels now adduced by Blommerde (*Northwest Semitic Grammar and Job*, pp. 50f.) support the traditional reading, which is quite in line with the parallelism.

[4] On the Wisdom character of this kind of riddle see the commentary on 6:5, 6. *Cf.* Gordis, pp. 178f.

godless (13).[1] At first 'he swells up with sap in the sunshine' (Delitzsch) 'and his suckers[2] run all over his garden'(16). Such prosperity is no better than *a spider's web* (14a). His own community (*place*, 18) will disown him, unless the words '*I have never seen you*' represent God's rejection (*cf.* Mt. 7:23). Here the word *place* seems to link back to 7:10, hinting somewhat maliciously that Job's course looks like that of the wicked.

It is a pity that the climax of this strophe in verse 19 is clouded by textual obscurities that nobody has been able to penetrate. Nearly every word involved has more than one meaning or connotation. Translations consequently offer the reader a wide range of choice. Irony has been found in the word *joy*, but various minor changes can yield quite different results, such as NEB 'its life withers away'.

20–22. Bildad sums up his analysis of the contrasting fate of the wicked and the righteous along the usual lines of Wisdom teaching. Comparison with withering grass and a healthy tree is popular imagery. Those who trust the Lord are like a flourishing plantation beside the irrigation channels (Ps. 1:3, reading collectives). The person who trusts in himself is like a stunted desert shrub (Je. 17:6). The jubilation of the *blameless man* (verse 20) will be enhanced by an additional proof of God's favour, the humiliation of his enemies (22).

This is Bildad's wisdom. Helpful as a general guide to life; but trite, and even cruel, when the friends of God are the ones with the most trouble. Job has long since left far behind Bildad's simple classification into good and bad. He knows that all men are sinners, including himself. He hopes for blessedness with God through forgiveness (7:21). He has already enjoyed that relationship and, as God's 'servant' (1:8), has already achieved that very different kind of wholeness (1:1; 8:20) possible only through faith. Bildad's assertion that *God will not reject a blameless man* (20a) makes him the precursor of those who mocked Jesus with the same logic: 'He trusts in God; let God deliver him' (Mt. 27:43). Job has a lesser Calvary, and each person has his own. But

---

[1] This word, important in Job, where it is used eight times, has various connotations. Here it seems to be general, since no specific sins are listed.

[2] There could be a play on this word, since collective *yōnaqtô* is an easy figure for progeny (*cf.* Jb. 5:25), meaning both shoot and sucking child.

when we know about God's rejection of Jesus, our dereliction
can never again be as dark as Job's.

iv. Job (9:1 – 10:22). This speech of Job abounds with
difficulties which beset the reader on every page. There is
the usual quota of individual problems arising from obscurities
in the text and ambiguities in the meaning of rare, sometimes
common, words. Even if we do not follow those commentators
who take the easy way out by emending or excising the
troublesome passage, it is not enough to deal with each instance
piecemeal. The accumulation of such results can make quite a
difference to the total outcome. In fact, our step-by-step
decisions are influenced by our prior, general impression of
the main thrust of the speech.

We need, accordingly, to find our bearings by asking what
is the trend of Job's thought at this point. Even more important,
but more elusive, we need to discern his mood. Since we can
no longer hear the tone of his voice, and the author has
provided no comment on what kind of a temper he is in, we
can only guess. Such guess-work can be dangerous, since it
can lead us along a wrong track. Thus, many commentators
have found a lot of sarcasm in this speech, especially when Job
echoes or repeats things already said by Eliphaz or Bildad.[1]
The decision we make about Job's general attitude is very
important, because interpretation depends on it all down the
line. Some scholars have thrown Job into wide disagreement
with his friends by various expedients. Thus the poem on the
power of God in creation used by Job in 9:5–10 is so similar
to a piece in the same genre used by Eliphaz in 5:9f. that some
of it has been removed as out of place on Job's lips.

It takes the seriousness out of Job's speech to feel in it
'bitter irony'.[2] We have already insisted that Job and his
friends are in basic agreement about the character of God.
That is not where the debate centres. Their disagreement

---

[1] It has been observed that this speech of Job contains more reactions
to Eliphaz's first speech than to the immediately preceding speech of Bildad
in chapter 8. Indeed, since chapters 9 and 10 have more connections with
4–5 than 6–7 have, we have a kind of delayed response. This open texture
of the argument should restrain us from moving the text around so as to
bring related things nearer to each other, removing things because they do
not fit, changing things because they do not follow logically.

[2] Hölscher, p. 29. Gordis says of this speech, 'He now reaches the apex of
his bitterness' (p. 248).

concerns the whys and wherefores of God's dealings with Job, just as the story began with God and the Satan disagreeing over the character of Job. But Job's faith is stronger than theirs, more imaginative and adventurous, and, in consequence, more exacting and painful. Job will explore his way into God while the rest merely watch and talk. Job accepts what they have said and then goes far beyond it. He replies to Bildad's speech with a tribute to the magnificence of God that makes Bildad's easy-to-talk-about deity seem puny and trivial. His agreement with Bildad (9:2a) is genuine; his question (9:2b) is not derisive, but the starting-point of a most urgent quest.

2. *But how can a man be just before God?* The language is forensic. How can a man win a legal dispute with God? Eliphaz has asked almost the same question (4:17). His negative answer came from the immense difference between almighty God and mortal man. Job is fully aware of the difficulty, but he is not daunted by it.

3. Here the word *contend* is the technical term for conducting a law-suit. It is not clear who is plaintiff, who defendant: who is laying the charges, and who is unable to answer them? RV implies that God accuses man, whereas RSV implies that it is Job who would like to initiate proceedings against God. This interpretation appeals to commentators who wish to cast Job in the role of a radical who dares to indict God. But, however heroic, such a venture would be futile, because 'God will not answer one question in a thousand' (NEB). This implies that God disdains to give any man an account of His ways.[1] There could be two reasons for this. First, the infinite power of God leaves finite man a very unequal contestant. The recital in chapter 9 shows that Job is terribly aware of this vast difference. A second, and more sinister, reason could be that man's ideas of justice are so different from those of God that no man can expect his righteousness to receive any recognition from God. A man has only to take another step to say that, by human morals, God is altogether unjust. The man who takes that step has fallen into the

---

[1] NEB wisely supplies an alternative translation: 'If God is pleased to argue with him, man cannot answer one question in a thousand.' This is rather like what happens at the end of the book; but there, far from being frustrated by his inability to answer God's questions, Job finds reconciliation through them.

abyss. It is therefore very important to find out if Job's thought has such a trend. We do not believe that the key to this speech is supplied by the conclusion that 'the theme of the whole of this chapter is the impossibility of obtaining justice from God'.[1] If Job has already reached such a conclusion, he would give up. He would have already reviled God in his mind (*cf.* 1:5).

4. The reverent (not sarcastic!) way he speaks here about the wisdom and strength of God shows how completely captivated his thought is with the power and justice of God, even though his thought cannot capture these realities. His faith is still intact, even though he has been plunged into darkness, or, as he says more dramatically, into 'muck' (verse 31). He cannot see God; that is his trouble (verse 11). His question is *How . . . ?* and he asks it again and again. How can he secure his vindication with God? He has no doubt that he is eligible for vindication, but he knows he cannot secure it, he cannot summons God, using the simple formulas recommended by his friends. Job's God is altogether too great for such easy management. Job gives his question its proper dimensions by rehearsing the immense power of God in creation (verses 3–12) and His undisputed sovereignty in judging the world (13–24). Discouraged by a renewed sense of his own weakness, he expresses a longing for an *umpire* (33) between himself and God. With this thought his faith rallies. He calls out to the unseen and silent Mystery. If there is any defiance in Job, it is seen in the persistence with which he thrusts his prayers into God's heart (10:1–17). The pity he has not received from his human friends (6:14f.) he still hopes to obtain from the Lord, even though the most he dares to ask now is that God would leave him alone (10:18–22).

5–10. Job's speech is not easily divided into its constituent poems, but in these lines we have a soaring lyric in the same tradition as the great liturgical celebrations of the works of God in the Psalms (*e.g.* Ps. 147), in Amos (*e.g.* Am. 4:13), in Isaiah (*e.g.* Is. 40:21–31) and elsewhere. Genesis 1 is not far away, although Job 9 is replete with several quite distinct creation stories. Eliphaz's similar poem, which begins with the statement that comes at the end of Job's (*cf.* 5:9 and 9:10),

[1] *NBCR*, p. 427b.

is reassuring. Job's is disturbing. Volcano, earthquake, eclipse and other marvels of the sky are all brought about by God. Such acts are too numerous to count and too *marvellous* to comprehend (verse 10).[1] The constellations referred to in verse 9 have been much discussed, with results of varying certainty. Details may be gained from technical commentaries and works of reference. The fact that the meaning of *the chambers of the south* still eludes us does not lessen the point Job is making.

11. It is no wonder that Job is amazed. In spite of this abundance of evidence that God is present and active, Job cannot *perceive him*.

12. As other occurrences of the same question show, it is not so much *What doest thou?* as 'Why?' The preceding recital makes it plain that Job knows quite clearly *what* God does, and verse 24b will sum this up with the unqualified assertion that God is the only cause of every event.

14. Job wants to be able to talk to God, but to do this he must have some idea of the purpose of God's activities. Later on (10:9–13) he will insist that there must be some purpose in creation.

15. This verse presents several difficulties. It is important that they be resolved, if possible, for this seems to be the pivot of his argument. Comparison of the versions uncovers very divergent results, for translators must make quite basic decisions about Job's stand at this point. Although the MT uses 'if', making Job's claim to righteousness hypothetical ('Even if I were righteous [which I don't pretend to be] I still wouldn't answer [because, as the preceding argument shows, that would be a waste of effort], [all I can do is] *appeal for mercy to my accuser*'), translators prefer to find an assertion of his righteousness as a fact. As in verse 3, it is not clear who is making the response. AV 'my judge', which is literal, has been replaced in modern versions by such words as *accuser* or 'opponent' (*AB*), presumably God. But this seems like a surprising capitulation to Bildad's advice to 'appeal for mercy'.[2] This inconsistency

---

[1] Quite apart from the mythological origins of some of the images used here for poetic adornment, such as the *pillars* of the earth (6b) and the description of the universe as a spacious pavilion (8a; *cf.* Ps. 104:2; Is. 44:24), which use architectural figures, we have another reference to the chaos monster in verses 8b and 13b (*cf.* 7:12).

[2] The same verb is used here and in 8:5, hardly a coincidence.

can be removed if the negative *not* in verse 15a carries on into verse 15b. He rejects Bildad's proposal: 'I won't answer (any charges, because I know they would be unwarranted); and I won't appeal to my judge[1] for clemency (for it is vindication I am insisting on, not mercy).'[2] This is reaffirmed in verses 20f.

16. No matter how verse 15 is taken, the statement attributed to Job here is incredible if the translations like RSV are correct. For Job to say that, even if God did respond to his summons,[3] he still *would not believe that he was listening to my voice*, would be scepticism that he does not express anywhere else. On the contrary, this is just what he wants, and what he will insist on right up to the end: 'Let the Almighty answer!' (31:35).[4] When God Himself, no-one less, answers Job, then, only then, will he be convinced[5] that his prayer has been heard. The translation in NEB (*AB* is similar) implies an even deeper mistrust than unwillingness to believe even the direct voice of God. Even if God did make some kind of response, and give Job a hearing, 'I do not believe that he would listen to my plea.' Support for this is drawn from the following verse. God has already crushed Job 'for a trifle' (NEB), wounded him *without cause* (verse 17b). He is unfair, if not cruel. In view of Job's consistent eagerness to meet God personally, we think that such interpretations are on the wrong track. It is not misgivings about God's fairness that cause Job's anxiety. It is the fearful consequences of such direct exposure to the divine presence that fill him with terror (verse 34). Far from being desolate because God is remote, Job is writhing with pain under the finger of God (verse 17), and only when God tells him *why* this is happening will he

[1] I don't think that Rowley has any grounds for siding with modern translators and saying that here *šôpēṭ* means 'adversary at law' (*NCB*, p. 94) and not simply 'judge'.

[2] That this is what Job maintains is proved by Elihu's complaint that Job had 'justified himself' and that the friends had failed to prove him 'in the wrong' (32:2f.).

[3] The repeated use of the same key Hebrew words is often lost track of when a variety of English equivalents is used. In 5:1 Eliphaz has told Job that if he does invoke (God, or even an angel), no-one will answer.

[4] It is in keeping with this that Elihu will make a forlorn attempt to speak to Job 'on God's behalf' (36:2).

[5] The Hebrew word translated *believe* is the same as that used in Gn. 15:6 to describe Abraham's faith. It has a definite intellectual component, implying credence as well as trust.

find relief, and 'even exult in pain unsparing' (6:10). M. Dahood solves the difficulty in verse 16b by transferring the negative to the end of the preceding line, and reading it as a noun.[1] The effect is to transform the statement from mistrust to defiant faith, similar to Job 13:15 (AV, but not modern versions). The suggestion has merit, although the grammar is a bit precarious. The trouble clearly lies with the word *not*. This could be read as assertative, 'certainly', without changing the text.

20, 21. If we have rightly divined Job's mood, he is torn two ways. He believes he is in the right, but he does not know how to set about establishing this. So far no sin has been laid to his charge by God or by men. Indeed, the only accusation he will listen to will be one from God Himself. But if God does enter into litigation, then Job is worried that he will not be able to carry out his defence triumphantly. 'Job is afraid he will be overawed and confused by God's presence' (Rowley, p. 95). Such an interpretation is far preferable to NEB 'though I am blameless, he twists my words', which is even worse than RSV *he would prove me perverse*. God has certainly not done anything like this to Job so far, nor has he any reason to expect God to behave like this when he is eventually able to work out what has gone wrong in their relationship. While Job will evidently struggle with doubts about the goodness of God, it is going too far to paint Job as a cynic who *knows* that, when they meet, God will use sheer irresistible might to brush aside Job's palpable innocence. There could be no indictment of God more extreme than this. This is the sentiment of a God-hater, and in view of what Job constantly says about the integrity of God, it is impossible to believe that he is here impeaching Him. Far from being arrogant, Job is subdued, even to the point of self-loathing (verse 21b).

The focus is not on God's suspected malice and perversity, but on two features of a man's place before God. First, no man can establish his own righteousness. Job can insist on his innocence without self-righteousness. He cannot, without dishonesty, parade a fictitious depravity for the sake of theological theory. Secondly, a man's highest perfections do not give him any control over God. Only such an insight makes sense of verse 21, where the staccato clauses betray great emotion. RV has translated this well:

[1] *Biblica*, XLVII, 1966, p. 408.

'I am perfect;
I regard not myself;
I despise my life.
It is all one.'

22. Job is consistent. He is not accusing God of failing to appreciate the difference between a good and a bad man. He adopted from the outset the attitude that a good man will receive both good and bad from the hand of God with equal blessedness (2:10). He was quite emphatic on this point. So here he recognizes another aspect of this, in contradiction of what Eliphaz and Bildad have said about the opposite fortunes of good and bad men: *he destroys both the blameless and the wicked.* The other side of this coin is found in the teaching of Jesus: God 'makes his sun rise on the evil and on the good, and sends rain on the just and on the unjust' (Mt. 5:45). The inequity of the one matches the inequity of the other. If God is to be charged with unfairness, He must be charged on both counts.

24. Job highlights the side he has most recently experienced. The occasions of men's suffering are all too frequently crime (verse 24a) and corruption (verse 24b). But, no matter what the human instrumentalities, Job has no doubt that it is God, and God alone, who orders the world in this way (verse 24c). The Hebrew of verse 24c is somewhat of a conundrum; but, in spite of continuing attempts to clarify it, including its removal to a footnote in NEB, RSV has probably got the gist of it.

25–31. The brevity and flimsiness of human life has inspired many sad passages in literature. The similes of the dream and the grass are found in Psalm 90:5. James uses the mist (Jas. 4:14). Job has already compared the swiftness of life to a shuttle (7:6). Here he uses three figures: the sprinter, *skiffs of reed*,[1] *an eagle swooping on the prey.* A famous passage in Bede's *Ecclesiastical History* uses the imagery of a bird's flight, 'as though a sparrow flew swiftly through the hall, coming in by one door and out by the other.' In the *Wisdom of Solomon* 2:1ff. such reflections serve as a pretext for licentiousness, and are rejected as 'unsound reasonings'. Job's personal ambivalence is clearly seen in this matter. It is trivial to remark on his inconsistency, longing one minute for his life to end

---

[1] An Egyptian speedboat made of light papyrus.

speedily, complaining the next that life is too short for consolation. Job's confidence in the stability of life has been shattered.
He is *afraid* to make an effort to *be of good cheer*, for there is no
guarantee that a new bout of *suffering* (28) will not soon follow,
so long as he does not know where he stands with God. He
will be depressed so long as God treats him like a *condemned*
man. This would seem to be the meaning of verses 28b and
29a; it is not that God thinks he is wicked for trying to be
cheerful.

As against the friends, who will constantly recommend
religious remedies to repair Job's relationship with God, Job
sees, in spite of his conspicuous piety, that self-cleansing is
impossible, indeed, a presumption. While hand-washing (30)
can be ceremonial, doubtless Job intends it here to represent
a thorough moral purification.[1] To no avail. Job says horribly
that God will dunk him in a slush-*pit*. Some commentators
see in this disgusting statement Job's pessimism at its lowest
point. Since God does everything, He is the one who makes
men filthy. But the following words correct this one-sided
impression.

32-35. The lament in verses 25-31 was addressed to God.
The next reflection resumes the theme of verses 14-21, the
difficulty of sorting out the issues between Job and God. Job
can neither initiate nor conduct the necessary negotiations.

The usual translation of verse 32a, *he is not a man*, is in line
with statements made elsewhere in the Old Testament
(*e.g.* Nu. 23:19). A serious difficulty is the lack of a subject
in the Hebrew. It is more likely that the phrase 'a man like me',
used as in Nehemiah 6:11, is the subject, and that the negative
covers both lines of the poetic verse.[2]

> 'A man like me cannot answer him;
> We cannot come together for adjudication.'

This expresses once more the thought of verses 3 and 14.

---

[1] The Hebrew of verse 30 needs more attention. Commentators have
been distracted by arguments about whether *snow* was considered to have
special cleansing properties. Viewing the bicolon as a whole removes the
false notion that two distinct acts are in parallel. The final word ('my
palms') is the common object of both verbs. Since *qal rḥṣ* describes the
simple act, the *hitpaʿel* used here is iterative, rather than reflexive. This
gives a vivid picture of repeated efforts to clean the hands by scrubbing
them with snow(-water?) and *lye*.

[2] Unless *lū'* is being used to express a wish (RSV mg.).

This is the persistent problem, the real problem of the book: not the problem of suffering, to be solved intellectually by supplying a satisfactory answer which explains why it happened; but the attainment of a right relationship with God which makes existence in suffering holy and acceptable. *Cf.* 4:17; 9:2. Job's question is, 'How?' He sees the need for an *umpire*, whether he states it as a longing (RSV mg.; *cf.* NEB 'If only there were one to arbitrate between us') or as regret that there is none (RSV). The Hebrew word *môkîḥ* does not mean a judge, who merely decides who is in the right; he is a mediator who settles the quarrel by reconciliation, a negotiator who brings both parties together, by laying *his hand upon us both* as a common friend. This interpretation is more natural than the idea that Job is thinking of some power greater than God who could 'impose his authority on us both'.

Besides the handicap of human inadequacy, Job is unable to *speak without fear of him* (35a) as he wishes, because of God's apparent continuing hostility. Once more Job recognizes that the initiative rests solely with God to *take his rod away from me* (34a). Unfortunately verse 35b is unintelligible; perhaps it should be joined to 10:1a (*cf.* 9:21, but the Hebrew words translated *loathe* are different).

10:1-7. Although there is no clear break at this point, Job reverts to direct address to God, and continues in prayer to the end of the speech. Many of the ideas have already been expressed. Among their reiteration emerges a new thought which gives him fresh hope. Job is a sick man. He cannot believe that God made him to end up in such a state. He must have had something better in mind, even though at present the only outcome Job can imagine is the gloom of death (verse 22).

'When we were in Asia', Paul wrote to the Corinthians, 'we experienced terrific pressure. We were so utterly, unbearably crushed that we despaired of life itself' (see 2 Cor. 1:8). So far does the apostle fall short of the image of the cheerful evangelist whose happy choruses promise believers nothing but peace and joy all the time, and who push the legitimately dejected into deeper depression by their pious disapproval of any downcast mood. Paul has more honesty, and more humanity. More theology, too. He connected such agony with the passion of his Lord. He was carrying the death of Jesus around in his own body (2 Cor. 4:10). The gospel of

Christ has not brought to any man a guarantee of less misery than Job's.[1] It has brought rather the sharing of Christ's sufferings (Phil. 3:10), without which a person is but half a Christian. For God's own Son did not hold the anguish of our life at arm's length; He embraced it and lived it and made it glorious as the instrument of man's salvation. And every distinguished forerunner of Christ in the Old Testament had to become 'a man of sorrows' (Is. 53:3) – Abraham, Jacob, Joseph, Moses, Ruth, Hannah, David, Hosea, Jeremiah – the list is long. Job is in this succession, and there is something he will find out about God as his Saviour which is much more than protection from harm or rescue from trouble. It is much more important for God to be with him in his trouble. This is what he is seeking in his prayer. It is a remarkable fact, apparently unobserved by commentators, but very revealing of Job's mind, that in none of his petitions does he make the obvious request for his sickness to be cured. As if everything will be all right when he is well again! That would not answer the question which is more urgent than every other concern: 'Why?' In the present passage Job focuses this question on the discrepancy between the care with which God had fashioned the human body, and the neglect now showing in his own diseased body. In the Old Testament it is affirmed again and again that God cares tenderly for His creatures, especially those who are cast down. Some of the most moving lyrics in the Bible are the songs of sorrow in which a worshipper tells the Lord how unhappy he is. Such a poem is called a *complaint*, a moaning appeal to God's compassion. The parallel phrase *the bitterness of my soul* describes misery, but not sourness.

2. In these questions Job seems to concede what the friends have inferred. *Condemn* implies that God has treated him as if he were wicked. His request to be told *why thou dost contend against me* expresses Job's genuine puzzlement and hurt, not arrogance and defiance.

3. Much depends on how the word *good* is interpreted here. It does not often have the meaning of 'right' in the sense of 'just'; if Job wished to question God's rectitude, a clearer word could have been chosen. NEB 'advantage' suggests that God might possibly gain some benefit 'in oppression', as if

---

[1] For sustained treatment of this theme see S. Kierkegaard's discourses on *Gospel of Sufferings* (Eng. tr. 1955).

God derives pleasure from torturing a helpless human. In view of the clear echoes of Genesis 1-3 in verse 9, we suggest that the word *ṭōb* (or *ṭôb*) comes from the same source. God was delighted that everything He had made was 'so good'. It is then unaccountable that He should *despise*[1] *the work of His hands.* This reversal of values is seen in His apparent preference for *the designs of the wicked,* an idea that Job will enlarge upon in chapter 21.

4-7. The chain of ideas in the complete poem is arranged in an intricate pattern of introversion which creates the initial impression that the ideas are not connected. Thus the lack of parallelism in verse 7 has occasioned scholars considerable perplexity, and has driven some to touch up the text to their liking. This is unnecessary when verse 7a is seen to match verse 2a, as the use of the identical root shows:

> 'Don't treat me as a wicked person . . .
> When you know that I'm not wicked.'

More detailed analysis along these lines will show that verses 4 and 5, which contain the heart of the matter, are enclosed, like the filling of a sandwich, between verses 2 and 3 and 6 and 7, which make up the other major thought. A possible explanation of God's upside-down treatment of a good person like Job as if he were a sinner (verse 6), while apparently smiling (NEB, verse 3) on the wicked, could be that God sees things differently from men, or that a man's brief life (9:25; 10:20) gives the matter a completely different perspective from God's endless *years*. Here Job has hit on a truth which, for the moment, gives pain. Later he will find contentment in it, and will say 'I loathe myself' in a completely different spirit.[2]

8-13. If some of Job's more frantic outcries have made us afraid that he is in peril of tumbling into unbelief, this exquisite poem on creation makes it clear that Job is basically confident that God's intentions were good (see commentary on 10:3) in making man. He uses three or four quite different images, drawn from technology, to tell the story of man's

---

[1] The word Job has used to express his feelings about himself in 9:21.
[2] The play on key words, which makes the entire book an intricate verbal tapestry, is generally lost on English readers. Thus the word for *man* in verse 5b is used with telling effect in 38:3 and 40:7. The word 'despise', used in 9:21 and 10:3, is used again in 42:6.

origins. Perhaps several quite lengthy creation stories lie behind these allusions. The use of Genesis 2 in verse 9 is clear. The craft of the weaver provides the comparison in verse 11 (*cf.* Ps. 139:13, which expresses a similar admiration of the wonder of it all). The most vivid figure of all, the curdling of the body *like cheese* (10), is unique in the Old Testament.[1] Nothing derogatory is implied, the way later writers expressed disgust at a person's derivation from 'a smelly drop' (*Pirqe Aboth* 3:1). The technique in verse 8 is the least clear; moulding, carving or joinery of some kind have all been suggested; but pottery (like verse 9) or plaiting (verse 11) would repeat the other illustrations. All such handicrafts have in common the deliberate design and careful construction of articles intended to be useful. Job's undisguised sense of the marvellous carries with it the confidence that God similarly had a purpose altogether intelligent and good.[2] God's very act of making mankind was a commitment. It is unthinkable that He would now undo His work and *turn me to dust again* (9b). God treasured in His *heart* a covenant promise[3] (*steadfast love*) that guarantees life for His creatures. *Life and steadfast love* (12a) is doubtless hendiadys. The affirmation of life by God through creation is all-important for Job. Here it is an expression of struggling faith, for the thought of death is still powerful, and dominates the end of this speech. It will come to clearer expression in the expectation of resurrection after death in Job's later speeches, especially chapters 14 and 19.

14-17. There seems to be an abrupt transition from the tranquillity of verse 13 to the agitation of the next section. But RSV does not provide a new paragraph, and NEB has a continuous text. Job's hope, which had risen to trust in the faithfulness of God, seems to sink back exhausted. He reverts to his previous misgivings, as shown by his return to the frequent use of the uncertain 'if', so plentiful in the earlier parts of this speech. He seems to be saying that it makes no difference to God whether he is good or bad. The first part

---

[1] Later writers speak of the coagulation of semen or blood into a foetus.
[2] Moffatt is surely astray when he speaks of a 'dark design' in God's mind, if he means something sinister, and not merely mysterious.
[3] The use of the great untranslatable word *ḥesed* at this point is of the utmost importance for the theology of this book. To call creation an act of *ḥesed* lays the groundwork for resolving Job's questions, which seem at first to require a covenant of redemption, by the surprising use of 'nature' poetry in the Lord's speeches at the end.

of verse 15 indicates that, if Job is wrong, he will be ashamed; but, if he is right, he will not be proud.[1] The rest of verse 15 is so cryptic that NEB relegates it to a footnote. In MT the verbs are imperative – 'Satiate my shame! And look at my affliction!' – as if he were once more appealing to God's compassion. Translators have turned it into a description of Job's state of distress, and the reason (RSV *for* has no basis in the Hebrew) why he is so abject.

But the real reason is given in verses 16f. In spite of difficulty in sorting out the picture in verse 16,[2] verse 17 shows that Job is still in terror at God's apparent hostility (*cf.* 9:34; the idea finds even more horrifying expression in 16:9–14). Job is assailed by accusers and, apparently, the army of God. The last line of verse 17 is another of those disconcerting places, so frequent in Job, where some clear phrases are followed by jumbled words which yield sense only in a loose translation guided by the general drift of the passage. It is literally 'changes and a host are with me' (RSV mg.). If the first phrase means 'relieving troops' (Rowley) or 'fresh forces' (NEB), then this resembles and illustrates the statement in verse 16b that God is full of surprises and His resources are limitless.

18–22. Job has now stated the issues more incisively than his detached comforters. The two great things he knows about God intersect and clash. God is powerful; God is good. In creation first, and now in Job's recent disasters, the might of God is seen. That God Himself did it all is indisputable. Job does not question God's right to do it. But God's reasons for His actions Job cannot detect. Why should He create only to destroy? His superb craftsmanship in a man's body is a supreme token of His commitment to life. But for Job it has become a burden and a horror (10:1a). The baffled sufferer retires to his first position, the lament of chapter 3, which is resumed in the closing lines of this speech.

---

[1] Since *lift up* the *head* can be used as a technical term for acceptance, or acquittal, Job could be saying that, even though he knows he is in the right, God is not acknowledging this, and Job has no way of making Him do so.

[2] Literally: 'And he grows tall [same verb as in 8:11] like a lion you chase me.' Some change this to 'if I am proud' (NEB) or the like; but Gordis (p. 250) makes God the subject: 'You take pride'. In NEB the lion provides the illustration of pride ('I am proud as a lion'). Some take the lion (Job) as the victim (*cf.* 4:8–11); others as a symbol of God's rapacity (Ho. 5:14; *cf.* commentary on Jb. 7:15). RSV preserves the ambiguity of the original in this regard.

The wishes have been expressed before. Job wishes he had never been born (18a), or had died in the womb (18b), or had not even been conceived (19a). Here he seems to be tracing his origins backward. Then he traces them forward. Since he did come to birth, he wishes he had died immediately (19b), or at least that his life had been short.[1] In his first lament, Job expressed envy of the dead, because they could relax. Here, however, he draws little cheer from the prospect of death; for he piles up a heap of gloomy terms, including four different words for *darkness*, to indicate how dreary Sheol is. His preference for *a little comfort* (20b) in this life points back to bodily existence in historical circumstances as the proper locus of the vindication of God and the fulfilment of man.

v. Zophar (11:1–20). The Naamathite is the least engaging of Job's three friends. There is not a breath of compassion in his speech. It is true that in Job's *multitude of words* so far there have been elements of impatience and exaggeration. Job will later regret this (42:6). But that is an apology to God, not men. Job has no obligation to keep to the prim conventions of pious talk just to satisfy people like Zophar. Zophar's cold disapproval shows how little he has heard Job's heart. His censorious chiding shows how little he has sensed Job's hurt. Job's bewilderment and his outbursts are natural; in them we find his humanity, and our own. Zophar detaches the words from the man, and hears them only as *babble* and mockery (verse 2). This is quite unfair. Zophar's wisdom is a bloodless retreat into theory. It is very proper, theologically familiar and unobjectionable. But it is flat beer compared with Job's seismic sincerity.

Zophar also exaggerates. He accuses Job of being garrulous (verses 2f.), self-righteous (4–6), opinionated (7–12) and recalcitrant (13–20).

3. As used in Isaiah 16:6 and Jeremiah 48:30, the word *babble* refers to the boasting of Moab, which is branded false. This would refer specifically to Job's claim to innocence. But,

---

[1] This is conjectural. The Hebrew of verse 20 has a rhetorical question which amounts to an assertion that life is brief. But the verb 'cease' (AV) does not fit in, unless it is parallel to the following request. But this also is obscure, literally 'put from me'. In 7:19 Job requested a brief respite, and there could be a similar idea here.

by calling Job 'a man full of talk' (2), Zophar seems to imply that, even if Job's previous conduct had been blameless, his recent speeches are reprehensible. He accuses Job of mocking, that is, deriding. Job has spoken alternately to the friends and to God, and we cannot tell which he is supposed to have scorned. We have already disagreed with commentators who find Job's words sarcastic; they deserve even less to be called derisive. Job has challenged God, but he has not mocked Him. He has expressed disappointment with the friends (6:14, 21), but he has not ridiculed them.

4. Zophar is blunt. 'He throws aside all mere hints and suggestions, and drives home the dart which the others have only pointed and brandished.'[1] Zophar is not quoting any extant words of Job when he accuses him of claiming to be *pure* and *clean*. Job has not applied these adjectives to himself. So as not to quibble about words, in fairness to Zophar we could concede that Job's insistence that he is in the right (or at least does not know where he is in the wrong) is tantamount to such a claim. The word *doctrine* is used in Deuteronomy 32:2; Isaiah 29:24 and in Proverbs for the instructive discourse of the sages. The word *clean*, although rare, refers in other places to 'hands' or 'heart', suggesting moral purity.

5. Zophar proceeds to express a wish that Job certainly shares. Only God can settle the issue; if only He *would speak*! But Zophar already thinks he knows what God will say. So much for his complaint that Job is arrogant!

6. A word from God is needed, because only His abundant *understanding* (this rare word is translated 'success' in 5:12) can report *the secrets of wisdom*. Unfortunately the many attempts of scholars to ease the difficulty of the word translated *manifold* (more literally 'twofold', suggesting perhaps the two levels of meaning in proverbial discourse) have not led to any agreement. The meaning of verse 6 is another problem. RSV reflects the consensus; but Zophar gives no reason for his harsh conclusion that Job, who has been punished to the limit of human endurance, is actually getting off lightly with *less than* his *guilt deserves*.

7–12. This poem expounds the statement made in verse 6a. The familiar rendering of AV – 'Canst thou by searching find out God?' – has been put to considerable theological use in declaring man's 'search for God' futile. Modern versions

[1] G. G. Bradley, *Lectures on the Book of Job* (1887), p. 92.

rightly emphasize that *the deep things* (NEB 'mystery') *of God*
is parallel to *the limit* (NEB 'perfection' is preferable) *of the
Almighty* and beyond the range of the human mind. It exceeds
the bounds of the four major realms of the universe – sky,
underworld, land and sea (8f.).[1] There is nothing wrong with
this, nor with the inference that God's power is irresistible
and His decisions irreversible. But there is no need to dismiss
men as *worthless* (11) or to call Job a donkey (12). Unfortunately
the difficulties in the language make it hard to tell just how
insulting Zophar's concluding words are. The statement in
verse 11b 'and he will not take notice' has been given an object
and turned into a question in most translations. This amounts
to an assertion that God can infallibly detect *iniquity*. Guillaume translates 'even though he considers it not', implying
that iniquity is not worth God's attention. But the associations
which this verb has with discernment suggest that the reasons
for God's judgments can be no more comprehended than the
extent of His world.

It must be admitted that the problems presented by verse
12 remain unsolved.

13-20. So much for Zophar's lecture. Now he preaches.
His remedy is simple: the usual string of pious advice. 'If
you get your thinking straight, and say your prayers,' and
so on. This is not cant. Let us assume that Zophar is trying
to be helpful in his blundering way. The prophets say the
same kind of thing quite effectively (*cf.* Is. 1:15). But this is
too glib; and it is off base, because it assumes that Job's
problem is his sin. Zophar falls into the common evangelistic
error of applying the categories of guilt and pardon to every
human problem. This is not what Job needs.

Zophar's beautiful portrait of the tranquil life of the forgiven
person (verses 16–19) resembles Eliphaz's sketch in 5:17–26.
Verse 19b indicates that people will flock to such a man whose
prosperity is proof of his friendship with God, either for alms
(Pr. 19:6) or for intercessory prayers. It is ironical that in the
end Job will be doing such a *favour* for these very friends
(Jb. 42:10). In the meantime, the recital can only give Job
painful memories. It describes him as he used to be, before the
malice of the Satan moved the Lord to put his character to the
test. But, far from seeing this testing as proof of an even more

[1] The cosmology is like the scheme of Genesis 1; *cf.* Hg. 2:6, but with
different vocabulary.

privileged relationship with God, Zophar sees Job now in the place assigned to *the wicked* (20). Being contumacious, Job is in danger of losing his sight, so that *all way of escape will be lost* to him.

The friends have now had their first round. All the issues are exhibited. Job still stands where he stood at first (1:21; 2:10), submissive to the irresistible might of God, but strained in faith as he fights to win his way to new assurance of the goodness of God. He is neither docile nor patient. The friends can only conclude that Job is somehow in the wrong. God has exposed his secret sin, and now his worst fault is to keep on concealing it. Their duty is to help him back to God through repentance and confession (5:17; 8:20; 11:14). So far Job has stubbornly rejected their well-intentioned ministry. He insists on his integrity, admits no fault. He refuses to establish the justice of God by confessing fictitious sins. The friends can only regard his stand as pride and hypocrisy. They cannot see Job's anguish as he tries in vain to discover the 'smiling face' hidden behind God's 'frowning providence'.

vi. Job (12:1 – 14:22). Job's response, which is exceeded in length only by his final speech in chapters 29–31, comes at a significant point in the dialogue. It marks the end of the first round and leads on to the second. An important change of mood can be observed at this point. Hitherto, Job's rapidly-changing emotions of outrage and despair have imparted to his utterances a turbulence that sometimes borders on incoherence. His attainment of a greater measure of self-control is reflected in the calmer tone and lucid thought of his next discourse. The chapter divisions mark the three major sections of the speech. In chapter 12 Job counters what the friends have said with his own interpretation of the activities of God.

2. Up to this point, we have disagreed with commentators who have found sarcasm in Job's statements. Here, however, it is unmistakable. He is justified in repaying scorn with scorn, for he feels, 'I am a laughingstock to my friends' (verse 4). The significance of his taunt *you are (the) people* (the article is not present in the Hebrew, a fact which makes the interpretation even harder) is not clear, since the word *people* is quite common. Some have changed it to another word which they think is more suitable. Others have found a facet of meaning with connotations of superiority – 'gentry' (Pope), 'correct people',[1] *etc.* Many alternate roots have been proposed, yielding meanings such as 'perfect', 'strong',[2] *etc.* The solution still evades us. Since God alone possesses wisdom, and all human wisdom is but a little share of this which He gives to a privileged few, the friends' claim to a monopoly (2b) means that they think they are like God, an attitude similar to that of the wicked described in verse 6.

3. Job rebuts the slur that he is a 'donkey' (11:12) by retorting that he is at least as intelligent as his friends. The pronouns are plural; he is speaking to them all. In fact, what they have said is common knowledge, and there is no need to disagree. What he says about God seems to express this shared belief. But, on closer inspection, it can be seen that Job has given it an emphasis of his own.

4-6. It is not clear how these lines serve as a transition from his opening rebuke to the main poem in verses 7–25. The point seems to be this. The friends' wisdom has not explained the contradiction between Job's condition (*a just and blameless man,* the victim of ridicule) and that of *robbers* who *are at peace.* The contrast is all the more extreme because Job has *called upon God,* whereas the robbers *bring their god in their hand.* The interpretation of the first statement as a reference to Job's good relationship with God in the past seems pretty straightforward, but Rowley thinks 'that these words are Job's representation of the derisive words of his friends, who think God has answered Job by his afflictions' (p. 112). But this is over-subtle; the participle used here does not have to refer to a present condition. Job's prayerfulness contrasts with *those who provoke God,* but what is meant by *bring their god in their hand* is quite unclear.[3] It could be a polemic against *robbers* who attribute their *peace* and security to their hand-made gods; or the idolatry in which a man's own strength is his god.

Verses 4 and 6 thus set out the contrast that contradicts the friends' theories. Criminals are safe, while the devout

[1] Jb. 12:2 is the only instance of this nuance recognized by K-B, but it has been adopted by Fohrer.

[2] M. Dahood, *Psalms I (AB),* p. 113. Dahood finds Wisdom connotations in the word, which he also considers to be a divine title.

[3] NEB relegates this line to a footnote, with a completely different translation.

man is in disgrace. The intervening verse (5) presents considerable difficulty. According to NEB 'prosperity and ease'
(which could be the *robbers* of verse 6) look with *contempt* on
'the man who is already reeling' (presumably Job). Job's
misfortune only goes to show that their way of life is better than
his (*cf.* Ps. 73). On the other hand, some think that Job is
criticizing his friends, continuing the thought of verse 4a,
saying that it is easy for them to adopt a superior attitude to
him, when they are not under any strain. Note that Job's
description of the peace and security of *the tents of robbers*
contradicts the promise made by Zophar in 7:11–19 that, if
only Job would pray to God, he would be safe. Job throws the
word *secure* back at him.

7, 8. There is a change at this point from plural to singular,
as if Job has now fastened his attention on one of his friends.
But another possibility is that Job is quoting something which
one of them has said to him, as preparation for his refutation
which occupies the rest of the chapter. The identification of
alleged quotations when a formula of quotation, such as
'You say . . .', is not used, is a tricky business. The effects on
interpretation are far-reaching, for the quoted words need
not represent the opinion of the speaker at all. Verse 12 a
little further on is considered by many to be another belief
of the friends, not shared by Job, but refuted in what follows.
So far none of the friends has suggested that Job might learn
wisdom from animals and other creatures (but see 5:23).
The proposal anticipates the end of the book, where Job will
find his answer through such enquiry, under the direction of
God.[1]

The possibility of unmarked quotations cannot be dismissed
out of hand; but we are inclined to think that verses 6f. are
integral to what follows. Job's point is that all the activities
of God, dealing with both animals (7–10) and men (14–25),
show the same traits. Job dwells on the destructive acts,
which manifest the irresistible power of God. They seem to be
so indiscriminate that it is hard to find any moral pattern
in them.

---

[1] The possible occurrence of quotations in Job has been thoroughly
studied by R. Gordis in chapter XIII of *The Book of God and Man*. See also
his 'Quotations as a Literary Usage in Biblical, Oriental and Rabbinic
Literature', *HUCA*, XXII, 1949, pp. 157–219; reprinted in Robert Gordis,
Poets, Prophets and Sages (1971), pp. 104–159.

9, 10. The fact that *the hand of the Lord has done* everything is not in dispute, so far as *the life of every living thing* (10a) is concerned. But when the same truth is applied to *the breath of all mankind* (10b), the results are more disconcerting. It is always pointed out that verse 9 is the only place in the poetry where the name Yahweh is used for God. For this reason its authenticity has been doubted by many. Its removal in the interests of a theory that this word distinguishes a prose original from poetic additions is a circle of reasoning. Viewed in a different light, the word acquired enormous importance because its rarity makes it so conspicuous. At this key point Job is still insisting on what he said at first in 1:21, where the sacred Name was used.

11, 12. Since these lines interrupt the continuity between verses 10 and 13, NEB places them in parenthesis.[1] There is some sense in this, for the question sounds like an aside flung at the friends, and the opinion about wisdom as the prerogative of *the aged* seems to be one which Job does not hold. The proverb quoted in verse 11 could be a plea for a testing of opinions (*words*) as fastidious as the tasting of food. (The figure of the taste of words has already been used in 6:6f.) But it could be a complaint that his friends are just enjoying the taste of fine words, his reprisal for Bildad's attack in 8:2.

13. The long description of the activities of God given in verses 14–25 suggests that there is no discrimination between good and evil. While most of the examples illustrate God's demolition of the achievements of men, the key thought seems to be that 'the deceived and the deceiver are his', equally (16b). In case this might suggest that God is whimsical, or a blind force, Job insists that God's *might* is coupled with *wisdom*,[2] *counsel* and *understanding*. There is an intelligent purpose. The acts are deliberate, even if man can barely see their meaning or moral justification.

14, 15. No line is drawn between nature and history. Just as

[1] It is a pity that NEB has also transferred verses 11f. to a new location between verses 9 and 10. This interrupts the continuity between these verses. Verse 10b is the text for the exposition in verses 14–25. But verse 12 and verse 13 also have a close connection, which NEB has lost by inserting verse 10. The verbal patterns are in fact quite intricate and closely interwoven. They are seen to advantage if MT is left as it is. Thus verse 9 has further connections with verse 13, since the *wisdom* of God must be affirmed as strongly as his *might*.

[2] The point is repeated in verse 16a.

in Genesis the events of creation pass without a break into the story of Abraham, so this awareness of the unity of the one world in which men live, with ground, sky and water as their environment, is found in God's absolute sway over it all. If any particular event is in mind here, it is the Flood. For instance, the verb for *shut . . . in* is the one used in Genesis 7:16. But the word *overwhelm* is characteristic of the overthrow of Sodom and Gomorrah.

17–25. With the exception of verse 22, which sounds rather like a phase of the original creation, the rest of the poem deals at length with the pageant of human history. The parade of *counsellors, judges, kings, priests, mighty, those who are trusted, elders, princes, strong, chiefs* is a series of disasters. No specific historical events need be sought, for the examples would be quite numerous. These destructions are not explained as judgments on the wicked, so that God's justice is vindicated. The emphasis is that all these great ones are puny figures in the fingers of God. Furthermore, the destructive forces of history are not just natural calamities, such as floods (15b). Job has analysed the break-down of society and traced its cause to a more inward activity of God in the minds of men. *He takes away understanding* (24a), depriving leaders of their powers of *speech* (20) and *discernment*. While an occasional act of liberation (18) or aggrandizement (23) is noticed, this is not traced to any moral cause, and it is offset by matching acts of imprisonment (19) or collapse (23). What Job describes are common facts. The use of participles in this poem makes it a recitation of the attributes of God which are virtually titles. It is a mock creed. If it is an imitation of Eliphaz's similar hymn in 5:18ff., it has been twisted into a parody. The positive side described there (healing after hurt, release after captivity) is either omitted by Job, or inverted. The downfall comes after the rise to power, and men finish up *in the dark* (25).

Here Job shows himself to be a more honest observer, a more exuberant thinker, than the friends. The mind reels at the immensity of his conception of God. The little deity in the theology of Eliphaz, Bildad and Zophar is easily thought and easily believed. But a faith like Job's puts the human spirit to strenuous work.

13:1–3. It is not enough to talk about God. Job can do this as well as anyone. Verse 2b repeats what was said in 12:3b; but it should not be deleted for that reason. It is needed to

163

complete the poetic bicolon, and it makes an important point. When Job says to his friends (the pronouns are plural), *What you know, I also know,* he is not only claiming to be their intellectual equal. He is also conceding that they have much common theological ground. But this is not enough for Job. He has still to find out how these truths apply to himself. This requires direct dealing with God. While *argue my case* has primary reference to the settlement of a legal dispute, the use of the same root in Isaiah 1:18 (where 'let us reason together' is God's offer) includes the desire, not to win the suit, but to reconcile the offended party by sorting out the misunderstanding. Job is willing to confess to any sins that may be proved against him (13:23), but so far neither his memory nor his friends have done this. His own vindication and God's will go hand in hand, but what he needs more is understanding of the ways of God through rational discussion. So far the friends have failed to supply the needed explanation (4–12). It must come from God.

4. Before talking to God again, Job deals some heavy blows to the friends, heaping reproaches on them. The similarity between verses 4 and 12 marks them as the boundaries of the speech. As often happens in Wisdom literature, a lot of incongruous imagery is thrown together; the wise men were not worried about mixing metaphors. All that the friends have done is to plaster over *with lies,* whether it be cracks covered with *whitewash* or sores covered with useless dressings by *worthless physicians.* LXX interprets both parallel participles as 'healers', artistically using slightly different Greek words, so that the whole verse draws its imagery from medical science. NEB has moved in a different direction, translating 'smearing' and 'stitching'. In any case, Job clearly brands them as incompetent; and, by calling them liars, charges them with fraud. They cover their ignorance by diagnosing an imaginary illness in Job (his dreadful, hidden sin) and prescribing a *worthless* cure (repentance, and so on).

5. If this is all they have to say, there would be more wisdom in silence. *Cf.* Proverbs 17:28.

6. In spite of his censure, Job shows here a remarkably perceptive pastoral concern for the spiritual safety of his friends. The tables are turned. He reasons (the same root as in verse 3 – it is deplorable that English translations lose the subtle inter-play of Hebrew words which is seen at its best in the composition of this brilliant chapter) with them first. By presuming to *plead the case for God* (8), *falsely, deceitfully* (7), and with *partiality* (8, 10), they are in grave danger.

8. Literally, 'will you lift up his face?'[1] That is, show favouritism in judgment, a thing God detests, even if it is showing favouritism to God!

10. The word *rebuke* is another translation of the root rendered 'case' in verse 3 and 'reasoning' in verse 6.

11. Job is terrified (*e.g.* 9:34). It would be better if the friends felt the same way. Perhaps the question should be translated ' Should not . . . ?' rather than *Will not . . . ?*[2]

The grounds of Job's assault on his friends should be appreciated, for his attitude has been commonly misconstrued by commentators. In particular, they often say that Job doubts the justice of God. But the warning he gives his friends is based on certainty that they cannot deceive God (9), or get away with things done *in secret* (10). God will deal with them in strict justice, and their 'defences will crumble like clay' (12, NEB).

13–19. Job is now fully alert and quite intrepid. The thunderstorm of words has cleared the air. He is able to express his present mind. He is prepared to *speak* out, no matter what the consequences (13). He is prepared to *defend* his *ways to* God's *face* (15). He is certain of his vindication (18b). The latter is a particularly strong statement, with *I know* and the prominent use of the pronoun *I*. Verse 16b, which makes him sure of *salvation*, could state a general rule. God rejects *a godless man*, but Job knows he is not such. But since the action is 'coming before God' rather than reception by

---

[1] The *inclusio* of the same words at the beginning of verse 8 and the end of verse 10 shows structurally that this block is an exposition of verse 7.

[2] Job thus disqualifies all theologians who try to 'persuade men' without 'knowing the fear (terror) of the Lord' (2 Cor. 5:11). Here Kierkegaard's writings are pertinent, in particular *Fear and Trembling* and *The Concept of Dread* (whose last chapter is entitled 'Dread as a Saving Experience by means of Faith' and contains the statement 'He who has learned rightly to be in dread has learned the most important thing'). The following words, from the essay 'Tremble – for God is in one sense so infinitely easy to hoax!' in *Attack upon 'Christendom'*, may serve as a comment on Jb. 13:11: 'He disposes it in such a way that those whom He loves and who love Him must suffer dreadfully in this world, so that everyone can see that they are forsaken of God. The deceivers, on the other hand, make a brilliant career, so that everyone can see that God is with them, an opinion in which they themselves are more and more confirmed.'

God, Job probably means that *a godless man* would never dare to do what he is doing now, coming to God with the most solemn asseverations of his innocence. Verse 17 is plural, addressed to the friends as solemn witnesses of his portentous words. He expects no contradiction (19). He knows the risks; this seems to be the meaning of verse 14, but the language is very obscure. A false word, and *then I would be silent and die* (19).

15. This summary of the content of Job's protestation permits us to look once more at the famous translation of verse 15a: 'Though he slay me, yet will I trust in him' (AV). This has been widely abandoned in modern versions. Thus RSV transforms Job's determination to *defend* himself into a futile gesture of defiance, which he knows will be fatal: *Behold, he will slay me; I have no hope.*[1] There are several difficulties in the text which have led to this turn-about in meaning.[2] The main ones are: (i) First, whether *hēn* must mean *Behold*, or whether it can mean 'if', possibly 'although'. The reasons given by Dhorme and others for retaining 'if' show that this word cannot be permitted to determine the meaning of the rest. (ii) MT has two possibilities: *ketib*, 'not' (what is written) (followed by RSV, *etc.*); *qere*, 'to him' (what is to be read) (AV, *etc.*). Again an ambiguity of this nature cannot be used to resolve the problem; it must be resolved by the context. (iii) The verb translated 'trust' (AV), 'wait' (RV), 'hesitate' (NEB), 'tremble' (Graetz, followed by several moderns: for details see Rowley, p. 123, and Dhorme, *ad loc.*) is the chief problem. Here the decision is influenced by the reader's impression of the mood of the surrounding context. Thus Rowley (p. 123) dismisses AV as 'irrelevant' because the context 'speaks of challenge, not trust'. But we have maintained above that this speech expresses the strongest confidence of Job in both his innocence and God's justice. Verse 15b is very much in this vein. He expects to be vindicated; this is 'hope'.[3] A positive meaning is absolutely required. As Dhorme observes (p. 187), the pessimism of RSV and the like 'does not fit'. It is of less consequence whether Job's confidence

[1] Such a desperate forcing of God's hand would amount to doing what his wife proposed in 2:9.

[2] Guillaume (p. 93) disposes of the objections one by one, and 'confidently' retains RV 'yet will I wait for him'.

[3] Calvin's exposition of this verse is superb, and has a singularly modern ring (*COCR*, XXXIII, p. 627), spoilt only by a slight tincture of Stoicism.

is expressed as 'hope', 'trust' or 'wait'.[1] The MT *l'*, 'not', can now be dealt with. Calvin accepted *ketib*, 'not', but made it an assertion by reading a rhetorical question.[2] *Qere lw* is supported by the occurrence of the same idiom in other places. It supplies the object 'him'. Dhorme felt that LXX pointed to *lû*, but Dahood has now explained the presence of the subject 'the mighty one' in the Greek as a translation of *lē*'.[3] This is possible, but we prefer his earlier suggestion,[4] followed by Mejia,[5] with the further proviso that *l'* is a normal spelling of assertative *la*' (to be translated 'certainly') rather than a full spelling of 'emphatic' *l*. We conclude that AV should by all means be retained.

20–28. Job's will to fellowship with God is strong, and finds expression in the remainder of this chapter, when once more he speaks directly to the Lord. It is not clear what are the *two things* Job wants (20a). The difficulty is increased by the fact that the Hebrew says, 'Don't do two things with me!' Several requests follow. Job wants relief (21) and an explanation in the form of a specific bill of indictment (23–25). There is no warrant for the translation of *nipʿal 'essātēr* as reflexive: *I will . . . hide myself* (20). Job has never hidden from God and has no intention of doing so. On the contrary, it is the hiddenness of God that is horrifying him. Cain's identical words in Genesis 4:14 describe his expulsion by God from His company. This is what Job thinks has happened to him (24 – clearly God's act), and he can neither understand nor endure it.

So little does Job deserve Eliphaz's criticism that he has despised 'the chastening of the Almighty' (5:17)! So little does he need the advice of both Bildad (8:5) and Zophar (11:13) to seek God!

22. Since the rare conjunction *or* is used here, perhaps these are the two alternatives which Job requested in verse 20. He is prepared to take the initiative in prayer, but he sees this as a man's response to the prior call of God.

23. Job never pretends that he is sinless. He freely admits

[1] 'Wait' (in hope) is to be preferred, because this is precisely what Job says he will do in Sheol – using the very same word. See 14:14, another high point of faith.
[2] *Qu'il me tue, n'espererai-ie point? Ouy i'espererai.*
[3] *Psalms I (AB)*, p. 144.
[4] *CBQ*, XVII, 1955, p. 24, note 23.
[5] *Estudios Biblicos*, XXII, 1963, p. 183.

being sinful in his *youth* (26). But he must know what particular sins warrant God's present hostility (24). By naming three kinds of sin – error, failure, rebellion – he lays himself wide open.

24, 25. The word *Why* embraces all the following questions. We met the same thing in chapter 3. The continuity of the passage is thus secured. RSV needlessly divides it up, making verse 25 an enquiry about the future, and verses 26f. statements about the present. They all describe things that God is doing to Job, and he wants to know, *Why?*

25. If Job is referring to himself as *a driven leaf* and *dry chaff*, we have once more a poignant admission of his own frailty and helplessness before the irresistible power of God.

26. Various attempts have been made to explain the *bitter things*. The key is supplied by the act of writing, and by the parallelism of the next line. The suggestion has been made that God is a doctor, writing a prescription for bitter medicine; or a judge, prescribing bitter punishment (NEB); or recording Job's bitter crimes. If we confine our speculations to what Job knows, he has complained that his spirit is poisoned (6:4) ('poison' is a possible meaning of *bitter*), and that his soul is bitter (10:1 – same root as here). Naomi changed her name to Bitter (same root) because the Lord sent her grief and poverty (Ru. 1:20). Job had the same experience. The writing is the decree allocating *bitter things* to Job.

27. The picture is not clear. If Job's *feet* are immobilized *in the stocks*, God can hardly watch *all* his *paths*. Perhaps the middle line has no connection with the others, but it could be quite general, *paths* meaning 'behaviour' not 'journeys'.[1] There is no need to make the figures congruous, but, if Hebrew *sad* is a lump of wood designed to hinder a prisoner's movements, then spying on his limited freedom as well would be doubly humiliating. The word translated *soles* ('arches' in NEB) is literally 'roots', and this strange expression has aroused its share of speculation. Since Hebrew *regel* is the fore-leg, including the foot, its roots might be the ankles, bringing verse 27a and 27c into parallel. Dhorme argues that the 'roots' are the places where the feet press into the ground (p. 192), and, by translating 'My footprints Thou dost examine', he brings verse 27c into parallel with verse 27b.

---

[1] LXX supports this. NEB tidies the text, quite unnecessarily, by demoting this line to a footnote.

28. If this verse really belongs here, Job is no longer talking to God about himself, but has switched to another subject. Hebrew 'and he . . .', which RSV interprets as *man*, has no obvious reference, unless Job has already begun the poem in chapter 14. Many scholars think so, and have incorporated the verse into chapter 14 at various places.

14:1–22. Job's utterances seem to oscillate between hope and despair. A uniform mood cannot be imposed on them, nor can a steady trend be found. We have, however, detected in the present speech a movement to a calmer, clearer and more confident position. See, in particular, the commentary on 13:15. Many scholars, however, find in chapter 14 a regression to his earlier hopelessness, in spite of a remarkable surge of faith in the middle (verses 14–17). The chapter opens with another reflection on the misery and brevity of human life (verses 1–6). Further illustrations of God's destructive power are added to the remarks on this subject already made in chapter 12. They are the lopping of trees and the drying up of lakes (verses 7–13) and soil erosion (verses 18–22). These are among the finest poems in the book. In the first instances, there may be subsequent renewal; in the last, the wastage is permanent. Water is the common element in all this, but we have already seen that its use by God is both beneficent and devastating. The question is, which of these opposite figures applies to man: the tree, whose life is renewed, or the mountain, which is never restored? The question is, *If a man die, shall he live again?* (14), and the answer usually given is a decided 'No!' It is recognized that, in the middle section (14–17), Job gives clear expression to the belief that, even after he lies down in Sheol, God will call him out into life again. But this hope of personal resurrection is dismissed by many scholars as a fleeting fancy on Job's part, an idea impossible for a person of his time, and a thought rejected in his concluding words. In arriving at this result, scholars are influenced, not only by their *a priori* belief that the idea of resurrection arose quite late in Israel's thought,[1] but also by expecting Job to use western logic in constructing his

[1] We believe that this opinion, commonly held by Old Testament scholars, is mistaken. On the contrary, belief in the continuation of personal human life with God after death was, we believe, part of Israel's distinctive faith from its beginnings. We cannot prove this here, but some idea of the new approach needed can be gained from Nicholas J. Tromp, *Primitive Conceptions of Death and the Nether World in the Old Testament* (1969).

discourse so that an argument is followed through step by step until the result is reached at the end. By this analysis, it is the final word of despair that has the upper hand.

We suggest that this approach is wrong. The author's real convictions may be stated in the middle of a poem, flanked before and after by contrasting opinions which he rejects. Verses 14–17 then constitute the high point of the speech, and reaffirm the faith already expressed in chapter 13, especially in verse 15.

1–6. Job dwells once more on the misery and brevity of human existence. 'The life of man is solitary, poor, nasty, brutish, and short.'[1] We have already noted a conflict in Job's thought on these points. The burdens of life are so intolerable that a speedy death is the most desirable thing; yet, far from rejoicing in the swiftness of life, Job finds its short span its ultimate mockery. This paradox puts side by side the phrases *of few days* and *full of trouble*.

2. Job gives some more[2] poignant similes of this transitory life. Man is like *a flower, a shadow*, 'a hireling' (6; *cf.* 7:1).

3. The introverted structure of this little poem brings this verse alongside verse 5, just as verses 2 and 6 match. Job is praying. To lament before God preserves legitimate sorrow from embitterment. He is more puzzled than aggrieved. The sovereignty of God in appointing each man's life-span is not questioned (5). But a man's complete helplessness at this point only shows how powerless he will be when God brings him *into judgment*.[3]

4. Far from deleting this verse, as some have done, we insist that its position at the apex of this poem makes it all-important. There are problems, however. The introduction of the idea of *clean* and *unclean* in a passage that otherwise highlights man's frailty should not be considered a difficulty in a book that delights to make full use of an abundant vocabulary. The thought has already been used (*e.g.* 8:6;

[1] Thomas Hobbes, *Leviathan*, Part I, Chapter 13.

[2] See commentary on 9:25; *cf.* 13:28.

[3] The prominent position of the object ('me' in Hebrew, not *him* as in RSV and numerous versions, to their loss) shows the pathos of Job's position. Also his torn mind; for he clamours for a hearing (chapter 13), confident of acquittal, yet also, as here, mistrustful of his ability to stand up against God. Hence his contradictory requests for God to pay attention to him, but also to leave him alone! Compare *desist* (6, RSV) with 7:19.

9:30; 11:4) in various connections, and there is no need to explain it with reference to 'woman' (verse 1) or child-birth as such.[1] Rowley replaces the question *Who can bring . . .?* by a wish. It is true that *mî-yittēn* is the usual way of expressing ardent desire in Hebrew, but this book is full of questions, and the following words, in spite of their difficulty, seem to be an answer. This answer, *not one*, is not satisfactory, in view of Job's insistence on the limitless power of God. Obviously He can do it. Ancient versions which paraphrased to the effect 'None, save God alone' might have been influenced by such theological considerations; but Blommerde, taking a leaf out of Dahood's book, has found a reference to God in the otherwise problematical[2] negative, which he reads *le'*, 'The Mighty One'.[3] This certainly merits attention, but we are not fully convinced, for reasons too technical to be given here. We shall restrict ourselves to the observation that the word *one* might be the name of God here, a reference to God's uniqueness appropriate to belief that He alone can perform the impossible.

7-12. The author's poetic artistry reaches one of its highest points in this elegy. The poem has two stanzas, in each of which a man's irreversible movement into the grave is compared to natural things. First *a tree* (7-10), apparently dead (8), has an astonishing capacity to revive at the mere *scent of water* (9). Not so *man* (10). The illustration suggests that a person might deliberately lop a tree in order to rejuvenate it. Is this why God has cut Job's life back to the roots? Since *the earth* and *the ground* (8) can be used for the underworld as well as for the soil, the image of human burial is not far away.

11, 12. A dead man is more like a dried-up *lake* than a dried-up root. The picture is more like that of the eroded mountain (18-22), never restored. As with the use of a similar figure for disappointed hope in 6:14-21, there is no thought that the waters will be replenished next season. The biblical hope of resurrection does not come from the fertility cults or the cycle of nature. The plurals in verse 12b, c (glossed over in the translations) probably mean that the three

---

[1] Rowley (p. 127) refers to Ps. 51:5.
[2] In normal Hebrew one would expect the negative existential predicator *'ên* to be used rather than 'not'.
[3] A. C. M. Blommerde, *Northwest Semitic Grammar and Job*, p. 69.

different words translated 'man' in verses 10 and 12 are collective. The deft switch to the new picture of sleeping and waking up, for death and resurrection, shows how little our author worries about the rule that metaphors must be congruous. In this respect he is quite a Shakespeare.

13–17. These verses shine brightly against the dark ground of the surrounding passages. The question which the poem answers does not come first (14a), but is embedded in the discussion.[1] The climactic importance of the poem is shown by numerous verbal clues. These show that threads that have been running through the preceding discussion are here gathered into a single knot. Most of the key words in these five verses have key functions elsewhere, and their use in other places has to be studied in order to clarify their meaning here. We have already drawn attention to the word 'wait' in 13:15 and 14:14. What Job said there is carried further here. Even if God kills him (before his vindication?) he will *wait* in hope. His readiness to go down into death in faith transforms his ideas of Sheol from those expressed in chapter 3, in 7:6–10, and in 10:20–22. It is now seen as a temporary hiding-place (13), answering the plea of 13:20. It is another period of contracted *service* (14; *cf.* 7:1, the same word). Even if silent now, God will be heard then (15a), answering the prayer of 13:22 (using exactly the same words). The basis of Job's expectation is a belief that God will *long for the work of his hands* (15b), because of the point already made in 10:8–13. The scrutiny of God, which seemed sinister in 13:27, sounds kindly as God now keeps an eye on Job in Sheol (16). Best of all, Job's troublesome sins will be disposed of once for all (17). The imagery of the last verse is elusive, but Pope has written a lengthy note (pp. 109f.) connecting verse 17a with ancient methods of accounting. Even if God has a full tally of Job's 'rebellions' (collective or plural should be read for RSV *transgression*), the tenderness of God's attitude makes it difficult to believe that they will be produced later to harm Job. The idea that the sins are *sealed up* to hide them, rather than to keep them for a time of reckoning, is supported by the parallelism of verse 17b. God will *cover over* Job's iniquity, a job which his friends have botched (same root as 'plasterers' in 13:4).

---

[1] NEB ruins the poetry by moving this line into verse 12, so that verse 12b is its negative answer.

All Job's hopes are summed up in the belief that God will *remember* him (13). God's thought names people into real existence and remembers them from continued being.[1] Job as creature has no existence, in fact or detail, except in the continued willing of his Creator. Here is no doctrine of immortality as an intrinsic and inalienable property of the soul. For any person to live is ever the act and gift of God.[2]

18–22. The final poem of the speech, which returns to a dismal note, we have already explained as the antithesis of the faith expressed in verses 13–17. Many commentators, however, see it the other way around. Revitalization after death is too much to hope for. Man is not like the tree of verses 7–9; he is more like the mountain of verses 18–22.

The contrast is brilliantly selected. For, to appearances, a tree is perishable, whereas *the rock* is a name for God, the unassailable one. The everlasting hills are a favourite symbol of the eternity of God (Gn. 49:26); one glance at their strength revives trust in God's constancy (Ps. 121:1f.). But even they are not permanent (verse 18).

19. *The waters*, so beneficial to a drought-stricken tree, destroy a rock. So God destroys *the hope of man*. Rowley says, 'this can hardly be the hope of a return to life' (p. 132). But the use of the same word in verse 7 links the two poems together in a single scheme, and gives it the same meaning in both places. The point is not that men are worn away, but that the mountain is never rebuilt. *Cf.* Job 10:21.

20. The placement of the phrase *for ever* occasions difficulty.[3] Dhorme should have been heeded, for he is certainly correct in identifying the conjunction as 'transposed', that is,

---

[1] Some idea of the richness of the root *zkr* can be gained from Brevard Childs, *Memory and Tradition in Israel* (*SBT*, XXXVII, 1962), and Willy Schottroff, '*Gedenken*' *im Alten Orient und im Alten Testament* (*WMZANT*, XV, 1964).

[2] Is Sheol a place where Job may find shelter *until* God's *wrath be past*, which was not possible in this life? Or is it a place where he must endure God's wrath for *a set time*? It is doubtful if any such ideas were connected with Sheol in the Old Testament. *Cf.* N. J. Tromp, *Primitive Conceptions of Death*, pp. 190–195. In view of the reference to creation in verse 15, we suggest that God's act of 'turning back his nose' (Hebrew, literally) is a repetition of Gn. 2:7, when God breathes life back into Job once more (*cf.* Ezk. 37).

[3] D. Winton Thomas finds here an example of the use of the phrase as a superlative: 'utterly' rather than 'permanently' (*JSS*, I, 1956, p. 107). *Cf.* NEB 'finally'.

post-positive (p. 205): 'And he goes off for ever.' Comparison of Genesis 15:2 with Genesis 25:32 shows that *hlk*, 'walk', as used here, is a laconic euphemism for *hālak lammāweṯ*, 'go to death', *i.e.*, 'die'. *Cf.* Job 19:10.

21, 22. The sadness of death is its loneliness. Unlike the dying patriarchs, who seemed to be looking forward to rejoining their ancestors, Job thinks only of separation from his family, in which alone he has his humanity in the relationships of life. We need not quibble about the fact that at this moment Job has no children. In Sheol a man can no longer rejoice or grieve with them. *He mourns only for himself.* There is no hint of extinction. If this state is the end, it is the ultimate horror.[1]

c. Second round of speeches (15:1 – 21:34)

The problem of dividing the dialogue into cycles has been discussed in the Introduction. We have assumed that Eliphaz begins each round, but we do not insist on it. Without attempting to list all opinions, we note that some scholars draw the boundaries at other places. Thus Fohrer (*KAT*), who understands the debate to consist of speeches by Job with replies from his friends, begins the second cycle with 12:1 and the third with 21:1. Snaith, on the other hand, has Job both ending and inaugurating each cycle, by dividing the intervening speeches in the middle.[2] In our opinion there is no need to look for such boundaries. While the net of argument is not tightly knitted, there is enough continuity in the flow of discourse to make separation undesirable. And just as within each cycle a speech does not necessarily deal with the one just before, so material in one cycle may deal with points raised in another cycle.

i. Eliphaz (15:1–35). As Job becomes more vehement, his friends become more severe. At first Eliphaz was gentle and courteous (4:2). Now his politeness diminishes, and he bluntly accuses Job of folly and impiety. If at first, with his great reputation (4:3f.), there had been doubt about Job's need for divine correction, now his irreverent words (verses 2–6) show how empty are his claims to wisdom (7–16). He needs a fresh reminder of the fate of the wicked (17–35).

---

[1] C. S. Lewis, 'Hell', Chapter VIII of *The Problem of Pain* (1940).
[2] The second cycle begins with 14:1, the third with 21:22 (*SBT*[2], 11).

1–3. The asperity of Eliphaz's response suggests that he has been personally hurt by Job's biting remarks. Job is a wind-bag. The poetic parallels 'wind' and *east wind* constitute a single phrase, common elsewhere. There is no need to dwell on the peculiarities of the east wind as hot and stifling, hinting at an equivalent of our vulgar 'hot air'.[1] The emphasis is on wind as something light and elusive (TEV 'empty'). The word translated *himself* is literally 'belly' (AV). An intriguing possibility arises from the use of the pi'el verb *fill* as privative. This would reverse the meaning to 'empty', which suits the context. Eliphaz has become coarse. Job's speeches are an excretion of belly wind. Eliphaz casts himself in the role of *a wise man*, while Job is the fool. He thus contradicts Job's claim of 12:3 and 13:2.

The initial question *Should a wise man . . .* embraces verses 2 and 3 together. Eliphaz dismisses Job's tremendous speeches as *unprofitable talk* which he will not dignify by debating.

4. Job is not only stupid; he is dangerous. His words are a threat to sound religion. The Hebrew has simply *fear*, but this is certainly short for the stock phrase 'fear of God' which is attributed to Job in 1:1, 8; 2:3, and equated with wisdom in 28:28. NEB makes Job sabotage his own religion ('you even banish the fear of God from your mind'), while TEV makes Job undermine other people's religion ('you discourage people from fearing God'). If in fact here 'Eliphaz brands Job's dangerous ideas as a menace to society' (Rowley, p. 134), the point is not developed. The emphasis is on the harm Job is doing to himself.

5, 6. So far, when the friends tried to charge Job with particular sins, they were shooting in the dark. Now they have something to pin on him – his guilty speech, which points to deep-seated *iniquity*. If Job's recent words are his only failing, clearly they could not be the explanation of his original troubles. Hence modern translations trace the words back to a hidden deceitfulness, brought out into the open by the testing. We think that this misses the irony of tracing Job's troubles back to a sin he committed as a result of them. Translation is improved once it is recognized that the speech organs – *mouth, tongue* and *lips* – are all subjects of four clauses in parallel:

---

[1] Rowley (p. 133) finds an indication of Job's 'passion' and 'mischievous sentiments' because the east wind is violent and destructive.

'For your mouth increases[1] your iniquity;
Your tongue chooses deceptions;[2]
Your mouth (not mine) condemns you;
Your lips testify against you.'

Eliphaz thus contradicts the statement in 1:22.

7–10. To belittle Job's utterances further, Eliphaz subjects him to a string of humiliating questions. It is an irony that his interrogation hits the style of the later interview with the Lord that Job will find so healing (chapters 38ff.). The present passage stands in chiasmus with the preceding, as Eliphaz's initial charges of folly (verses 2f.) and irreligion (4) are elaborated in inverse order: iniquity (5f.) and ignorance (7ff.).

The unique phrase *the first man* has occasioned much discussion. 'An allusion to the myth of the primeval man, who existed before the creation of the world' (Rowley, p. 134) has scarcely been proved. By linking verses 7 and 8 together, it is suggested that this pre-creation man 'learned the plans of God in the divine council' (Rowley, *ibid.*). The chiastic structure of the strophe shows that two sources of knowledge are in mind: antiquity (7 and 10) and initiation to God's secrets (8 and 9). Job has neither qualification. Two further clues are needed to solve the problem of verse 7. The same idea is found in Psalm 90:2, where similar verbs but different nouns are used. Only God is 'older than the hills'; there is no talk of a primal man, and it cannot be Adam, for he was made after the mountains. The second clue comes from the parallelism of the verse itself. Instead of *man* read 'earth' as a parallel to *hills*.[3] The preposition does double duty. The question is:

'Do you think you are the First[4] –
born before the earth,

[1] The usual translations make *iniquity* the subject, *mouth* the object, and this is supported by the word order. But normal syntax gives way to the intricate patterns of chiasmus which unify the four lines of poetry. The verb *teaches* (RSV), 'dictates' (NEB), 'prompts' (Pope), which is used elsewhere in Job, supports the result, since the *mouth* is the organ of instruction. But, in view of Ps. 144:13, perhaps it means 'increase a thousandfold'.

[2] The near-by suffix 'your' does double duty. 'Tongue' can be feminine (*ZAW*, XVI, 1896, p. 78).

[3] In view of the copious evidence adduced by Dahood (*Psalms III, AB*, 1970, pp. 40, 205) this meaning of *'ādām* is an undeniable possibility which the parallelism clinches to near certainty.

[4] In view of Ps. 90:2, we might recognize a name for God in 'First'.

brought forth before the hills?'

The charges are not deserved. Job has made no such exaggerated claims. He had claimed only to be as intelligent as his friends (12:3), not to have a monopoly of knowledge (verse 8).

11-16. Eliphaz's supply of ideas is beginning to run out. There is little new in his continuing remonstration. Although the meaning of several rare words in the speech is not known, Eliphaz's reproof suggests that his vanity has been injured. Job should be satisfied with *the consolations of God*, presumably the inspired words he conveyed in 4:12ff. Verse 11b might then be another reminder that he had spoken *gently* to Job. But other translations suggest that the 'word whispered quietly' (NEB) is a similar revelation which Job might receive if his attitude to God were less defiant. The rare word translated *flash* (12; AV 'wink') sustains the idea that Job's spate of words (13) betrays reprehensible anger (NEB) with God. But Eliphaz puts Job down by denigrating all men.

Job has already asked 'What is man?' (7:17; *cf.* 15:14). While their answers have much in common, there are important differences. While agreeing that men are fragile and dirty (14:1-4), Job nevertheless thinks that people are precious to God (10:12f.). Eliphaz goes to the extreme, dismissing man as *abominable and corrupt*. Job has admitted (14:4) that it is impossible to bring clean from unclean, but not for God! In verses 15f. Eliphaz repeats what he has already said in 4:18f.

17-35. Eliphaz's first sketch of the good man's happy death (5:26) has been contradicted by Job (7:9f.). Bildad's picture of the camp of the wicked (8:22) is the opposite of Job's (12:6). Eliphaz rebuts with the theme that the wicked have a miserable life and a premature death. His appeal to traditional belief (verse 18; *cf.* verse 10) suggests that this kind of poem was common in the curriculum of the *wise men*, a deposit from the ancestors, uncontaminated by foreign influence.[1]

While the broad outline is clear, numerous details are obscured by textual and grammatical difficulties. The *terrifying sounds* (21) may be the report of terrorism, as in

---

[1] It is not certain that this is what verse 19 means. A reference to the gift of *the land* to the patriarchs, or its conquest under Joshua, has been suspected. But such knowledge of Israelite history does not appear in Job.

chapter 1. But *qôl*, 'voice', can be read as an infinitive absolute, yielding the better parallel, 'Terrors sound in his ears.' If *the destroyer* is 'the raider' (NEB), another reference to chapter 1 may be intended, clearly identifying Job as a wicked man because such things had happened to him.

22. Perhaps the idea is that the wicked fear to walk in the dark because they are scared that those they have wronged are lying in wait for them with *the sword*. But *the sword* is often the instrument of God's vengeance (again an echo of 1:15, 17), and it is possible that *darkness*, as so often, stands for 'dark death' (NEB).

23. NEB 'he is flung out as food for vultures' has something to be said for it. It goes back to LXX and has found wide modern acceptance. Such a fate is another sign of divine retribution. So it is death, not just danger, that terrifies him as *a day of darkness*.

25, 26. At its base, the wicked person's attitude to God is one of insane hostility, 'pitting himself against the Almighty' (NEB). Eliphaz paints a comical picture of the insolent

> 'acting like heroes[1] against Shadday,
> charging against him in full armour,
> neck-mail and thickly-bossed shield.'[2]

27. Eliphaz's next portrait shows the self-indulgence of the wicked, whose 'sides bulge with fat' (NEB; *cf.* Ps. 73). NEB correctly translates *kî* as 'though' rather than *because* (RSV).

28. All this bravado and luxury is transient, for, so Eliphaz claims, their fine cities and houses will become uninhabitable ruins. The difficulties in this verse are so numerous that detailed discussion must be left to larger commentaries. TEV sees the destruction here as an act of rapacious men, whose conquests will, in turn, be wiped out by war. Others see deserted ruins as the habitat of the wicked. Others, such as NEB, read a threat, continued in verse 29a with the prediction that *his wealth will not endure*. RSV, by being more literal, is almost as obscure as the original.

---

[1] Although the words are singular, it is not an individual but the class that Eliphaz describes.

[2] There is disagreement as to how concrete the imagery is here. The phrase 'with a neck' could be abstract (*stubbornly*, RSV) or more concrete ('head down', NEB). Pope, following Tur-Sinai, finds a reference to armour to go with *shield*.

29, 30. Here once more is the favourite image of the wicked as a rank growth quickly withered, already used by Bildad in 8:16–19 (*cf.* Ps. 1; Je. 17:5–8). Eliphaz sprinkles scraps of this simile through the remainder of his speech.

31–35. It is a subtlety of our author that Eliphaz, who began by calling Job a wind-bag (verse 2), ends his own speech with a pile of verbiage. With tedious repetition, assertion not argument, he presents the doctrine 'you reap what you sow' in several forms. Key statements are verse 35a (the birth image) and verse 31a, where the word *emptiness* (which Job has used in 7:3) is played on as the *recompense* of the man who trusts it.[1] The mixing of metaphors need not disconcert us. It might well be intended by the author to make Eliphaz's ornate peroration somewhat ludicrous. The wicked are like palms, grapes, olives that never come to fruitage (32f.). He is back to where he started in 5:3ff. Eliphaz cannot even admit the fact – the frequent fact – of the untrammelled prosperity of the bad and the unrelieved misery of the good, let alone reconcile it with the justice of God.

ii. Job (16:1 – 17:16). The inferences from Eliphaz's words to Job's case are obvious. If Job has been as good as he claims, he would never have had such troubles. Since troubles have come, he must be wicked. And if he does not admit it, he is a hypocrite besides. Against these insinuations, barely concealed in Eliphaz's latest speech, Job protests with even greater indignation. He holds more tenaciously to two facts: he is guilty of no grave fault, and God is entitled to do what He pleases. But it is infinitely painful to Job that God is now inexplicably acting like an enemy. Eliphaz's trite words do not even begin to touch on this awful fact.

This speech is an instance, rare in Job, where the thought matches the ideas of the preceding speech, but more by outright contradiction than by debate. First Job hurls Eliphaz's taunt back at him (16:2–5; *cf.* 15:2–6). It is God who is hostile to Job (16:6–17), not Job to God (15:7–16). Far from having a tormented conscience (15:17–26), he is confident of acquittal (16:18 – 17:9). The meaning of death

---

[1] There is no need to remove this verse as 'incongruous with the series of figures of plant life' (Pope, p. 119). Instead of repetition, NEB finds a pun, translating 'trusting in his high rank'. This is precarious.

for him (17:10–16) is thus quite different from Eliphaz's interpretation (15:27–35). This analysis is, however, far too neat. The themes we have identified are interwoven. For example, 17:10 echoes the opening rebuke, and the rich images for God's onslaught (as warrior or wild beast) are reiterated. On top of all this, as we have already seen in chapter 14 and shall see again in chapter 19, a titanic assertion of faith is embedded in the lamentations (17:8–10).

2–5. Assuming that Eliphaz has spoken for the others, Job dismisses them all contemptuously as *miserable comforters*, which Rowley (p. 144) explains as 'comforters who increase trouble instead of ministering comfort'. In the Hebrew phrase 'comforters of trouble' Job has picked out the word translated 'mischief' in 15:35 to throw back at Eliphaz. It is easy to talk; but, Job asks, how would they feel if they were in his place and he spoke like that?[1] If there is antithesis between verse 4b and verse 5, Job is claiming that, if their positions could be exchanged, he could do much better than they have done in the role of comforter. But verse 5 could be sarcastic.

6. Job finds no relief in either speech or silence.

7, 8. Job is assailed by both God and men. RSV has turned the direct address of the Hebrew text, which uses 'thou', into the third person, and NEB has taken greater liberties. RSV at least supplies the word *God*, but NEB leaves the impression that Job is talking only about human persecutors. This greatly weakens the effect. It is God who *has made desolate all my company*. NEB has made the last word refer to the 'fellows' of Job's 'friend', but the entire translation bears little resemblance to the Hebrew. Starting with the pedestrian observation that Job has no company, some change the word to 'calamity'. But the 'community' could simply be Job's family. In verse 8 the tradition embodied in AV, RSV, which presents a horrifying picture of Job as emaciated and shrivelled, is to be preferred to NEB, which identifies the one who testifies against Job as 'the liar', not his *leanness*.

9–14. Only literal translation can do justice to the savagery of Job's description of God's vicious attack. He is like a ferocious beast (9f.), a traitor (11), a wrestler (12a, b), an archer (12c, 13a), a swordsman (13b, 14). Verse 11 explicitly

---

[1] The second phrase in verse 4 is literally, 'Would that your soul was instead of my soul!'

names *God* as the assailant; but the plural in verse 10[1] suggests
that Job is also complaining about God's human allies (his
'friends' he calls them in verse 20, heavy with sarcasm).
Since the word *torn* is commonly used to describe the mutila-
tion of the prey of a rapacious animal, including God's
mauling of His people 'like a lion' (Ho. 5:14; 6:1), the concrete
imagery requires that the word *wrath* (lit. 'nose') be taken
physically.

> 'With[2] his snout he ripped me and chased[3] me,
> He slashed me with his fangs;
> My opponent[4] glared[5] at me with his eyes;
> They[6] gaped at me with their mouth.[7]
> With insolence they punched me on the jaw,
> They are completely united against me.'

The story gives no hint that Job was physically assaulted. The
blows he has received are the words of his friends. But if they
do not deserve to be called *wicked* and *ungodly* (11), this
complaint might be lodged against the vilification Job received
from the dregs of society (chapter 30).

Verse 12 reverts to the singular. Only a literal translation
can bring out the appalling cruelty of God's attack.

> 'I was at ease, and he shattered me;
> He grabbed my gullet, and smashed me.[8]

[1] NEB normalizes verse 9c to plural; but this, and the break it makes at
this point, spoils the poetry.
[2] The preposition that goes with the word *teeth* does double duty for
both nouns. The words for these organs come in chiasmus which confirms
the parallelism.
[3] The illogical sequence should not bother us. The meaning 'hunt'
rather than 'hate' is supported by Tur-Sinai.
[4] In spite of the striking Ugaritic parallel adduced by Dahood, the
meaning 'sword' remains a speculation (*Psalms I*, *AB*, p. 46). Furthermore,
it would mean a switch to a military figure at this point, whereas Ps. 22
shows that the animal imagery continues into verse 10.
[5] Ps. 7:12 shows that the verb describes the whetting of a sword; hence
RSV *sharpens*, NEB 'look daggers'.
[6] The clash in number in the sudden change from singular to plural is
ineradicable. *Men*, supplied by RSV, may be correct, identified as *the ungodly*
and *the wicked* in verse 11.
[7] The four organs – nose, teeth, eyes, mouth – link this line with the
preceding, and support our literal translation of verse 9a. But verse 9 has
three lines in the singular, while verse 10 has three in the plural.
[8] The reduplicated verbs *wayᵉparpᵉrēnî* and *wayᵉpaspᵉṣēnî*, coming in
sequence with assonance and rhyme, have terrific poetic force.

He set me up as his target,
His archers[1] encircled me.
He chopped my kidneys unsparingly,
And spilt my guts[2] on the ground.
He wounds me with wound upon wound;[3]
He rushed against me like a champion.'

15–17. Job's terrifying description of the treatment he has
received from God does not include any sign that he had
fought back. He has not submitted to his suffering bravely,
knowing that it is punishment well deserved. Nor has he tried
to placate this angry deity by the standard means of sacrifice.
He will not budge from his position that he is guilty of *no
violence*. While this word refers primarily to physical violence,
it can be extended to cover any 'violation' of the moral
code. Job insists, *My prayer is pure*. Although he has already
claimed to be 'blameless' (9:20f.), only now does he use the
word that contradicts what Bildad said in 8:6. He wears
the tokens of grief, not penitence, defiling himself by sitting
in the dust with no other lower garment but a loosely fitting
rough bag (*sackcloth*). His piteous appearance – *face . . . red
with weeping*, eyes[4] sunk in 'dark shadows' (NEB) – must
surely move God to compassion.

18–22. Job supports his self-vindication by an appeal to
the earth and the sky (*cf.* Is. 1:2), the sleepless watchers of
men's actions and guardians of ancient covenants, as witnesses
of his murder. His use of the word *blood* implies that he expects
to die (22) before his *cry* for redress is heard.

19. Job is confident that he has a *witness . . . in heaven*. The
identity of this advocate has been carefully sought. Job is
clearly hoping for some agent to help him to settle his dispute,
to secure *the right of a man with God* (21a). The Vindicator of
19:25 is the obvious candidate. But whether this is God or
someone else is a matter for dispute (see commentary on

---

[1] This means, not single combat, but the use of supporting troops, so
that verses 9 and 10 might be a single picture of a pack of animals. But by
translating 'his arrows' (NEB), God is Job's sole foe in this section.

[2] The Hebrew word, which is found only here, is generally assumed to
mean *gall*.

[3] The root *prṣ* is used three times. Since it is a technical term of siege
warfare (or forcible entry by a burglar), Job thinks of himself as a beleaguered
fortress. Repeated stabbing, if not dismemberment, is pictured as *breach
upon breach* (RSV).

[4] Lit. *eyelids*.

19:25). Here we note two important features. God is the one who hears the cry of shed blood; and God is the one who is said to be *on high*. And Job has consistently appealed to God.

20, 21. On first sight verse 20, in AV, RSV at least, intrudes between verses 19 and 21. The thread is hard to trace when the verse itself is so full of difficulty. One problem is the unequal length of the lines, which has led some to transfer the phrase *to God* to the first half (*cf.* NEB). As it is, the statement 'my scorners my friends' has almost as many interpretations as there are commentators. Although the same word means 'translator' in Genesis 42:23, the idea that 'my mediator is my friend'[1] seems to be ruled out by the fact that Job has lost faith in his friends. His position is complicated by the fact that he is simultaneously in dispute with both God and men. This seems to be recognized in verse 21, where, in spite of the parallelism, the *neighbour* is probably not God. This is the same Hebrew word as *friends* in verse 20, and the meaning is probably constant. In his speeches Job argues alternately with his friends and God. He feels the need of someone to assist him on both fronts.

22. In view of Job's longing for a speedy death, it is strange that here he does not seem to be expecting the end for *a few years*. Instead of seeking a completely different meaning in the phrase, perhaps it is enough to find here another expression of the thought that a man's short life-span does not give enough time to solve the problems of life. With increasing clarity Job is seeing that satisfactory answers might be gained only when he has more direct dealings with God after death.

17:1–4. There is no break between the chapters. Thoughts already expressed crowd together in brief, jumbled sentences. Verse 1 contains three clauses of two words each. Job's sense that death is imminent confirms our interpretation of 16:22. His *spirit* is already *broken* (the word means 'ruined'). His 'life-span' (literally *days*) complete. (The Hebrew word translated *extinct* occurs only here, and some scholars have replaced it with something more familiar.)

In a swift change, Job returns to the theme of 16:18–21. Most translators have not been able to handle the oath formula 'if not' that begins verse 2, except as an assertion, *Surely*. More is involved. It has the force of a curse binding upon God, and in making it, Job puts his own life to hazard.

[1] W. A. Irwin, 'Job's Redeemer', *JBL*, LXXXI, 1962, pp. 217ff.

It ends with the penalty for perfidy: 'That's why you mustn't let them triumph!' (4b). It is a formal act of handing the 'friends' over to the tribunal of God. Compare the similar manoeuvre in 27:2–6. The charge is that they are *mockers*. In Israelite jurisprudence the penalty for malicious prosecution was to apply to the false accuser the punishment assigned to the crime he wrongly alleged (Dt. 19:15–21). Job is prepared for that risk. And there is another twist. The penalty, when the matter is left to God, matches the fault, so the culprit is exposed by a divine act. A Wisdom teacher, guilty of malpractice, has his 'counsel' turned to 'foolishness' (2 Sa. 15:31). So Job takes heart from the evidence of God's disapproval of the attempts of these 'wise' (Jb. 12:2) to solve his problem, shown in their stupidity. God has already deprived their *minds* of *understanding* (4a; *cf.* verse 10b). Job does not spare his friends the insult, and Bildad's angry reply in 18:3 shows that the blow went home.

Verse 3 is another example of surrounding the main thought with its background ideas, even though this breaks the close connection between verses 2 and 4 which we have just pointed out. Job appeals confidently to God to give him a favourable verdict in his dispute with the friends, using an image taken from business practice. The *pledge* he wants God to keep safely (*with thyself*) is some material token of commitment to a commercial transaction (Gn. 38:18). 'Striking hands' (so verse 3b, literally) is the gesture that confirms the agreement. The question, *Who is there . . . ?* (NEB 'Who else . . . ?'), implies that only God can do it, supporting the conclusion that God Himself is the advocate Job is searching for in 16:19ff. and elsewhere.

5–9. It is hard to find a path through the profusion of ideas in this speech. If verse 5 goes with the preceding, it continues the accusation of the friends. A proverb is suspected (*cf.* TEV). Since the *friends* are the victims of treachery, it is not easy to find the application to Job. Perhaps, as a general rule, it applies to everybody. The failure of *the eyes of his children* would be a fit punishment for a person who gives false eye-witness testimony in order to defraud *his friends'* children of their inheritance. This is a grave charge to fling at the friends, who have not betrayed any such motive for discrediting Job. Perhaps he is using this proverb simply as an example. On the other hand, Job's reference to the failure of his own eye from *grief* (7) suggests that he is now suffering for the misuse of his eye. The importance of the eyes as the starting-point for sin is recognized in 31:1, and in 17:2 Job has given eye-witness testimony to the 'provocation' he has endured. Hence TEV links verses 5 and 6 closely, saying 'now they use this proverb [*i.e.*, the one in verse 5] against me'. In the following verses his extreme illness (7), far from arousing pity, evokes contempt, since they 'spit in my face' (TEV).[1] This leaves verse 8 open to more than one interpretation, including the removal of verses 8–10 altogether. Job could be saying that decent people would be *appalled* at the way his friends are treating him (so NEB). But others think that he is still talking about the friends ('who claim to be honest', TEV), who wrongly 'condemn me as godless' (TEV). If, as LXX worked out, verse 6 describes an action of God, then there is a break at this point (RSV).

While despairing of any convincing solution to these tangled words, we venture to suggest that the general impression is this. Job is outraged because he, the man after God's own heart, has made matters worse for himself by maintaining his own integrity. He has laid himself open to the charge of hypocrisy on top of secret sin. As a person now obviously deserted by God, he is unprotected prey for any hunter. *Cf.* chapter 30. And worse, while people with base minds may make him a target of popular obloquy, with no fear of divine retribution, for such a damned soul has no longer any claim on the protection of God, those who are on God's side (*cf.* commentary on 13:7f.) may feel that they are helping God in His work by treating Job as a miscreant. So Job is forced to defy them *all* (10a), as devoid of wisdom, even if everyone else admires them as sound men.

What can Job do? Nothing, except cling to his belief in the rightness of his cause, of which he is more convinced than ever (9). There is hardly a place in the book of Job concerning which commentators are in wider disagreement than this statement. Delitzsch (I, p. 300) compares it with a rocket burst of light.[2] Others find the thought quite out of place, and either transfer it to another position, or leave it out al-

---

[1] An alternative interpretation of 'portent' rather than 'spit' has been adopted by NEB.

[2] Calvin's sublime exposition (*COCR*, XXXIV, pp. 54ff.) is a penetrating synthesis of pastoral and theological insight.

together. We see no need for this, although the difficulties are acknowledged, and dogmatism either way is no solution.

10. Because this verse completes the idea in verse 4a, we have connected it with the preceding. Some, however, such as NEB, find here a detached statement. Others, like Rowley (p. 155), begin a new section at this point.

11–16. Verse 11 continues the thoughts of 16:16 and 17:7. His diseased body is on the verge of death. The taut language – three lines of two words each – is just like verse 1, and the ideas also are similar. NEB, with some support from LXX, has succeeded in turning it into two lines of three words each.

12. This verse is quite obscure. It was omitted by LXX, and is treated with suspicion by modern scholars. It is hard to say what to do with it. RSV is literal, but self-contradictory. If the unidentified *they* (the highly interpretative *they say* of verse 12b is not present in the Hebrew) are the friends, then Job is accusing them of a complete inversion of moral values, like the blasphemers of Isaiah 5:20. NEB, on the other hand, taking considerable liberty with the prepositions, and reversing the chiasmus of the Hebrew, makes the lines synonymous and brings them into agreement with the remainder of the poem. Job is moving from life (the light of day) to death (the darkness of night).

13. It is impossible to tell what Job's mood is here. Translations are quite tendentious. Is Job eager for death, as in chapter 3? Does he fear death (chapter 10)? Does he see it as the next step into a new possibility for life (chapter 14)? The word *look* has the same root as 'hope' in verse 15, and this has already been expressed several times in key passages. RSV continues the questions into verse 16, as if they have no answer in the mind of Job.[1] NEB and TEV make verse 16 a negative answer, with no warrant whatever from the Hebrew, which makes a simple statement of fact. The plurals are difficult, but Dhorme takes them literally to reach the conclusion that Job's hope and happiness will go down to Sheol

---

[1] At this point the Qumran Targum comes to our aid. First, it supplies the interrogation, lacking in MT. Secondly, it does not confirm MT *bars*, but agrees with LXX 'with me'. This weakens the case for Dahood's proposal 'into the hands of' (Pope, p. 131). Thirdly, the translation *go down . . . descend*, although supported by LXX, which has the same verb in each line, requires a change in MT. But 11QtgJob supports MT by reading [we will] 'lie down'.

with him. This may be fanciful, and could mean that hope will die when Job dies. But the greetings in verse 14 sound like a joyful entry into one's home. Job calls Sheol *my house* in verse 13. In ancient usage, the title *my father* could be formal recognition of an overlord, especially in treaty formulations.[1] *My sister* is a declaration of love.[2] Their association with *My mother* makes one cautious in applying either of these clues to 17:14. But there is no mistaking the note of acceptance and confidence, as in Proverbs 7:4, in spite of the disgusting references to 'decay'[3] and 'maggot'.

iii. Bildad (18:1–21). Bildad's second speech is straight-forward. It is no more than a long diatribe on the fate of the wicked (5–21), preceded by a few reproaches addressed to Job (2–4). While covering the same ground as Eliphaz's earlier speech (15:17–35), the differences reflect the contrasting temperaments of the two men. Eliphaz is gentle, and a good pastor, according to his lights. Bildad, a traditionalist, is content with the old ideas, and has obviously failed to appreciate Job's thoughts, because they do not agree with his own. While Eliphaz emphasizes the mental worries of the wicked, Bildad focuses on their outward troubles.

2. The plural *you* is used when addressing Job. 11QtgJob reads singular; but MT has a plural pronoun in *your sight* (3b), ruling out the possibility that Bildad is addressing his two companions, not Job. The cryptic LXX 'stop' and also Vulg. have left their mark on AV, 'How long will it be ere ye make an end of words?' Modern replacements of 'end' by *hunt* (RSV), 'bridle' (NEB), 'shackles' (Dhorme), 'snares' (Guillaume, Pope), *etc.*, are attempts to come to grips with the unique word *qnṣy*. The vocabularies of other Semitic languages have been ransacked in the search for a suitable cognate, with varying results. The context suggests that Bildad is trying to curb Job's speech, rather than hindering the friends, or setting traps for them. Hence the reading *qēṣ*,

---

[1] For theological assessment of this familial language in covenants, see Dennis J. McCarthy, *Old Testament Covenant*, (1972).

[2] Johannes C. de Moor, 'Frustula Ugaritica', *JNES*, XXIV, 1965, p. 361.

[3] Evidence from both Ugarit and Qumran indicates that AV 'corruption' should be rehabilitated to displace 'pit' or 'grave' favoured by modern translations and commentaries. See N. J. Tromp, *Primitive Conceptions of Death*, pp. 69ff.

although it leaves the Hebrew unexplained, is an obvious solution which had already caught on in pre-Christian times, as 11QtgJob *swp*, Aramaic for 'end', now shows.[1]

3. Bildad is more concerned for his own reputation than for meeting Job's need. Of course, Job has asked for this with his derogatory remarks (*e.g.*, 12:2; 17:10). But Bildad continues to do what Job has rightly complained about; he kicks a man when he is down (6:14, 21; 12:4; 13:4; 16:2).

4. A speaker who has run out of ideas can always resort to satire. No pastor mocks a sufferer by throwing his own words back at him. Yet this is what Bildad does. In 16:9 Job had identified God as his torturer, tearing him to pieces. Bildad replies that it is Job (assuming, with most interpreters, that the words are vocative) who is tearing himself to pieces by his needless rage. In 14:18, Job spoke plaintively of the erosion of the most solid cliff. Bildad jibes, 'Do you want the whole universe to be reconstructed to suit you?'[2]

5–21. According to Bildad, the moral order, which Job is overturning, is as fixed as the earth and the hills. The fate of the wicked equally follows a strict law. Bildad recites a long poem about the troubles that overtake evil men. There is a touch of extravagance; what the argument lacks in substance it makes up for with rhetoric. It is also ironical that in the end Job will rediscover God's justice by contemplating His works in nature. Here a bunch of incongruous images is assembled in five or six distinct poems: darkness (verses 5ff.), hunting (8ff.), illness (11ff.), brigandage (14), drought (16), childlessness (17ff.).

5–7. This darkness is not the gloom of Sheol, as often in Job, but the extinguishing of the household lights of everyday life. Verse 7 may contain a different figure, with a picture of the wicked tripped up by *his own schemes*, a platitude of the more superficial 'Wisdom' mongers. The change from 'cast him down' (AV; *cf.* RSV) to 'trips him up' (NEB; *cf.* LXX)

---

[1] Since LXX is a paraphrase, this new evidence falls short of proving that *qṣ* ever stood in a Hebrew MS. The reading might have come from Jb. 16:3.

[2] NEB has no right to remove verse 4a. Verse 4b may contain a reference to Sheol as *the earth*, so MT *be forsaken* could be Bildad's way of describing the depopulation of Sheol by resurrection, which is what Job wants (14:15). The translation 'rearranged' is accepted cautiously on the basis of Dahood's discussion (*JBL*, LXXVIII, 1959, pp. 303–309). The etymological arguments may be strained, but the parallelism is improved.

requires a rearrangement of the Hebrew consonants. A better translation of verse 7a would be 'His athletic pace becomes a shuffle', an anticipation of the illness in verses 11ff.

8–10. Six different names of hunting-devices are used in these verses. Precise identification of all these items of equipment is still not possible, as a comparison of current translations quickly shows.

11. If this verse continues the imagery of hunting, we need not boggle about a man who has already been caught in six different traps still being on the run. If the *terrors* are external foes, they could be animals, men or demons. If they are inward fears, Bildad is repeating Eliphaz's point from 15:20ff. Although the poem begins with the plural (verse 5a), it switches to the singular. But, if 'he' is collective or generic, the literal meaning 'scatter' (AV mg.) can stand. Otherwise *chase* is all right. A conceit advanced by Ehrlich in his celebrated *Randglossen* that it means 'piss over his feet', although dismissed by Dhorme (p. 263), has been revived by Driver,[1] and has regrettably found its way into NEB.

11–13. If demons cause the *terrors*, they are the demons of famine, disease and death. It is a grisly picture.

> 'His plump body becomes emaciated,
> His ribs stick right out,
> Disease corrodes his skin,
> Death's eldest son swallows his organs.'

The first-born of death may designate the titular god of some particularly destructive illness. It can hardly be leprosy, which is not dramatically fatal.

14. If the body is a *tent* whose collapse means death, see commentary on 4:21. The incomparable phrase *the king of terrors* is another reference to death, and the repetition of the same Hebrew word for *terrors* marks verses 11–14 as a single unit.

15. Since this speaks of enforced residence in an alien encampment, this, together with verse 14, could imply captivity by brigands, and verse 15b refers either to the devastation left behind by raiders, or it begins the ensuing sketch of a natural disaster, like that in Genesis 19.

16–20. By dragging in once more the hackneyed comparison of the bad man with a blasted tree (*cf.* 8:11ff.), used

---

[1] *ZAW*, XXIV, 1953, pp. 259f.

also by Job (14:7ff.) and Eliphaz (15:30), Bildad gives a transparent allegory which is singularly cruel in its obvious reference to Job's bereavement. The last state, having *no offspring, descendant* or *survivor*, is the worst. Bildad has listed the things most dreaded by an Israelite in life and in death as the tokens of rejection by God. Such events distinguish the godless from the good, and serve as warnings to the rest (verse 20). The references to *west* and *east* might equally well suit the old and the young (AV).

21. Bildad's description of *the dwellings of the ungodly* shows how preoccupied he is with externals. The catalogue is too similar to Job 1 and 2 for the point to be missed. But the sermon is wide of the mark. It might take effect in a man with a bad conscience; but this, for all their efforts to develop one, is what Job does not have.

iv. Job (19:1–29). In this speech Job's audacious faith reaches its climax in the famous words, *I know that my Redeemer lives* (verse 25). He leaps to this height from a state of despair caused by the reproaches of his friends (verses 2–6), his devastation by God (7–12), and his sense of utter forsakenness (13–22). His certainty of final vindication (23–29) shines all the more brightly against this dark background.

On first reading, Job's description of his present plight does not seem to add anything new. It reiterates what he has already said in chapter 16, and parallels much of Bildad's last speech, admitting that his condition is just like that of a bad man overtaken by retribution. The facts are the same for all eyes, but Job places them in totally different relationships. In modern terms, the friends are detached, Job is involved; they are on the balcony, he is in the street.

Bildad's description of the fate of the wicked is academic. He does not think how horrible it must be to be God, doing such things to helpless men, however justly. He does not stop to think how horrible it must be to be a man suffering such things, whether justly or unjustly. Bildad recounts the disasters as the outworking of moral laws which control the movements of men around the central God as gravitation governs the movements of planets around the sun. God's justice consists of His maintenance of these laws, natural and moral. This is a common opinion of philosophers, whose god is a factor in a formula.

Job's point of view is totally different. He does not see God dealing with him through laws. He is vividly aware of God's direct contact with him, and openly names Him as the sole agent of all that 'happens'. Morality is no connecting link. Job cannot understand why God is now acting so completely out of character with what he has always believed. He must somehow recover his friendship with God by means which supersede the theological calculus of the friends. He boldly claims God as his nearest relative.

2. The friends have completely misinterpreted Job's experience, and their harassment only makes his suffering worse.

4. If Dhorme is right in his interpretation ('Even if it were a fact that I have gone astray, that would remain my own business'), Job is rejecting their interference in a matter strictly between a man and God. They are acting 'like God' (verse 22).

6. Since many commentators say that Job openly accuses God of injustice, the meaning of this verse is crucial for discovering what Job really thinks. Although the hunting *net* mentioned here is not one of the items listed by Bildad in 18:8ff., Job picks up the image. It is not enough to say that the wicked is caught in his own trap. It is God who has ensnared Job. The verb translated *put me in the wrong* is the one Bildad used in 8:3 to ask, 'Does God *pervert* judgment?' It will be used later by Elihu to insist that God never does such a thing (34:12). Here Job says, 'God has made me crooked.' What he means by this must be explained by what he says about God in verses 7-12. It is not that God has 'subverted' (Pope) Job. Nor does Job accuse God of caprice, as Rowley claims (p. 167). The judge has not pronounced Job guilty; at this stage that is no more than an inference that the friends have made by applying their theories to Job's experience. Job is still waiting to hear from God, and has maintained all along that, when God does speak (even if he has to wait until after death for that), He will declare Job innocent. It is not a miscarriage, but a denial, or at least a delay, of justice that Job has had to endure.[1] *Cf.* 27:2.

7. It is the silence of God that Job complains about, so

---

[1] In Ps. 146:9 the verb describes a perfectly righteous act of God. The best solution is to identify *me* as the indirect object, and supply 'judgment' as the object understood.

long as there is no response to his plea for redress. To say that *there is no justice* does not mean that there is injustice. The verdict has not yet been given.

8–12. This description of God's unsparing attacks on Job resembles that in 16:7–14, with a similar mixture of metaphors. In poetry of this kind, it is the cumulative effect that counts. One can only smile at commentators who are bothered by the picture of *siegeworks* built up around a *tent*.

13–19. People ally themselves with God in the assault on Job, just as their forces are combined in the warfare described in chapter 16. The realism with which Job's words reveal his inner mind is seen at its best in this speech. Job's burning concern for God does not make him insensitive to human relationships. On the contrary, the two are inseparable in the life of any person who attains wholeness as a human being. Job's list of *brethren, acquaintances, kinsfolk, close friends, guests, maidservants, servant(s), wife, children* reveals his capacity, his enjoyment, and equally his hurt when denied the solace of company, the respect of employees, the intimacy of family. When urchins are impudent to a helpless old man, one of the most sacred courtesies of Israelite society is flouted. It is even worse when the bonds of moral obligation and affection (verse 19) are shamelessly severed. Like the Servant of the Lord (Is. 53), Job is treated as an outcast. He is God's reject, so he may be abused without fear that God will come to his aid – the attitude also of the persons who taunted Jesus on the cross.

20–22. Job is a shocking spectacle that might yet claim some shred of pity. He describes his own physical condition, a horror of emaciation and ugliness. The unforgettable phrase *escaped by the skin of my teeth*, although retained by RSV, does not fit the context, since Job is not rejoicing in a narrow escape. Numerous attempts have been made to secure a more suitable meaning. A selection is supplied by Rowley (p. 170). For the time being this must be left as one of the many unsolved problems of the book.

Job's dignity and self-composure are lost. He lies broken under the blows of God and the words of men. To men he appeals for pity (verse 21),[1] to God for justice. But both alike hound (*pursue*) him.

---

[1] Concessive 'even though' is better than 'for'.

23–27. This passage is notoriously difficult. Much depends on the authenticity and meaning of its central affirmation, *my Redeemer lives.* Unfortunately it is followed by several lines which are so unintelligible that the range of translations offered is quite bewildering.[1] Two extremes should be avoided. There is no need for the loud note of Job's certainty of ultimate vindication to be drowned by the static of textual difficulties. But too much of later resurrection theology should not be read back into the passage, as in AV. Because of the numerous problems in the passage, the scholar who looks only at the insoluble difficulties might overlook much that is clear and strong. It is better to find the firm ground first, and use this as a foothold for venturing into less certain places.

Proceeding thus, we observe first that Job stakes his honour on his future justification by providing a permanent written record of his protestation of innocence (verses 23f.). This is certain, even though we do not know whether his *book* is a scroll or a tablet of clay, metal or stone. All have been suggested, but the use of the verb *inscribed* suggests carving in some durable substance, like a monument. This would make the engraved *rock* of verse 24 part of the same image, even though we do not know what technique used *an iron pen and lead.*

Secondly, there is a tremendous emphasis on 'seeing God'; the point is made three times in verses 26f. Hitherto Job has indicated a need to hear God speaking. Sight is more immediate, more physical, harder to doubt. *Cf.* 42:5. The references to *skin, flesh* and *eyes* make it clear that Job expects to have this experience as a man, not just as a disembodied shade, or in his mind's eye. What he says should not be watered down by the biblical teaching that no-one can see God. The Old Testament records several notable instances where people such as Abraham, Moses and Isaiah 'saw' God, and Job doubtless has something similar in mind. To underline his belief that this will happen with full possession of his personal identity, Job uses *I* three times in verse 27a, once on the verb, once as the emphatic pronoun subject, once as the 'ethic

---

[1] A sample of a dozen or so renditions, with references to many more, was given by H. H. Rowley in his lecture 'The Book of Job and its Meaning' (*BJRL*, XLI, 1958, pp. 167–207; see p. 203, n. 5), reprinted in *From Moses to Qumran* (1963), pp. 180f.

dative': AV 'Whom I shall see for myself' cannot be improved on.[1]

Thirdly, verses 25–27 are so tightly knit that there should be no doubt that the *Redeemer* is *God*. NEB is to be commended for securing this, and also for bringing out the forensic connotations: the 'vindicator' who 'will rise . . . to speak in court' as Job's 'witness' and 'defending counsel' is none other than 'God himself'.

So far, so good. Beyond this the ground becomes unfirm. The phrase *not another* can hardly mean that Job expects to be the only person who will ever see God. The word means 'stranger' (RV mg.): either Job will not be a foreigner to God, or God will no longer act like a stranger towards Job. Leaving aside other minor points, the great matter for disagreement is when Job thinks this event will transpire. Some, appealing to the end of the story, especially 42:5, and relying also on a general belief that the hope of personal resurrection is not present in the book, maintain that Job still expects vindication in this life, in spite of all that he has said about the imminence of his death. Others, while admitting that the passage falls short of a full statement of faith in personal bodily resurrection, find in it the hope of a favourable meeting with God after death as a genuine human being. We think that there are several good reasons for accepting the second position. First, there would be no need for Job to deposit a written testimony, if he expects to be vindicated before he dies. Secondly, the word translated *earth*, as used in Job, is constantly connected with Sheol, and the statement that the Redeemer *lives* is a direct answer to the fact that a man dies (14:10). The repetition of the word *after*(-wards) in the prominent position at the beginning of verses 25b and 26a suggests an interval, or even, with the meaning *at last*, something eschatological. Finally, the argument that Job does not expect personal reconstitution as a man, because this idea entered Judaism only towards the very end of the biblical period, can be dismissed in the light of much recent research that shows interest in the after-life as an ancient concern for Israelite faith. In particular, the outcome of our study of such passages as Job 14:13ff., if valid, shows that the hope of resurrection lies at the very heart of Job's faith.

[1] It is recognized that some scholars interpret *lī*, literally 'to me', not as dative, but as benefactive 'for me', *on my side* (RSV). This is possible.

28, 29. Job's concluding words, addressed to the friends, sound like a warning that they, too, must face judgment. Unfortunately these verses are largely unintelligible, including verse 27c, which reads 'my kidneys have ended in my chest'.

v. Zophar (20:1–29). Zophar's opening remarks (verses 2f.) are a retort to Job's concluding warning, which he considers an insult. After that he plays his own variation on the theme of the fate of the wicked (verses 4–29). Their happiness is short-lived; their wrongdoing is self-destructive. All three friends dwell on this fact, incontrovertible to their mind, in the second round. Job, having refuted their argument in chapter 12, restricts his discourse to the contrary fact of the suffering and death of the righteous, a problem on which the friends have nothing to say, for in their theology this would never occur.

2, 3. The clarity of mind which Zophar claims for himself is lost in the heat of his words. His statement about his *thoughts* and *spirit* answering him suggests a capacity for dialogue with himself of which we are now to share the benefits. The difference between AV 'reproach' (reinstated by NEB) and RSV *insults* involves an interesting problem.[1] A reproach is personal and produces private shame; an insult causes public disgrace.[2] Zophar is stung by the way Job has discredited his claim to be 'wise'; hence his parade of *understanding*. That RV 'shame' should accordingly be discarded is proved, not only by the work of Klopfenstein, but also by the remarkable reading 'curses' in 11QtgJob.

4. The addition of *not* seems justified. In spite of the claim to have worked things out by his own *understanding*, Zophar bases his assertion on common and timeless knowledge, expressing surprise that Job does not know such things.

5–11. Zophar's first point is that *the joy of the godless* is brief. But Job has already argued that the life of all men is transitory, whether they are good or bad. By his evasion, Zophar has conceded that present experience might not give

[1] The later translations are not consistent, since the same root in 19:3, which doubtless accounts for Zophar's use of it here, is rendered 'reproach' by RSV and 'insult' by NEB.
[2] The matter has now been thoroughly studied by M. A. Klopfenstein in '*Scham und Schande nach dem Alten Testament: Eine begriffsgeschichtliche Untersuchung zu den hebräischen Wurzeln bôš, klm und ḥpr, ATANT*, LXII, 1972. The present verse is discussed on pp. 135f

the final answer. He has moved nearer to Job's position that confidence in God's justice is not based on observation, but is a matter of trust and hope. For Job, this hope might have to be postponed until after death. Zophar evidently thinks that retribution will be swift (verse 8) and dramatic (verses 6f.). The death of the godless will be premature (verse 11).

The picture of destitution in verse 10 may include the thought of poetic justice: *his children* will have to beg from the poor who had begged in vain from their father (*cf.* Tobit 4:7–19).

12–18. There is a certain realism in Zophar's remarks. They are not without foundation in fact. If judgment is a slow process, it is because God uses a person's own wickedness to bring about his downfall. Using a vivid image, he says that the delicious food relished so self-indulgently by the rich makes them vomit, because God turns it to poison in their stomach. The seven lines of this poem have an introverted structure: A B C D (verse 15) C′ B′ A′ which accounts for the remarks about snake venom before (14) and after (16) the climax (15), in which the name of God significantly occurs. With poetry of this fanciful kind we need not look for snake-bite as a punishment different from food poisoning (itself a figure), nor be worried by the scientific difficulty that vipers do not sting with their tongue.

19. Scholars are not sure about the boundaries of this poem. Zophar reflects common Israelite belief in highlighting neglect of the poor as the worst fault of the rich. Since verse 19 matches verse 10 in this regard, the introverted structure of verses 10–19 is completed if verse 11 corresponds to verse 18b, in which RSV has found two lines of poetry, both affirming that the wicked person does not live long enough to enjoy his criminal gains, nor to build a house on the land he has snatched.[1]

20–22. Some editors find a break at this point. These verses are not as clear as the rest of the poem, and a comparison of current translations will show how divergent the results can become when this happens. Verse 22 in RSV seems to contradict itself, for how can he be *in straits in the fullness of his sufficiency*? NEB suggests that he will experience a dramatic reversal of fortune at the very moment when he seems to have

---

[1] Proof that *house* in verse 19 means 'land', not a building, requires technical arguments for which this commentary does not provide room.

attained the height of success. Others imply that when he falls into want his suffering will be all the greater because he is so used to indulging his greed. But death, not poverty, seems to be his end, with poverty for his children (verse 10).

23–28. This seems to be a distinct poem. The verb forms express wishes, as if Zophar is calling down God's wrath on the wicked, like the curse in 5:3. In the references to various weapons there are painful echoes of Job's description of God's savage attack upon him (chapters 16 and 19). We recommend a translation: 'Let him flee from an iron weapon. Let a bronze arrow strike him through. Let it go right through and come out at the back. Let a javelin come out through his gall-bladder.' And so on.

Although verse 26 changes to the familiar figures of darkness, a symbol of disaster and fear, and fire, an agent of destruction like the cosmic blaze of Amos 7:4, the picture is not entirely clear. Once again the word *tent* is used to include all a person's property.

In 16:18f. Job had appealed to earth and heaven to support his cause. Here in verse 27 Zophar could be turning these words back upon Job. But the language is so conventional that no connection need be intended. What is important is the idea of a final public assize, a decisive *day of God's wrath*. Since the name *God*, which Zophar has used sparingly, is used twice in verse 29, it is rightly supplied in verse 28.

29. Several speeches in Job are summed up by means of a final bicolon of this kind. *Cf.* 18:21; 28:28.

It is worth pointing out, as a sign of the narrowness of Zophar's beliefs, that his speech contains no hint that the wicked might repent, make amends and regain the favour of God. Zophar has no compassion and his god has no mercy. By contrast Eliphaz is more humane and evangelical. And Zophar is at heart as much a materialist as the wicked man he condemns. He sees the carrying off of 'possessions' (verse 28) as a judgment. The loss of fellowship with God, in this life or after it, does not strike him as a far worse fate. Yet it is precisely this loss that fills Job's mind with horror, and this need that arouses his most desperate longings.

vi. Job (21:1–34). This speech is unusual for Job on several counts. It is the only one in which he confines his remarks to his friends and does not fall into either a soliloquy or a prayer. The time has come to demolish their position. Secondly, in making this counter-attack, Job reviews a lot of the preceding discussion, so that many cross-references can be found to what has already been said. These are a valuable guide to interpretation when they can be discovered. Thirdly, by quoting their words and refuting them, Job comes nearer to formal debate. While his words are still quite emotional, there is less invective in them.

In one place (verse 28) Job explicitly labels the quoted question as one which the friends have asked. But the question ascribed to them cannot be found in this form in any of their speeches.[1] Bildad (8:22), Eliphaz (15:34) and Zophar (20:26) have all referred in one way or another to the 'tent' of the wicked, laid waste by the wrath of God. This, then, is the point Job is referring to, without quoting verbatim. He is quoting freely, but not unfairly. This leads to the further question: When we find Job saying things which seem to be the opposite of what he believes, and sound like what the friends have said, or might say, should we identify such remarks as further quotations of the same kind, even though Job himself does not label them as such? Most scholars are convinced that verse 19a is another such quotation, and translators supply 'You say', which is not in the Hebrew. Gordis finds the same kind of thing in verses 22 and 30 (pp. 267f.), and he may well be right.

2–6. Job is angered by the friends' lack of empathy. A more fitting response to such a sight would be to *be appalled* (verse 5) and to be silent (5b) as they were at first (2:13). Just to *listen* (verse 2a) would be *your consolation* (2b), that is, 'the comfort you offer me' (NEB). They have not seen the real cause of his *shuddering* (6). Although verse 4a is not altogether clear,[2] it seems to imply that God, not man, is the cause of the trouble. But the friends have been approaching the problem all along on the supposition that God is the cause of Job's troubles, and Zophar has even dared to say that 'God exacts of you less than your guilt deserves' (11:6). Perhaps Job is saying that, even if the friends could manage to convey some solace, this still would not meet his need. His appeal for pity (19:21) was treated by Zophar as an 'insult' (20:3).

---

[1] The rare word 'prince' has actually been used only by Job (12:21).

[2] With RSV *complaint* contrast NEB 'thoughts', which is a more accurate translation of *śîḥ*, which refers to inner agitation.

In a parting shot (21:34) Job says that their words are empty and false. They can keep on mocking if they like (verse 3b), for that is what their comfort amounts to.[1]

7–16. The friends' thesis is that sin produces suffering. Their inference is that suffering proves sin. Job denies both. His attractive sketch of the carefree life of the wicked resembles the picture of the good man painted earlier by Eliphaz (5:17-27).

7. Zophar has just asserted that the wicked die prematurely (20:11). Job maintains the opposite: they reach old age and even improve in health. The Hebrew word translated *power* can refer to both physical prowess, managerial efficiency and material prosperity. In the introverted structure of the poem, verse 7 is matched by verse 13, where *spend their days* means 'complete their life-span'.

8. Bildad had asserted that the wicked die childless, as Job looks like doing (18:19). Job contradicts this. It is the wicked who have large, happy families, just like anybody else. Again the introversion places the description of the frolicking children (four different Hebrew words are used) in verses 8f. and 11f. around the reference to livestock in verse 10.

9. Eliphaz had asserted that Job's 'tent' would be safe (5:24). Job denies this. The *houses* (it could mean either families or estates) of the wicked are secure. The *rod of God*, which Job is feeling (9:34), does not fall on them.

10. The friends do not seem to have specified fertile bulls and fecund cows as God's gifts to His favourites, with sterility and miscarriages for the herds of the wicked. But the idea is a commonplace (Dt. 28:4, 18) and the people whose God is the Lord are promised flocks of incredible size, with successful pregnancies for the cows (Ps. 144:12-15). Job sees the wicked, not the righteous, in this happy state. The verse curiously reads 'his bull' and 'his cow', which most versions, including the Qumran Targum, have pluralized. Dhorme (p. 311) correctly explains the singular pronouns as attracted to the singular nouns. All may be left, so long as they are seen to be collective.

Since the clean introverted structure of verses 7–13 shows

---

[1] The *hiphil* verb implies the highest degree of derision. English does not bring out the switch from plural *bear* to singular *mock*, as if Zophar alone is singled out as a mocker. Unfortunately 11QtgJob fails just at the point which would tell us how it read this word.

them to be a single unit, the initial question *Why?* should be applied to each individual statement. Job does not consider the facts to be open to question. It is the reason for them he seeks.

14, 15. The wicked enjoy all this while practising the most presumptuous profanity. They will have none of God. In their experience, prayer is a waste of time.

16. The meaning of this verse is unclear and its place in the speech uncertain. NEB begins a new paragraph here, but RSV attaches verse 16 to the preceding. RV mg. adds 'Ye say', making it a quotation that Job attributes to the friends. It sounds like something Job said in 12:6, to the effect that the wicked make their own 'hand' their God. But such a sentiment could be part of the godless person's scorn, and Gordis includes it with verses 14f. Verse 16b sounds like a disavowal by Job, or even the horrified ejaculation of a pious reader,[1] but why this should occur here is not clear. In 10:3 Job had accused God of favouring 'the designs of the wicked'.

17–22. When the friends say that the wicked do not prosper, Job replies, 'But they do!' The friends have an answer for that: 'But not for long!' (20:5). Job retorts, *How often . . .?* Bildad had claimed that 'the light of the wicked' is extinguished (18:5). The Psalmist had said that the wicked are blown away *like chaff* (Ps. 1:4). Job asks, *How often . . . ?* If punishment is delayed, the friends can fall back another step and say that the children will pay for their fathers' sins (5:4; 20:10). Job considers this to be monstrous, encouraging a further depravity: 'We can sin; our children will pay!' *What do they care?* Job indignantly asks. This theory of the friends, that God is saving up *their iniquity for their sons* (verse 19a), is a blatant evasion, useless as a demonstration of God's justice (verse 22).[2] Justice will be seen to have been done, only when the wicked experience in themselves *their destruction* as *recompense*.

23–26. Job's point is not that the good always suffer, while the wicked are always at ease. This generalization is no more true than the formula of his friends that the righteous always prosper and the evil always fail. Life is more complicated than

---

[1] TEV, 'But their way of thinking I can't accept.'
[2] This is a guess. Where verse 22 fits in is not clear. Gordis thinks it is a quotation of a question the friends have asked Job, to put an end to his investigations.

that, and it does not disclose any patterns. And death always has the final say, and it says the same thing to everyone. At this stage Job's realistic observations come close to those of the Preacher (Ec. 2:14; *etc.*). Rowley sums it up well: 'In life no moral differences explain their diversity of fortune; in death as little do they explain their common fate' (p. 189).

27, 28. Job finds the thinking of the friends is so dishonest that it can only arise from malice.[1] Although they have rarely come out into the open with their accusation, their logic is obvious: the wicked suffer, Job suffers, therefore Job is wicked.

29. Zophar had airily appealed to universal knowledge (20:4). Job retorts that he cannot have been around much. Any traveller could tell him that things are just the opposite of what he says.

30–33. Verse 31 is difficult, but NEB, by identifying the interrogative *who* as negative 'no one' (there are plenty of other examples in the Old Testament), has probably got it right. The wicked are not exposed (31a), not requited (31b). On the contrary, they are actually *spared* and *rescued* on *the day of calamity*. This seems to point to an act of God. The rest of the poem observes that the public likes to flatter the rich (32f.), shutting its eyes to their crimes. Far from an ignominious death, with no memorial (Bildad in chapter 18, Zophar in chapter 20), the wicked ends his life with a flourish: a sumptuous funeral, accompanied by vast crowds, a lavish tomb, all the marks of honour and respect.

34. What Job is offered for *comfort* is *hebel*, the Preacher's favourite word for the 'vanity' (*empty nothings*) or futility of everything human.

d. Third round of speeches (22:1 – 26:14)

We have already observed that steady progress cannot be traced through the dialogue. There is a considerable amount of repetition and some back-tracking. Sometimes there is delay before a statement made by one speaker is taken up by another. Nevertheless, a certain movement can be detected. In the first cycle the friends are content to talk in generalities, without venturing to apply their doctrine openly to Job. In the

---

[1] 11QtgJob seems to confirm RSV emphasis on scheming rather than physical violence.

second round the main theme is the fate of the wicked and Job's point of view comes into open contradiction with that of his friends. Their relationship noticeably deteriorates and there is a certain amount of vituperation. The inference from Job's resemblance to the state of the wicked, namely that he must be a sinner, has been made, obliquely at first. Now it comes into the open and the breach between them is complete. Once this point is reached there can be no further dialogue, and the discussion grinds to a halt.

From the point of view of the friends, Job's persistence is incomprehensible. The idea of a good man suffering never enters their thoughts. It would demolish their theology, or, as Eliphaz has already said, undermine religion (15:4). The reader, who happens to know what is really going on, understands that Job is neither stubborn nor arrogant. He is honest and tenacious. From the depths of a sick body and broken mind, his spirit is still thrusting its faith into God, even though his blind cries sound wild to his friends.

i. Eliphaz (22:1-30). Eliphaz is a good man. No trace of malice appears in his words. The irony of his final speech lies in his failure to see Job's problem with Job's eyes, or more, to feel it with Job's feelings. How can he, when he thinks Job is self-deceived? He does his best, and he talks well.[1] He makes a more drastic attempt to bring Job face to face with his sin (verses 2–11), pays another tribute to the greatness of God (12–20), and makes a final appeal to Job to repent (21–30).

2-4. Eliphaz thinks that Job has charged God with moral indifference to the conduct of wicked men, saying, 'What does God know?' (verse 13). This alleged quotation is not found in any of Job's reported words. Job has never questioned God's knowledge. But it seems to Eliphaz that Job feels that God doesn't care.[2] Eliphaz is shocked at the idea, and is genuinely alarmed for the spiritual safety of a person who can say such a thing. Here is proof of Job's impiety, if any had been lacking before. Far from being apathetic (2f., a belated reply to 7:20), God is active in judgment (4). Eliphaz is

---

[1] With *belles sentences, et sainctes*, as Calvin says (*COCR*, XXXIII, p. 23).

[2] Jb. 21:22 could be in mind. If so, it disposes of the idea that that verse is not Job's idea, but one of his quotations from the friends. In any case, Job has said that the wicked prosper with the connivance of God.

emphatic that God could not possibly be reproving Job *for your fear of him*, that is, for Job's celebrated 'piety' (NEB; *cf.* 1:1). We know, in fact, that this is precisely why Job is suffering. But Eliphaz, reacting against Job's blasphemy that God is indifferent to human wickedness, has fallen into an opposite blasphemy of his own, that God is indifferent to human virtue (2f.). Again we know that Job's righteousness was a matter of immense pleasure to God.

5–11. Eliphaz now openly brands Job a sinner more bluntly than anyone has so far dared to do. He accuses him of extreme wickedness. The list of crimes enumerated in verses 6–9 is very revealing. None have to do with religion in the formal sense. Job is not charged with any failure in his duty to God, nor is he blamed for having done anything wrong. To that extent, Eliphaz can still find no flaw in Job's conduct. Instead, he tests a person's goodness by the way he treats his fellow-man. The acts Eliphaz describes are not elicited by legal or even moral obligation. Here, too, Job had never failed. For superlative righteousness, a person should be humane towards the needy, not from duty, but from compassion. The destitute were protected from neglect and exploitation (6) by Exodus 22:26f.; Deuteronomy 24:10ff. Job later denies any failure here (31:19). The hungry and thirsty (7) should be succoured. Job insists that he did this (31:17). A woman or child left without the protection of a man (the terms are wider than widow and orphan) (9) are constantly commended to the compassion of the Israelite, especially of rulers (Dt. 10:18; 14:29; *etc.*), and their neglect is condemned again and again in the Old Testament as the worst social evil (Ex. 22:22; Dt. 27:19; *etc.*). Once more Job is innocent (31:16f.).

8. Some commentators have removed this verse because it interrupts the continuity, and is in the third person. But, as we have seen so often, this more general statement is enclosed in, and sums up, the particular items that surround it. The common wrong done to the poor (6), the starving (7) and the defenceless (9) is to abuse one's power by seizing and occupying their family *land*.[1] This also Job had never done (31:38–40).

[1] The enormity of this crime is illustrated by 1 Kings 21. See the writer's treatment in *JBL*, LXXXV, 1966, pp. 46–57.

10, 11. The sins Eliphaz traces to Job explain why the *snares* that Bildad had spoken about (18:8ff.) have now caught him. The oft-used images of *darkness* and *flood of water* are also applied to Job (11), for these are the best examples of God's judgment, even though they do not match the events of chapters 1 and 2.

12–20. Everyone agrees that God is great. Neither RSV (*high in the heavens*), nor NEB ('at the zenith of the heavens'), nor any other translation we have seen has grasped the point that 'tall' is an attribute of the Lord, not of the sky. He is higher than the heavens. The comparative preposition is often omitted in poetry. This agrees with the further statement that God *walks on the vault of heaven* (14). This removes God from the world, and by saying that Job holds the view that God *does not see through the deep darkness* and *thick clouds*, Eliphaz perverts Job's position. For Job has complained about being under God's constant surveillance, without himself being able to see God.

15, 16. This description of the wicked fits mankind before the Flood, but it could apply to any age. The reference to a 'river' (a word not used in the Flood stories) has been taken as a simile by NEB and some other translations. Since the verb translated *snatched away*, found only in Job, is rendered simply 'they died' by 11QtgJob, we may doubt if it is an Aramaism, as hitherto alleged.

20. While the reference to *fire* may take us back to Genesis 19 (thus strengthening the suspicion that verse 16 refers to the Flood), it could be no more than a general reference to one of the traditional destroyers used by God (*cf.* Jb. 20:26). If verses 16 and 20 belong together by introversion, the word *saying*, supplied by RSV, but not present in MT, may not be necessary.

In verses 17f. Eliphaz is tackling what Job had said in 21:14–16, but just how he is handling it is not clear. The general impression is this. The impiety Job there describes receives punishment by water (verse 16) and fire (20). Perhaps verse 18 should be seen as Eliphaz's quotation of Job's words in order to refute them. The judgment which Job denies is seen and enjoyed by the righteous. In Psalm 2:4 the Lord similarly derides the wicked.

21–28. There is no mistaking the earnestness of Eliphaz's closing words. He is a diligent soul-winner, doing his best.

What he says about God is correct. Its warmth is an improvement on his earlier severity. In spite of what he has just said about God's terrifying judgment and the gratification this brings to the righteous, Eliphaz (unlike Zophar, whose rigour never softens) obviously prefers the mercy of God, which will generously accept any sinner in his penitence. It is pleasing that his final statement encourages Job with such a hearty evangelistic appeal.

The only thing wrong with Eliphaz's exhortation is that it is completely irrelevant to Job's case.

21, 22. The exact meaning of Eliphaz's initial advice, *Agree with God*, is not known. Many proposals are available. The purport is clear. Job will find *peace* and *good* by accepting *instruction*[1] from God's mouth. It is a common opinion of commentators that Eliphaz is here affecting to be God's mouthpiece (*cf.* his appeal to revelation in his first speech, 4:12ff.). But it is more likely that he is echoing Bildad's wish that Job would 'seek God' (8:5), and Zophar's expectation that God would speak (11:5). What makes this so fatuous is their assumption that this is easy to arrange, and their presumption that they already know the outcome. God does speak in the end, but what He says is a surprise to everyone, including modern readers.

23-25. These are the conditions that Job must satisfy. Verse 23 is a conventional description of repentance in general terms. Verses 24 and 25 abound in difficulties and, in spite of the industry of many scholars, seem to be as far from solution as ever. RSV is probably close to the truth in keeping the verses together, and making the *if* of verse 23 blanket all three verses.[2] By mentioning only *gold* as needing Job's attention, Eliphaz hints that wealth was the cause of his downfall and that, to be right with God, Job must renounce it and make God alone his treasure. Some commentators have found this idea too spiritual for acceptance; but wisdom is prized as better than wealth in Proverbs 3, to mention only one place. *Ophir* is the legendary source of the best gold. Its location is not known (*cf.* Gn. 10:29). There is no need to

---

[1] This is the only place in Job where the word *tôrāh* is used. The terminology of the Mosaic 'law' is surprisingly absent from the book as a whole.

[2] Some commentators make verse 23 the only condition, so that verses 24–28 describe the happy consequences for the penitent. NEB begins the description of the outcome with verse 25.

supply the word *gold* in verse 24b, since its occurrence in verse 24a is sufficient to complete the phrase.

27, 28. Eliphaz echoes promises made in many parts of the Bible in this forecast of the happy results of reconciliation with God. It is a tribute to his own spirituality that, whereas in 5:17-26 he had emphasized the material advantages of religion, here intimacy with God and success in prayer are of chief importance. While it is hurtful to remember that Job has already made these his supreme values, the irony will be felt at the end when Eliphaz will be the chief beneficiary of Job's power as an intercessor (42:8).

29, 30. Eliphaz falls back on some commonplaces of Wisdom teaching to end his speech. At least so it seems. The Hebrew text is a thicket of thorns, and AV pays the price of honesty by being largely unintelligible. Solutions are almost as numerous as commentators. If RSV is right in saying that God *delivers the innocent man*, then Eliphaz has annulled his call to repentance (verse 23) and fallen back on a sterile legalism of salvation for the righteous alone.[1] Pope (p. 164) has done better by translating literally 'one not innocent' (*cf.* footnote to NEB), but he concurs with Gordis that this guilty person is not Job himself, but someone saved by Job's purity (Gordis, p. 271). This is, of course, what does eventually happen in chapter 42, and we have already pointed out the irony that it is Eliphaz himself who stands indebted to Job for this patronage with God. But in the context of the present speech Eliphaz is treating Job as a sinner (5-11) in darkness (11), for whom he has a remedy that will bring him to the light (28). All this would be wasted if Eliphaz were locked in to Zophar's position (chapter 20) of reward for the good, affliction for the bad, no troubles for the good, no relief for the bad; and no way, it would seem, for a bad person to become good. Eliphaz is more evangelical, and his words would be good news for anyone suffering from a guilty conscience. If Eliphaz had not misjudged Job (22:5), his proclamation of salvation through forgiveness of the penitent would have been the brightest word that any of the friends have said. As such they

---

[1] Harmonization might be secured if Eliphaz is teaching that Job must first make himself 'clean of hands' by self-abasement, which still means that he has no real gospel of forgiveness for sinners. Unfortunately RSV *humble yourself* in verse 23 is a guess (*cf.* other translations) and the word translated *lowly* in verse 29 occurs only here, so that its meaning has to be guessed.

have an intrinsic truth that need not be denied. If Job does not accept them it is because they do not apply. Not everybody's need can be met by preaching the gospel.

ii. Job (23:1 – 24:25). The first part of this speech is superb. The option placed before Job by Eliphaz has clarified his thinking. He has come to quite different conclusions, and he expresses them in a soliloquy, for he does not appear to be addressing either Eliphaz or God. Job is not at all reluctant to 'come to terms with God' (22:21, NEB). On the contrary, there is nothing he desires more (23:2–7). But it is not as easy as people seem to think. God is inaccessible (verses 8–17). Job's acknowledgment of this fact is less complaining, more admiring, than some of the things he had said earlier.

In chapter 24 we run into all kinds of problems. First there are textual difficulties, which render many lines almost unintelligible. While many translators have patched them up to their satisfaction, NAB has admitted defeat with verses 18–24, and is content to supply a translation from the Vulgate in a footnote. Secondly, the speech as a whole seems incoherent to many readers. Numerous solutions have been offered. Some scholars blame the most troublesome verses on later scribes, who inserted them to improve the doctrine. Whether modern scholars have now improved the text by removing these suspected intruders, we must leave the reader to judge. The failure of research to agree on which verses deserve the surgeon's knife should make us pause before accepting their shortened version as original. Others have tried to tidy up the chapter by shuffling the verses around into a different sequence. What Pope has done in the *Anchor Bible* is a good example. Others again (and here we have quite a line of scholars from Duhm to Fohrer) gave up the search for order in this chapter, and viewed it as an uncoordinated bunch of little poems. An extreme result along these lines is represented by Snaith's conclusion that the whole of chapters 24 to 28 constitute 'a collection of miscellaneous pieces, not placed in any recognizable order and not arranged according to any recognizable plan'.[1] According to this hypothesis, the dialogue ends with chapter 23.

Thirdly, chapter 24 is said to express sentiments that Job could never have uttered. They would sound better on the

[1] *SBT*², XI, 1968, p. 62.

lips of his friends. Verses 18-24 in particular would, in the opinion of many scholars, represent a complete reversal of Job's beliefs, if he really declared these words as his own conviction. Hence it would be better to assign these lines to someone else. This problem is generally connected with two other curious features of the third round of speeches, namely the brevity of Bildad's third speech in chapter 25 and the complete lack of a third speech by Zophar. Some of Job's words in chapters 26 and 27 are said to resemble 24:18-24 in being out of character. Such passages have been culled out and given to Bildad or Zophar or both, in various ways. The confidence with which the Jerusalem Bible, to mention only one instance, has reorganized the text along these lines shows what an attraction such a solution has, even for scholars with a high view of biblical inspiration. Since the scope of the present commentary does not permit more than this to be said, we shall have to be content with taking the text at its face value, and do the best we can.

2. The problem of finding drinkable water in the desert made the Israelites contumacious, and the similar sounds of the Hebrew words meaning 'rebellion' and 'bitterness' provided the tradition with a popular pun. This word-play seems to be used here, and from ancient times translators have chosen between the two possibilities, such as 'defiant' (Gordis) or 'resentful' (NEB). Since Job's mood in this chapter is somewhat subdued, he is probably denying that he is 'rebellious' (RV), but admits being *bitter* (RSV). The word has exactly the meaning that Naomi gives it (Ru. 1:20), for similar reasons. MT reads 'my hand', but 'God's hand' (NEB) is certainly meant, as Mesopotamian parallels show. There is evidence that the suffix 'my', which can mean 'his' in Phoenician, was sometimes so used in Hebrew as well. This solves the problem without changing the text.

3-7. Here Job's courageous honesty is seen at its best. His consuming desire is to come face to face with God (3), not by a contrived penance, as Eliphaz recommends, but in fair trial (4). Job has abandoned his earlier hesitation and self-mistrust (9:14-20, 32; 13:18). He is now confident that he will be able to state his case persuasively (4).[1] He is confident of acquittal (7). He is prepared to answer charges (5; *cf.* 13:22). Earlier, when everyone had been emphasizing the infinite

[1] This is what he does in chapters 29-31.

power of God, Job had dreaded such a meeting, even while he was demanding it. Fully aware that God is 'not a man' (9:32), he expected to be paralysed with terror (9:34; 13:21) when it was his turn to speak. Behind this anxiety lay an even more shattering thought. What if the difference between God and man is so great that each has a different moral code and Job finds that there is no common ground to argue on? The friends' songs in praise of God's justice, instead of making Job feel guilty, have had the opposite effect. Now he is certain that he is in the right (7a: the key word of Jb. 1:1), and equally sure that God will not take unfair advantage of His superior strength (6a), but will give him a fair hearing (6b). The acquittal he expects is not the pardon of a guilty man by grace, but the vindication of a righteous man by law. This does not mean that the book of Job is ignorant of the truths that were later enshrined in Pauline theology. The justification of which Paul spoke is attested by 'the law and the prophets' (Rom. 3:21), including Job. What Job is seeking is confirmation from God, in contradiction of what his friends have been saying, that his right relationship with God, which, throughout his whole life, had been grounded in 'the fear of God' and not in the merit of his own good deeds, was unimpaired. Job's expanding faith will now embrace his sufferings as something between himself and God within that right relationship.

8-12. To see all this is not to achieve it. Job is powerless to arrange the confrontation he desires. He has searched in every direction: *forward, backward, left* and *right*.[1] But even when walking as if without God (8f.), Job has trodden assiduously in God's footsteps (11f.). It is a daring claim, self-annihilating if not true. In the construction of this little poem the key thought (10) resolves the paradox in the two units (each a tetracolon) that embrace it. Faith keeps a dry skin in the water. Job's faith combines these opposites – a vivid consciousness of an intimate personal relationship with God through obedience to *his way*,[2] and an equally vivid awareness of being denied fellowship with God. The latter is entirely God's doing: 'The Lord gave, the Lord took' (*cf.* 1:21). Job has done nothing to forfeit God's favour. Therefore he sees his

[1] Perhaps the points of the compass are intended.
[2] The words *lips* and *mouth* bring out the vital fact that Job's righteousness is not ethical obedience to moral rules, but personal faithfulness to a living Lord.

experience for what it is: not punishment, not chastisement, but a test. *He knows the way* . . . (10a). The word *way* in the Hebrew has neither article nor suffix. It is traditionally referred to Job's conduct, and the ancient versions already read 'my way'. But, although *he knows the way that I take* has gathered a lot of devotional sentiment over the centuries, it has blurred the Hebrew 'with me'. It is more likely that the missing suffix refers to the subject of the verb, God, and that *way* equals *his way* in verse 11. A more literal translation then yields: 'But he (God) knows (his) way with me.' Because God knows what He is doing with Job, Job is coming to a point where he will be satisfied even if God never explains the reason for His strange conduct. Earlier Job had demanded to know why God was dealing with him thus, and he found his trial insufferable (7:18). Now he accepts the testing, because he knows: *I shall come forth as gold.* This image, drawn from metallurgy, does not necessarily imply purification. It could mean simply that the test proves that Job had been pure gold all along. The comparison of Job with *gold* at this point may be an echo of 22:24f., where the reference was less clear. There Eliphaz urged Job to make God his most precious thing; here Job is saying that he is precious to God. Only valued metal is put through the fire.

13, 14. Israel's highest confession of faith was that the Lord is One (Dt. 6:4). Once the preposition is recognized as *beth essentiae*, it is obvious that Job is saying the same thing here. There is no need to interpret it as *unchangeable* (RSV), or to add the word 'mind' (AV); and many modern translations (*AB*, NEB, *etc.*) have (wrongly, I think) been encouraged by the parallelism to adopt an emendation of the text that leads to 'he chooses' or 'he decides'. The statement that 'He is One' carries with it an affirmation of God's sole sovereignty. 'He does what his own heart desires' (NEB). And the plans of God are multifarious beyond human comprehension (14b). Job is already coming close to the point he will reach at the end of the story. And how different his God is from the domesticated God of his friends. Yet Job's God is not lost in His own vastness. Job cannot scale the heights of 'the steep and trifid God',[1]

---

[1] 'Pontifical Death, that doth the crevasse bridge
  To the steep and trifid God; one mortal birth
  That broker is of immortality.'
  　　　　　　　　　　Francis Thompson, *An Anthem of Earth.*

but he knows that God's plans are focused on himself personally (14a).

15–17. In view of the structures we have often found in earlier chapters, we should not suppose that these words represent an eclipse of the faith of verses 10–14, just because they come later, as if 'his terror returns' (Rowley, p. 203). If the word *therefore* is taken seriously, his *dread* is an essential part of his faith (see commentary on 13:11). The sense of being *hemmed in by darkness* corresponds to the experience described in verses 8f. But too much should not be made of verse 17 in view of the fact that the Hebrew text is almost unintelligible.

24:1–17. The next poem returns to a familiar theme. Job's own experience of being left in the dark (23:17) and the impossibility of bringing his cause to God for redress (23:3–9) is but one instance of many. The claim of the friends, that God regularly enforces justice in the world, is not borne out by facts. According to RSV Job asks why God does not have a fixed schedule of court sessions so that *those who know him* can resort to Him. The implication is that there should be such an arrangement and that Job is finding fault with God's administration because there is not.[1] Such a hasty conclusion would be unwise when the text is far from clear.

In spite of what has been said about their incoherence, verses 2–16 are a fairly conventional inventory of crimes. Verse 17 can then be linked to verse 1 as the frame in which this picture is set. Just as in chapter 21 Job gave his version of the untrammelled prosperity of the wicked, in answer to the friends' quite opposite claims, so here he answers what Eliphaz had said about the ungodly in chapter 22. The point would then be that God apparently does nothing to prevent the wrongs that occur every day. What makes the list disturbing is that most of the evils, such as removing a landmark (verse 2), are things forbidden again and again in the laws that the Lord gave to Israel. Hence the question, why doesn't He enforce them?

---

[1] NEB, by cavalier removal of the first word *Why?*, arrives at a result more in harmony with chapter 23, to the effect that God has everything properly organized, even though men 'have no hint of its date'. But it is very doubtful if the book of Job contains the idea of a final 'day of reckoning'. A solution that leaves MT as it is is much to be preferred, but none is yet in sight. AV, RV, RSV, *etc.* all take liberties.

4. It is not clear why thrusting *the poor off the road* is serious enough to deserve mention. Something more culpable than 'jostle' (NEB) is required. Perhaps it is a figure for the denial of civil rights.

5-7. Job describes the pitiful condition of the helpless members of the community, victimized by the ruthless. Any decent person would be moved to indignation by such outrages, and Job's own compassion comes out in his protest.

8-11. At some point the description of the plight of the dispossessed changes to the wretchedness of over-worked labourers, exploited with low wages, clad in rags, hungry for the harvest they gather for the well-fed owner. Thirsty, they tread the grapes. (There is no need to move verse 6 up to verse 2 to bring the field near the boundary stone; nor to move verse 9 in between verses 3 and 4 to deal with poverty in one place. It is amazing that critics have thought that the poem is in disarray because it was not written in the way a storekeeper writes a docket. This is not the time for neat lists.)

12. The climax of pathos is reached with the groans of the dying. But the Hebrew reads 'men'. NEB turns the references into similes. The *wounded* could be mentioned in anticipation of verse 14.

Verse 12c is an excellent example of a single colon which serves an important structural purpose. It is the hinge between the list of crimes in verses 2-12 and the account of criminals in verses 13-17. God is (or seems) indifferent to it all. MT reads *tiplāh*, 'folly', as in 1:22. Since *śm*, 'put', is a synonym for *ntn*, 'give', the statements are essentially the same. God ascribes nothing improper to such actions. RSV, however, identifies *yāśîm* as laconic for the familiar idiom 'pay attention' (*cf.* 1:8), and reads *t^epillāh*, 'prayer', which has a little MS support.

God neither redresses the wrongs of the downtrodden described in verses 2-12, nor restrains the wickedness described in verses 13-17. It is easy to theorize, and to say that the former must be sinners, getting what they deserve (less, according to Zophar; 11:6), while the latter will get theirs later. Since God is infinitely holy, the slightest sin is an infinite affront for which no punishment would be too severe. Job, who identifies himself with the wretches of verses 2-12, cannot accept such a callous theology. The inactivity of God is no proof of His disfavour.

13-17. Job selects murderers, adulterers and burglars, because their crimes are committed under cover of darkness. Consequently they love the dark and hate the light, a point made several times in this poem. Like the depraved of Isaiah 5:20, their values are inverted. The coming of darkness is their *morning* (17a) when they must be up and doing. What holds *terrors* for others is their ally (17b). The worst part is that they think that the darkness, which prevents men from detecting them, also hides them from God. Like the ungodly described by Eliphaz (22:17) they think, '*No eye will see me*' (15), including God's. And so it would seem to be, contrary to Eliphaz's confidence that their exposure will bring public satisfaction to the righteous (22:19).

18-25. The problems attaching to this paragraph have been mentioned in the Introduction (see pp. 53f., 208). We should not too hastily remove these words from Job's lips, just because they don't sound like what we think he should say. This has been done in three ways: to remove them altogether as a pious gloss which makes Job sound more orthodox than he is; to transfer them to one of the friends, either Bildad (NAB), or Zophar (Pope); to take them as a quotation by Job of what his friends say (RSV, which adds *You say*, and identifies verses 21-24 as Job's rejoinder; or Gordis, who takes all of verses 18-24 as the quotation).

While admitting that the difficulties are compounded by problems of a textual character, we are not convinced that Job could not have uttered these words. Job has never maintained that the wicked never come to the bad end described by Eliphaz (5:2-7; 15:17-35), Bildad (8:8-19; 18:5-21) and Zophar (20:4-29). When he asked, 'How often is it that the lamp of the wicked is put out?' (21:17), his implied answer is not 'Never'. Rather his impression is that God treats good and bad alike. Among the prosperous are righteous and wicked. Disaster overtakes the vicious, but also the virtuous. In the end, death takes them all (21:23-26). In other words, Job does not counter the friends by a one-sided exaggeration of his own, claiming that God is hostile to the upright and an accomplice of the crooked. His position is more balanced, but more baffled. He simply cannot see how God's justice works out in his own case, which he realizes is only one of many. There is therefore no reason why he should not flaunt this problem again by throwing together one poem about the immunity of criminals from divine intervention (verses 13–17) and another about the frustration of their enterprises by death or some other set-back. (verses 18–24). That some of the sentiments expressed here are compatible with Job's known views is shown by the willingness of RSV to let him have verses 21–24. The distinction that this implies will help us to disentangle the several threads in this little poem, or rather to see how they are woven together. This cannot be done with certainty, if only because it is often unclear whether it is God or the wicked person who is the performer of the action described. RSV has taken such liberties with the Hebrew text that it is not to be trusted. AV, although not without its faults, is much to be preferred, if only because its literalness reproduces the obscurities of the original. The Hebrew text supplies several clues, through its vocabulary, for connections with earlier speeches. Thus the vineyard scene in verse 18 goes back to verse 11. The imagery of *snow waters* and the broken *tree* has been used before. The allusion to the 'womb' and the 'worm' in verse 20 (unfortunately lost by RSV but happily restored by NEB) connects with verse 21, providing a glimmer of light on the genre of this piece. Once the troublesome *feed* is recognized as 'female companion' (Ps. 45:14) we may suspect that the whole is a string of curses, beginning with verse 18, where an imprecation, not a statement, should be read, as the grammar shows. Hence the variegated picture. Even if we concede that Job is here expecting an eventual devastation of the wicked after a temporary triumph, this does not represent capitulation to the friends' beliefs. It is only a small portion of the complex picture he presents, and by no means his last word on the subject.

iii. Bildad (25:1–6). The discussion is nearly exhausted. The brevity of Bildad's final speech and the absence of a third speech by Zophar are indications that the friends have run out of fuel. Attempts to enlarge Bildad's pronouncement by adding some lines gathered from near-by speeches of Job are not convincing, if only because the number and variety of competing solutions leave the student quite dizzy. Bildad's feeble ideas, most of which we have heard before, are the platitudes of theology common to all the protagonists.

2, 3. In one respect Bildad has made a significant retreat before Job's assault. He no longer speaks so confidently about the judgment of God on the wicked. According to LXX, the first word is a question, in line with the questions that follow. These anticipate, in a way, the questions that God Himself will soon ask on a more elaborate scale. Bildad has taken a flight to heaven and, by emphasizing its vast population, implies not only that God's limitless resources cannot be opposed, but also that no person can hope to comprehend God's enterprises.[1] Job has no quarrel with such assertions. But how different the inference! According to Bildad, puny man counts for nothing in the infinite space of God's mind. But Job thinks that God, precisely because of His boundless capacity for knowledge, can give to each individual the most complete personal attention.

3-6. In spite of the statements of some scholars that this poem is a fragment, these verses display a beautiful symmetry. There is alternation between the heavenly bodies (3, 5) and man (4, 6). We have returned to the first point made by Eliphaz (4:17ff.). The idea that the heavenly bodies (or angels), for all their magnificence, are dull compared with God's brightness throws man into an even darker shadow. If the heavens are not clean, how much less man who is abominable and corrupt (15:14ff.)? This sounds like a very pessimistic doctrine of total depravity. There is no way for any man to be *clean* or *righteous before God*.[2] Man is a *maggot*, a grub (6). On this disgusting and hopeless note the words of Job's friends end.

iv. Job (26:1-14). Job now holds the stage in the longest discourse by one person in the book: 26:1 - 31:40. At least, no other persons are named until Elihu appears on the scene in chapter 32. But it is not certain that Job himself says all this. It is not a single speech, for it is broken at two points by a formula not used elsewhere (27:1; 29:1). This is why we have identified chapter 26 as the last speech of the third round and chapter 27 as the conclusion of the dialogue as a whole. While chapter 28 could be a continuation of this, and

[1] While some find *light* (verse 3b) an acceptable parallel to armies, especially since it often means the 'sun' and the *moon* and the *stars* are mentioned in verse 5, NEB has followed LXX in reading 'ambush'.
[2] It is strange that the 'innocent' and 'upright' person, about whom the friends spoke so confidently at first (4:7), seems now forgotten.

Job's final statement on the subject of wisdom, we think it is more likely that it serves as an interlude between Job's dialogue with the three friends and his interchange with Elihu. It is thus spoken by the author (the only place where he declares his own mind), even though no speaker is identified.

Chapter 26 is one of the grandest recitals in the whole book. It is excelled only by the Lord's speeches, as is fitting. It sounds well in Job's mouth, and ends the dialogue, like the first movement of a symphony, with great crashing chords.

It is surprising that so many scholars have stolen parts of this speech from Job and given them to one or other of his friends. We have already touched on this kind of problem in connection with chapter 24. Similar considerations apply here.

The speech is in two parts. First there is a sarcastic response to Bildad's dismal last speech (verses 2–4). Then there is a magnificent description of God's power in creation (5–14). It is the latter that is considered out of place in Job's mouth by many scholars. But it seems to me that it is even more out of place in the mouth of Bildad, where it is often put. By tacking it on to the end of chapter 25, the impact of Bildad's last word (25:6) is lost. Furthermore, 26:2–4 makes sense as Job's retaliation to this insult, but it is inconceivable that Job would heap scorn on such a superb exposition of God's splendour as 26:5–14, if this is Bildad's final word.[1] We search in vain in the preceding discussion for ideas of this kind in the mind of any of the friends. It is true that Eliphaz has a lyric along these lines (5:9ff.), but it is nothing to the eloquence with which Job caps this (9:4–10; 12:7–25). This passage (26:5–14) is then Job's last and best treatment of this theme. Incidentally, this also shows that the Lord's speeches, which are almost entirely restricted to such topics, do not go off at a tangent, as some scholars complain. They

[1] We shall say nothing further about the dozens of mutually-contradictory 'solutions' by which scholars have unscrambled the allegedly disordered speeches at the end of the third round. We do not wish to disdain such efforts; by the very nature of textual criticism, certainty is hard to achieve in such matters and, by the same token, no-one can say dogmatically that the text has suffered no injury in transmission. But when there is so little sign of a consensus, it might be better to leave the text as it is, since the onus of proof rests with those who wish to alter it, and so far nothing like proof has been forthcoming.

have already been prepared for in the dialogue, and Job's mind has moved a considerable distance in this direction before the Lord speaks. Already Job seems to have left behind the problems of the fate of the wicked and the sufferings of the just.

2–4. The word designs in this little poem have a filigree exquisiteness. The pronouns are singular; Job is addressing one person, presumably Bildad. Job resents Bildad's attitude to himself as a person with *no power, no strength, no wisdom*.[1] Since poetry often omits prepositions, and *the arm* (2b) is always that of the deliverer, the question is, 'How have you saved with your arm the strengthless?'[2] Since Elihu speaks about 'the breath of the Almighty' in 33:4, Job is probably saying in 26:4 that Bildad's *words* have not issued from divine inspiration.

5–14. Since Bildad is abysmally ignorant of God and His ways, it is fitting that Job should instruct him. Their roles are reversed. The catechumen knows more than the catechist! The transition to this next poem is abrupt. It starts with the underworld (5f.) and expands until the entire universe is explored.

This is one of the most fascinating cosmological passages in the entire Bible. More than a dozen elements are listed: earth, water, cloud, sky, *etc.*, sometimes under the names they had in the old myths, such as Yam (*sea*), *Rahab*, and especially *the fleeing serpent*. A little of the vocabulary comes from Genesis; *e.g.*, *the void* (7a) is the word translated 'without form' in Genesis 1:2. But none of the creation verbs of Genesis is used. It would seem that more than one old creation-story has supplied the disparate imagery. The division of light from darkness is reported in Genesis, but the architectural imagery of *the pillars of heaven* (11a) and laying out the plan by inscribing *a circle* (10a) with cosmic callipers is not found there. The mention of Sapon (*the north*) in verse 7a (*cf.* Is. 14:13) takes us back to the primaeval world-mountain of Canaanite (and perhaps, behind that, Egyptian or Sumerian) creation-stories. The subjugation of Yam/Rahab is well known from Canaanite sources, as well as having a more distant connection with the Babylonian creation epic in which Marduk subdues

---

[1] NEB, adopting a suggestion of Driver's (*HTR*, XXIX, 1936, p. 172), completes the quartet by reading 'foolish' instead of *plentifully* in verse 3b.
[2] *Cf.* the Lord's question to Job: 'Have you an arm like God?' (40:9).

Tiamat. Whether *the fleeing serpent* (13b) is another name for
this sea monster, or whether we have a different story about a
flying dragon, is not known. We are hampered in our search
for the background of this allusion by the paucity of creation-
stories of Canaanite provenance, but the reference to *his
wind* (literally 'Spirit') takes us back to Genesis 1:2. It is not
certain that *the moon* is referred to in verse 9. MT reads 'throne'
(*cf.* AV). Clarification is likely to be found by comparing the
picture here with that in Psalm 104 and Isaiah 40. It is
worth adding that the points of contact that this poem has
with Genesis 1 seem to come in a sequence that is the reverse
of the events recounted there. This suggests that Job 26:5–14
is not a creation-story, but a pastiche of phrases from several
traditions.

14. These snatches from mysterious old poems create an
atmosphere of wonder. The mind is lost in the immensity of
God's world and the even greater immensity of the Power
behind it. But, Job says, this is but a glimpse, a whisper, a
fraction: 'these are only the boundaries of His realm'![1]
We should not wax too metaphysical over this statement. It
could be that Job is hinting that the visible cosmos, for all
its vastness, is but the outer boundary of the 'real' realm of
God, transcendent and quite hidden. From such a remote
distance, *the thunder of his power* reaches man as no more
than a faint *whisper*, communicating nothing intelligible.
Grand as this may sound, it is highly doubtful if Job was such
an agnostic. Although what we can see and hear of God in
His world (our world!) is but a fragment of all that He is,
it is not to be demeaned because our minds are so small. To
scrap these tiny insights because they might be deceptive,
or no safe guide to the remainder of God's unexplored infinity,
would be timid. And Job is doughty. The word *outskirts* does
not describe the visible world as an impenetrable frontier
behind which God is forever hidden. Rather it describes the
limits of a realm from the point of view of a person who lives
inside it. By mapping the universe from Sheol to heaven
Job has shown us the world *in* which God lives with people.

---

[1] It is now widely recognized that *drkw* in Pr. 8:22 is to be read as
durkō, 'his realm'. The same applies to Jb. 26:14, where the spelling is
identical, making the MT 'his ways' unnecessary. The common Canaanite
background supports this result. See below, p. 234, n. 2, and commentary
on Jb. 28:23.

He has said nothing about the 'manifold' and 'innumerable' creatures that inhabit this world (Ps. 104:24f.). When compared with, say, Genesis 1, Job's silence about all vegetation, all creatures of water, land and air, about man, is astonishing. The wise man delighted to talk about trees, animals, birds, reptiles and fish (1 Ki. 4:33). Very soon the Lord will do just that. Meanwhile Job admits that the subject is beyond human telling; but he does not draw negative conclusions from this awareness of his own limitations.

e. Job's conclusion (27:1–23)

1. A new formula is used to introduce this speech. This marks it off from the rest of the dialogue.[1] We suggest that it is a closing statement, balancing chapter 3.

Although we have frequently pointed out that the key statements of some speeches come at climactic points in the middle, on some occasions the punch-line comes at the end. Job's closing remarks are worth looking at as the debate draws to a close or, rather, falls to pieces. In 21:34 he says that the friends' answers are nothing but falsehood. In 24:25 he challenges them to show that there is nothing in what he says. These two thoughts come out once more in 27:2–6. Chapter 26 is Job's final recognition of God's great power, of which a complete account is impossible. The same applies to God's justice, which can be perceived only in bits and pieces. This limitation does not prevent Job from reaffirming the justice of God (27:7–23). He can only insist on his own righteousness (verse 6) if he is confident that God will endorse it. Hence his prediction of judgment on the godless is not a belated conversion to his friends' point of view; nor is it a slice of orthodoxy put into the text long after it was finished, by some worried scribe (much as the Christians converted Josephus posthumously in the manuscripts of *The Jewish War*). Nor need we relabel 27:7–23 as the lost third speech of Zophar, even though this proposal has enjoyed considerable prestige among scholars for two centuries. Since Job nowhere denies the justice of God, it is not inconsistent for him to affirm it here. The disagreement between Job and his friends is not

---

[1] Some scholars (*e.g.* Gordis, p. 275) think this is a late editorial addition intended to break up the long speech which had come about when the text of the third cycle became confused. See section III of the Introduction (pp. 19ff.).

over whether God is just or not; it is over how the justice of God is seen to work out in particular events, and specifically in Job's experiences. The friends think they know the answer, and they have offered it to Job. Job knows that they are wrong, not in affirming the justice of God, but in applying it to himself. But since he does not know *how* the justice of God is being fulfilled in his case, he is neither able to refute the friends nor able to satisfy his own mind.

2-6. In this adjuration Job takes the last resort of a man on trial. Using a powerful oath, he hands his case over to God. The name of God is solemnly invoked as the ultimate custodian of justice, the impartial punisher of all perjury. For a culture whose jurisprudence provided such a device, a trial could be stayed by this means. It might be an innocent man's only protection against false testimony, or the only way out of an impasse when insufficient evidence prevented a human tribunal from reaching a verdict. Both considerations could apply here. Only God can indicate that the friends' accusations are false; and to the extent that their debate resembles litigation, the controversy remains indecisive for want of an adjudicator. Job has already appealed to God many times. Now swearing 'by the life of God', he uses the strongest measure possible for forcing God's hand. It is in keeping with this procedure that the Lord, when He finally responds, does so precisely by declaring Job to be in the right and his friends in the wrong (42:7). This also makes it clear that Job's asseveration that he is (and will keep on) speaking the truth (verse 4), that his conscience is clear (6b) and *I hold fast my righteousness* (6a) is not a claim to sinlessness in relationship to God, but to the validity of the stand he has taken against the friends. Using another formula of self-cursing, he says, 'I'll be damned if ever I concede that you are right!' (5a).

The most arresting feature of Job's oath is that he swears by the God 'who has denied me justice' (2a, NEB), *who has made my soul bitter* (2b, RSV; *cf.* 7:11; 10:1; 21:25). What he says is a fact, and Job has consistently maintained it. His high trust in God becomes quite audacious in this paradoxical appeal to God against God. Many since Elihu (34:5) have been shocked by it. But Job is not shaking his fist at God. By his solemn gesture he stakes everything on a justice beyond this injustice. It is up to God to set right the wrongs which, in a world of which He is the sole Maker and Owner, must, behind all secondary causes, be His full responsibility. Just how responsibly God would take up this burden and, in the person of His Son, Jesus Christ, would carry, absorb and quench 'the sins of the whole world' (1 Jn. 2:2), Job could not know. But his faith is leaping the vast distance into God as 'righteous . . . and a Saviour' (Is. 45:21).

7-12. These words can be accepted as Job's once they are seen to be an imprecation, not a statement of fact. As such they continue to express Job's faith in God's justice. The opening verb *let . . . be* blankets the entire poem, making it a long curse. The *enemy* here is not God, and the Satan does not figure in the dialogue. The 'opponent', in this clearly juridical context, is the false accuser, here the friends. That Job is addressing them, 'instructing' them about *the hand of God* (11), is shown by the plural pronoun in this verse.[1] In Israelite law the penalty for malicious prosecution of the innocent was the punishment attached to the crime wrongly charged. Hence Job's repudiation of the charges with the oath, 'Let my hater be treated *as the wicked* person he untruthfully says I am.' Such a person has forfeited all right to call on God (10), as Job so confidently does.[2] We cannot emphasize too strongly the contrast between Job and his friends in this regard. He constantly calls upon God; they never do.

Once more and finally Job dismisses the friends as empty (*vain*, 12; the whole verse is consistently plural).

13-23. The concluding speech is like several others in the book. *The portion of a wicked man* (13) is an inheritance, suggesting future retribution. By wickedly blaming Job, the friends will now become the targets of their own predictions – if they are right![3]

The list of calamities is fairly conventional. War, famine and disease will lay his family waste (14f.). The statement that 'his widows' (MT) – the wicked man is apparently a polygamist – 'will not lament' reads strangely (11QtgJob confirms the text, so far as it survives), unless it means that

---

[1] It is a feeble expedient of critics to change this to singular (without support of manuscripts or versions) in order to make it something that Zophar says to Job.

[2] The verb *take delight* was used by Eliphaz in 22:26.

[3] As it turns out, ironically enough, they are not punished in the end, but pardoned for their cruelty to Job.

they are glad to be rid of him. This is the opposite of what Job said about the funerals of the wicked in chapter 20.

His wealth will be decimated. His secure house will prove as flimsy as the temporary shelter erected by a watchman in the fields (18). In verse 18a MT reads 'like a moth'. But the moth does not construct a dwelling. It could be an example of something fragile (see 4:19), but ancient versions already interpreted it as *a spider's web* (accepted by RSV), and some modern scholars have suggested a bird's nest.

Consistency is not to be sought in the total picture. The wicked man, who already has widows in verse 15, is going to bed in verse 19. But each item in the string of curses applies separately. MT reads simply 'and he/it is not'; RSV supplies *his wealth*, but it could mean that he wakes up in the morning only to discover that he is dead. The same is probably the meaning of *he is gone* in verse 21. The confusion reaches its climax in the closing lines, with the mixed-up picture of a person carried away helplessly by water and whirlwind, yet fleeing in terror before them.

The practice of Hebrew poets of using the opening and closing lines of a poem as a framework (*inclusio*) to enclose the rest invites us to link verse 23 with verse 13, and to identify God (not the east wind – *it* of RSV) as the One behind all these calamities, who *claps* His palms and *hisses at him*. While clapping can express anger (Nu. 24:10), and hissing can express horror (Je. 49:17), both can express derision (La. 2:15; Ezk. 27:36), which is often mentioned in the Old Testament as the best treatment for the ungodly.

III. INTERLUDE (28:1–28)

As already discussed in the Introduction, this chapter is a bit of an enigma. It stands complete in itself, and is not joined smoothly with the preceding and following material. Yet it does not interrupt the flow, as if it would be better out of the way; for there is a natural break at this point. Job's next speech (chapters 29–31) is also a self-contained work, balanced, we have suggested, with the speeches of Elihu. In this view, the dialogue with the friends ends with chapter 27, and chapter 28 provides an interlude which helpfully prevents Job's soliloquy in chapters 29–31 from following too abruptly on his peroration in chapter 27. Because no speaker is identified, chapter 28 could be a continuation of Job's words. (The chapter divisions do mark off distinct literary units, but they have no more authority than an editorial opinion, and are sometimes mistaken as a guide to structure.) Here, however, there is no doubt that chapter 28 is a relatively independent composition and, if spoken by Job, represents a movement of thought through quite different moods. The serenity of chapter 28 is a total contrast to Job's usual mood, but not impossible, in view of his highly temperamental responses to the situation.

But most scholars find it impossible to believe that Job ever recited this poem. They find it quite incompatible with what comes before and after. It would represent a premature conversion, and render any further speeches by Elihu or by the Lord superfluous.[1] But, if it is not Job's, whose is it? One solution assigns it to one of the friends: Zophar (especially if 27:7-23 also belongs to him and chapter 28 continues it), or Bildad. But it is too calm for them also, for everyone has lost his temper at the end of the discussion, and is far loftier than any thought they have expressed so far. It is so sublime that other scholars prefer to remove it altogether, because it competes with the following Yahweh speeches and lessens their impact. It is a poem, they suggest, which originally had nothing to do with the book of Job, but which was wrongly pushed in at this point because some later scribe recognized a real similarity to some of the ideas in Job. It has even been suggested, because of this great resemblance, that the poem is the work of the same author, although not intended by him to be part of the larger book. This observation, however, is a significant concession.

The objections to the presence of chapter 28 at this point are almost entirely structural, so, if it makes structural sense where it is, it can be left alone. By calling the poem an interlude, we find it appropriate to mark, by means of this meditation, the transition from the dialogue in three rounds between Job and his friends to the monologues in three rounds of Job, Elihu and God. Because we do not think that Job is a drama, we do not see any need to have a Chorus recite it. But there is value in this suggestion, since it preserves the poem, it recognizes that it must come from someone other than the known

[1] Hence the suggestion that it should come after 42:6.

characters, and it appreciates that the dramatic function of the piece is like that of a commentary supplied by a Chorus between the acts of a play. But, because we think that Job is a story, we find it appropriate that this interlude is spoken by the story-teller. It sums up the case as it stands at this point. It emphasizes the failure of the human mind to arrive at the hidden wisdom, and so, far from interfering with the Lord's speeches, it lays the foundation for them by showing their necessity. To complain that this gives the book two climaxes seems to us to have little weight. Why should it not have two, or even more, if this served the author's purpose? We suggest that here the author expresses his own point of view. As such the poem has key importance for understanding the whole book.

The poem is beautifully constructed around the question:

'Where shall wisdom be found?
And where is the place of understanding?'

This refrain, which comes in verses 12 and 20, divides the poem into three strophes: verses 1–11 indicate that human research has not discovered wisdom; verses 13–19 indicate that human wealth cannot purchase wisdom; verses 21–27 declare that God alone has wisdom, which remains His gift. Verse 28 completes the poem with the classical definition of wisdom. This statement, by picking up the language of Job 1:1, constitutes an *inclusio* which suggests that the book should be divided into Part I and Part II at this point.

1–11. The tranquillity and detachment of this poem, its almost scientific objectivity, matches the suspense in which the reader's thought is held at this point. The debate is done. Nothing is settled. The wit of men is exhausted, and God is still silent. The question does not have to be stated to enter our minds: 'Where can we find wisdom?'[1]

The last recorded word of the friends is that 'man is a maggot' (25:6). Job has more respect for mankind, and for God's good intentions for making him. There is no gain in glory for God by belittling His work. So here the author

---

[1] Some scholars would like to put the refrain at the beginning as well as in verses 12 and 20. This would ruin the artistic effect of the sudden, matter-of-fact onset – 'There are mines for silver' – which is at once an intriguing riddle in the true Wisdom mode.

expresses nothing but admiration for man's industry and ingenuity. He draws his example from mining technology and gives us several pen-sketches of ancient engineers at work. Tribute is paid to their persistence and courage, for digging treasures from the earth is one of the most dangerous of occupations. There is a hint that the getting of wisdom will be equally strenuous and hazardous. There is no suggestion that the author is disapproving, as if he thought that the energies spent on the search for material wealth would be better used in the quest of wisdom. His point is much simpler. Man's remarkable success as a miner shows how clever and intelligent he is; but, for all that, he has failed completely to unearth wisdom.

Other literature from the ancient world has given us little in the way of stories of prospecting for minerals or of the craft of the smelter. Hence there are several places in this poem where the exact processes involved are not clear. Verse 3 seems to describe the need for artificial light in deep mining shafts. All translations have to paraphrase somewhat to arrive at sense, but Duhm deserves Dhorme's censure (p. 400) for rewriting the text to solve its problems. Everyone is reduced to despair by verse 4, and, comparing several versions, such as AV, RSV, NEB, it is hard to believe that they all had the same Hebrew text in front of them. AV, taking the word 'wadi' in its usual sense,[1] develops the idea of water breaking into the mines. There is no evidence that *naḥal* can mean a mining *shaft*, although this is widely favoured by modern scholars. Those *forgotten* could be explorers far from home, or slaves in the mines. The epithet 'of the foot' (AV) is *travellers* in RSV, interpreted by some as meaning that people walking overhead do not suspect that there are men underground. Guillaume finds an accident that sweeps them off their feet. The picturesque *swing to and fro* has gained some favour because it suggests the dangers of lowering men down into holes.

5. The idea of bread coming out of the earth is found also in Psalm 104:14f.; but, since it seems a little out of place in the present poem, it could be that knowledge of Psalm 104:14 has influenced the Massoretes to make Job 28:5 similar. Those who are satisfied with this tradition find a contrast between what is produced on the surface (NEB even interprets

---

[1] Strictly the *naḥal* is the ravine, not the torrent.

bread as 'corn') and what comes from beneath. But *fire* is neither a parallel nor a contrast to *bread*, and the verb 'come out' equally means 'emerge from inside'. Since more minerals are mentioned in verse 6, perhaps *lûḥ*, 'stone(-tablet)', with enclitic *mem* could be considered. It is supported by the perfect symmetry of the first fourteen colons (verses 1–6); for the four periods consist of a tetracolon (verses 1 and 2, listing four metals), a tricolon (3), another tricolon (4) – admittedly both obscure[1] – and then another tetracolon (5 and 6, listing four minerals, with *gold* repeated). This observation removes the ground from beneath the feet of scholars who wish to remove (or transfer) verses 7 and 8 as interrupting the continuity between verse 6 and verse 9. The well-formed strophe (verses 1–6) is kept structurally separate from verses 9–11, even though the latter resume the theme of man's achievements.

7, 8. The *falcon* is celebrated for its vision, the *lion* for its courage. But neither is as observant or as intrepid as man, and neither bird nor beast has access to the remote places that men have penetrated in their lust for treasures. The function of these remarks in the middle of a poem about mining would seem to be another way of prizing mankind more than any other of God's creatures, however admirable. This is in keeping with the role the animals will play in the Lord's speeches in helping Job to accept and enjoy his place in the world and in God's schemes.

9–11. Although shorter, this unit of six colons probably balances the first strophe of fourteen colons, and the problems of one may be solved with the help of clues derived from the other. Thus verses 9 and 10 are probably a tetracolon (there is a certain amount of parallelism), matching the two tetracolons of the first strophe. For instance, the various minerals listed in such detail in verses 1, 2, 5 and 6 are covered by *every precious thing* (10). But verses 9f. are also climactic, in that they give more prominence to human achievement.[2] Verse 11, which does not show the same kind of parallelism (this has bothered commentators), has links with the two tricolons in verses 3 and 4, through the catch-words *streams* (parallel

---

[1] No excuse for trimming to bicolons the way NEB does to both.

[2] For these structural reasons, we think that the theme is still mining, and has not switched to some other enterprise, such as the construction of water-tunnels.

to *nḥl* in verse 4) and *light* (parallel to *darkness* in verse 3).
Another way of looking at this is to say that the separate
colons in verse 11 complete the tricolons in verses 3 and 4, so
that the complete poem of twenty-four colons consists of six
tetracolons. The pattern is so harmonious that nothing should
be disturbed. We might add that the integral place of verses
7 and 8 within the rest is shown by the contrast between the
eyes of man (10) and the falcon's eye (7).

12. Man's spectacular successes, here deservedly praised,
and his superiority to all animals make his failure to find
wisdom all the sadder. The implied answer to the question
is not negative. Scholars who think that the poem is agnostic
have deleted verse 28 to keep it so. But verse 23 will affirm
that 'God understands' and it is nowhere hinted that He
will keep His understanding to Himself.

13-19. The theme of this strophe is the impossibility of
buying wisdom. For this reason MT 'its price', followed by
AV and RV, is to be preferred to LXX *the way to it*, although the
latter is preferred by modern versions. This old mistake is
probably due to the influence of verse 23, which does read
'way', and a too-literal reading of the parallel *found*, whereas
'acquired' would suit better.[1] Verse 13b, as generally taken,
is palpably untrue. Job never asserts that there is no wisdom
whatever 'in the land of living men' (NEB). The point is that
it cannot be obtained from the world, nor from the most
primaeval and elemental powers of nature, Tehom and Yam,
the original watery chaos of creation (14). The logic of saying
in one breath, 'It isn't there, but, even if it were, you couldn't
buy it', is often met in the Bible.

The identification of the dozen or more valuables itemized
in verses 15-19, which one might think of using for purchasing
wisdom, has not yet been completed to everyone's satisfaction,
as comparison of translations quickly shows. Even when the
words are used several times in the Old Testament, the lack of
additional information leaves several possibilities open.
Fortunately the point being made does not depend in any way
on the results of such research.

20. The refrain separates the three strophes. The variation

---

[1] Now that Pope (p. 203) has accepted Dahood's new solution 'abode',
his reasons for doing so should be carefully weighed. This removes another
difficulty from MT, the contradiction between saying that wisdom has no
price, but that God knows its price.

comes here should not be levelled out.[1] By being more general, this second formulation comprehends both problems, how to discover and to secure wisdom. The third strophe gives the answer. Wisdom is found only in God, and man obtains it only by revelation.

21–27. An analysis of the structure will serve us as well here as it did with the first strophe; for here, as there, the thought does not proceed along a straight line. What God says in the end (verse 28) contrasts with the admission of *Abaddon* (the word means 'dissolution'; *cf.* 26:6) *and Death* in verse 22, and of *the deep* and *the sea* in verse 14. God's ability to see *everything* (24) contrasts with the concealment of wisdom *from the eyes of* every human being (21), even though man sees much (10) and finds hidden things and sees more than the birds (7).[2] If Abaddon and Death are elemental powers matching the chaos, then we ought not to find in verse 22 a contradiction of the idea that what is not available 'in the land of the living' (verse 13, which is another counterpoise to verse 22) might be found in Sheol, let alone a polemic against necromancy.

23. In parallel with *place*, *way* should probably be read 'realm', as has been demonstrated for Proverbs 8:22.[3] In any case, the statement should not be misunderstood. The place of wisdom is not simply in the mind of God. Wisdom is what God *understands* when He *looks to the ends of the earth*. Wisdom is observable in the universe because God embodied it in His creation when he 'saw', 'reckoned', 'organized' and 'fathomed'.[4] Men can see this for themselves, but only when God Himself shows it to them (Rom. 1:19). This is precisely

[1] Without making the reading the same, Dhorme (p. 406) has brought the meanings closer by means of impressive arguments which have some textual support.

[2] In view of the verbal threads that weave the poem into a tapestry, it is more likely that *all living* in verse 21, congruous with verse 10, refers to man (as it does in 30:23) and does not include animals (Rowley, p. 232), so that 'no creature on earth' (NEB) is not a desirable translation.

[3] See above, p. 218, n. 1.

[4] All the verbs in verse 27 imply more intellectual activity than the vigorous verbs 'create', 'make', 'form' of the creation-stories of Genesis. They also offer the translator a variety of nuances to choose from. RSV *declared* cannot mean 'revealed' (except in the technical sense that 'the sky reveals' (same verb) 'the splendour of God', see Ps. 19:1) because God has given visible expression to His thoughts, and so to Himself, in what He made.

what God will do for Job shortly, when He takes him on the grand tour of inspection.

25, 26. Only a few specimens of God's wise ordering are given – wind, water, rain, thunder – which, in all likelihood, are intended to comprise but one thing, the thunderstorm. We are close to some very ancient theology here,[1] and we shall meet it again in chapter 37 and in the Lord's speeches. *Cf.* Psalm 29. The point is sufficiently made by one example, especially one so ambivalent, for in the rainy tempest God is at once manifest and mysterious, destructive and beneficent. But it is not a chaos coming again. There was complete success and stability in God's creative acts. What *he saw* then is what he *sees* now.

28. Many commentators do not like this verse. They dismiss it as a platitude that replaces a noble agnosticism with a banal moralism. We have already insisted that there is nothing agnostic about the rest of the chapter. Rowley (p. 234) has trounced the argument that the solitary use of the word 'Lord' here betrays an alien source. Such a sudden twist is often met at the end of a Wisdom poem. Wisdom turns from reflection to action. Having caught a glimpse of God's wisdom in the marvellous terrors of the storm, the question follows: 'Can you thunder with a voice like his?' (40:9). Wisdom for a man cannot be contemplation, 'thinking God's thoughts after him'. How is that wisdom which is bodied forth in the storm to be realized by a man? By being – a man! And by realizing what is quite accessible to all men, and most difficult for them, *the fear of the Lord* which made Job himself the exemplar of wisdom, a clean and straight man, devoted to God, shunning evil (1:1).

IV. JOB AND ELIHU (29:1 – 37:24)

After the dialogue, rounded off by chapter 28, there are three main speakers: Job, Elihu and the Lord. Viewed in one way, Job's final speech (chapters 29–31) completes the discussion with the friends. The following utterances of Elihu and of the Lord could then be grouped together as a human

[1] Mythology too, perhaps, in the imagery, especially if scholars are right who find in the word *decree* something quite material, a sluice ('groove', Pope).

and divine adjudication. But too much similarity should not be found between them; it is better to detach the Yahweh speeches as a distinct act in the drama. Since Elihu deliberately reviews the preceding debate, his speeches can be paired with Job's concluding statement as an attempt to sum everything up. But again their character is not very similar. For these and other reasons the Elihu speeches could be marked off as a separate episode. Job's final declaration (chapters 29–31) is similarly self-contained.

a. Job (29:1 – 31:40)

This long speech is inappropriately called a soliloquy by many scholars. What Job says is integral to the whole debate. Even if the friends have now been reduced to silence, Job is not talking to himself. It is a public utterance, the final assertion of his innocence. The chapter divisions correspond to the three clear sections of the speech: Job describes his former happy estate (29) and contrasts it with his present lamentable condition (30). He concludes with a wide-ranging oath of clearance (31).

i. Job's former estate (29:1-25). The artistic structure found in this chapter has already been met several times in the book. A description of Job's admirable conduct (verses 11–17) and sense of security (18–20) is framed by memories of his place in society. Beginning with his relationship with God (2–5) and his family (5b and 6), Job dwells on the recognition he received in the community (7–10 and 21–25). Scholars who like to have all the remarks on one subject in one place have united these passages by inserting verses 21–25 between verses 10 and 11 (NAB, NEB, *AB*). This is to be deplored. 11QtgJob fully supports the MT in this regard. The design of chapter 29 serves to lock the next two chapters into the whole, for the parade of virtue in 29:11–20 corresponds to chapter 31, while the indignities described in chapter 30 are the opposite of the respect shown to him in 29:21–25. These verses must be left in their present position in order that *But now* in 30:1 might have its powerful effect. This is lost when 30:1 follows 29:20, as in NEB, *etc.*

Job's review of his life is one of the most important documents in Scripture for the study of Israelite ethics. His positive sketch of life at its best (chapter 29) and his negative confession (chapter 31) indicate the loftiest moral standards. For him, right conduct is almost entirely social; his private duty to himself as a man is not discussed, his duty to God in the cult is touched on only in the matter of idolatry (31:26f.), an important but negative matter. In Job's conscience, sins are not just wrong things people do, disobeying known laws of God or society; to omit to do good to any fellow human being, of whatever rank or class, would be a grievous offence to God.

Job's pride in his achievement should not be misunderstood. It was legitimate, not self-righteous. For Job to have adopted the posture of a cringing sinner would have been a species of self-righteousness for him. We need to keep this in mind when reading 42:2–6, for even then Job does not go back on the present speech by admitting to any known fault.

Chapters 29–31 grow out of 28:28, for Job is the wise man, and here we learn in detail what it meant to fear God and shun wrong.

2–6. Job's crown of sorrow was remembering his former life, so full and joyous. The secret lay in God's protection and friendship. The word *watched* (2b) implies kindly care (Ps. 121), although in Job 10:14; 13:27; 14:16 there is something frightening in God's ceaseless supervision. *Friendship* should be retained as the reading in verse 4, although 'protection' is preferred by both ancient and modern versions (changing one letter) and advocated by D. Winton Thomas without a textual change.[1] The nuance of 'secret' (AV, RV) is present, for the *sôḏ* of the Lord is the intimate circle of acquaintances, those who fear him (Ps. 25:14), the chosen few (Je. 23:18). It was in his home (*my tent*), not at a shrine, that he enjoyed this fellowship with God. These were his *autumn days* (4a), the time of ripeness and richness, not the sad decline into winter, but the fulfilment of summer's warmth and growth.

The traditional tokens of God's approval were a numerous family, prolific herds and productive fields. These Job enjoyed (5b, 6). *The rock* is either the olive press or the hillside with terraced groves of trees.

7–11. Wealthy men are not often loved. They are more likely to be feared, envied or hated. In the Bible there are numerous passages in which the rich are equated with the wicked. It is supposed that a person gets rich only by dishonesty,

[1] *JBL*, LXV, 1946, pp. 63ff.

at someone else's loss, and keeps his gains because he is selfish. Not so Job. He enjoyed the esteem of the whole town. The Greeks were not the only ancient people who saw the good life in terms of full participation in the affairs of the city. In Israel *the gate of the city* (7) was the community centre where public business was done. Here Job was shown the highest respect. It was courtesy in Israel to stand up in the presence of an older person (Lv. 19:32). There is no reason to think of Job as an old man, yet *the aged rose and stood* (8) in his presence. The most distinguished leaders paid attention to him (9, 10). His speech and demeanour won universal approval (11).[1] Such a status would be common knowledge, and in claiming it for himself Job would have been quite open to contradiction, if self-deceived.

12-17. All this acclaim was not just the obsequious honour given to a rich man because of his economic power and political influence. Job has already spoken about this with detestation (chapter 21). Job's reputation was squarely based on solid achievement as a benefactor, known to all. Besides the traditional claimants on charity – the exploited, the orphan, the destitute and the widow (12, 13; Job repudiates what Eliphaz had dared to accuse him of in 22:6-9) – Job went out of his way to help the handicapped, even to the lengths of seeking out folk quite unknown to him (15, 16). The poetic arrangement in these two four-colon units guides us to the structure of the strophe. Verse 17, which is climactic in a way, embraces the rest in showing what strong measures Job would adopt (to his own danger?) in combating crime. Verse 14 occupies a strategic position between the two matching tetracolons, and has its own inner design. Its considerable length can be explained once it is seen to be a tricolon of a kind common in old Canaanite verse, with incomplete parallelism, development (augmentation) and *inclusio*.

'Righteousness I wore
> And it clothed me like a cloak
>> like a mantle my judgment.'

18-20. This is a perfectly legitimate thought. It needs no retraction or apology. It was not presumptuous, but based

---

[1] It is not certain whether this verse ends the preceding passage or begins the next section.

on confidence that God would honour those who honoured Him. Job's adherence to this doctrine here silences the critics who had denied him similar beliefs in chapters 24 and 27, transferring such statements to other speakers. The poetry is somewhat lavish, the extravagant metaphors mixed, as we have already seen. One figure is not a guide to the next in a rhapsody of this kind. Hence the allusions continue to evade us. Job's *nest* could be his home, or children ('nestlings' enjoys some favour), but numerous other suggestions have been made, beginning with LXX 'old age', in tune with the idealized deaths of the patriarchs, and in parallel with verse 18b, if we take the obvious meaning of MT as in RSV, that Job's days will be as numerous *as the sand*. It is amazing how much discussion verse 18b has aroused. Already in antiquity several options were abroad, including the possibility of 'phoenix', which has taken on a new lease of life (as, perhaps, we would expect the phoenix to do) since Albright found the bird in the myths of Ugarit. The works of the many scholars who have cast their vote for the phoenix can be reached through the documentation in larger commentaries. There is a long and cautious discussion in Pope (pp. 214ff.) who remains undecided. We share his hesitation, if only because the idea of endless renewal seems contrary to Job's acceptance of death after a full life, and resurrection (once!) cannot be intended by this symbol of a quite different kind of immortality.

The common figure of the luxuriant tree (19) is not rendered less appropriate by Bildad's application of it to the wicked in 8:16f. Verse 20 shows how highly the Israelite valued the retention of his natural powers until the instant of death.

21–25. These verses complete the picture of Job's enjoyment of well-merited respect in the conduct of public business. He was the leading man of the town, whose every utterance enjoyed unquestioned prestige. Another extravagant figure is used in verse 23. Job's more recent words were certainly not welcomed like *the spring rain*, which, in the agricultural round of Palestine, was vital if crops were to survive enough of summer to be harvested. Verse 24 is difficult (*cf.* AV). NEB has completed the trend of RSV. Instead of meaning that Job's cheerfulness could not be spoilt by despondency in others, it makes his smile the certain cure for discouragement (4:3).

The last verse is the most difficult of all. This is a pity, for it seems to be a summary. The last colon, which some (*e.g.* NEB) delete as a homeless stray, might be echoing verse 24 with a reference to the comforting of *mourners*. The parallelism within verse 25a, however, permits a tetracolon to be worked out. Job is invested with the highest titles.

'I was chosen[1] as their governor,[2]
And I used to sit as their[3] chief,
And I dwelt like a king in his regiment
           like one who comforts mourners.'[4]

Such was the former greatness of Job.

ii. Job's present humiliation (30:1-31). The Lord gave (chapter 29); the Lord took back (chapter 30). The contrast could hardly be more extreme. Present loss made worse by past achievement; both complete. There is no one source of Job's misery. Several causes converge and reinforce each other. No remedy can be found by identifying 'the' explanation (sin, Satan, and so forth) and dealing with that. Yet there is one Source, Cause and Explanation, and He alone can be the Remedy.

In linking Job's closing statement (chapters 29-31) with his opening lamentation (chapter 3),[5] we had chiefly in mind the resemblance between chapters 3 and 30. But there are also many differences, and they are important. Job has come a great distance. In chapter 3 his attention was narrowly focused on his immediate pain. In chapter 30 he is more widely aware of the social and spiritual dimensions of his predicament. This is perhaps the most pathetic of all Job's poems of grief, and a fitting finish to all the earlier ones. It is more subdued, more reflective, less defiant. It shows Job in his weakness, no longer able to hope for even one touch of friendliness from men or God.

Growing out of chapter 29, Job 30 dwells on the complete

---

[1] Reading a passive, implying election rather than the imposition of authority.

[2] A good case can be made out for reading *dāriku*, as commonly used in Canaanite.

[3] The suffix on *darkām* (*their way*, RSV) does double duty.

[4] While taking this as a figure (*k*- marks a simile), and not as proof that Job was actually king of his people (*cf.* Ecclus. 49:9 and the LXX additions to Jb. 42:17 which link him with the royal line of Edom), the portrait of the king as both soldier and philanthropist is thoroughly Israelite.

[5] See Introduction, p. 22, above.

reversal of all Job's relationships. What God has done to him (verses 16–23) is set in the middle of what men have done to him (1–15; 24–31); but these are not two distinguishable experiences, and the whole poem is a tumult. Conflicting emotions gather in Job's soul. He is abject, scornful, outraged, forlorn.

1–8. Job has exchanged the respect of the most respectable for the contempt of the most contemptible. Something of patrician pride comes through Job's disdain for the dregs of society who *now* (1)[1] make him their laughing-song. Such despicable persons are in no position to look down on Job, for they are the lowest of society, living like animals (3, 4, 6, 7). Less than human, this gang is rightly expelled from where decent people live (5, 8).

The general picture is clear, although many details are obscure. rsv has replaced 'old age' (av) with *vigour* in verse 2, securing clarity for the price of a conjecture. It would imply Job's refusal to employ the useless; but it is unlikely that he is still talking about their decrepit *fathers* (1), for it would have been hard-hearted to spurn the crippled just because they could not be productive. Attempts to repair verse 3 have not succeeded. It seems (with verse 4) to be describing the degraded habits of these outcasts, gathering *leaves* and *roots* for food (neb; rsv identifies *the roots of the broom* as fuel by changing the Hebrew). 11QtgJob deviates considerably from mt in this section, and its readings, with more study, promise to lead us to some variants worth considering. It confirms the general theme of eating (thus obviating a lot of current emendations, including rsv), and points to a diet of desert herbage.[2]

The vocabulary of insult connects verse 8 with verse 1, completing the execration of these 'sons of an idiot, yea sons of an unperson' (literally 'nameless' in Hebrew, perhaps a person never to be named rather than one without a name).[3]

---

[1] The three occurrences of *But now* (verses 1, 9, 16) mark the strophic structure.

[2] Josephus's account of persons expelled by the Essenes comes to mind (*Wars* II. viii. 8).

[3] Budde and Bickell saw this when they preferred the removal of verses 3–7 rather than 1–8, or 2–8, still favoured by Fohrer (p. 411), for verses 3–7 break the continuity between verse 1 and verse 8. For details see Driver–Gray, Part I, p. 215. Recognition of *inclusio* makes all this unnecessary.

The word rendered *whipped* has not yet yielded its meaning to research.

9–15. The picture is exaggerated, but the irony is deep, for Job himself had been humane towards such scum. He had wept for them (verse 25), but who weeps for Job? A person's last claim to humanity has gone when he becomes a common jest of the most depraved (9) and *no one restrains them* (13). Job is now the outcast (10, 12), to be spat on. The identification of *God* as the agent (11a) has been supplied in translation. It is based on the contrast of the singular verb with the plurals used in the surrounding context. NEB makes it all refer to *the rabble*, but RSV could be right, with verse 15 as another remark about God's assault, which is, of course, simultaneous with that of men. We met the same mixture in chapters 16 and 19, and similar siege-imagery could be behind the very difficult language of verses 12ff., where *breach* and *crash* suggest the fall of a beleaguered city. The dramatic *roll on* (14b), however, suggests an onrush of waters, in line with the reference to *the wind* in verse 15. The metaphors could be mixed. Here the reading of 11QtgJob is interesting, since it uses the same verb to translate the end of verse 14 and the beginning of verse 15, as if it were a more direct statement about Job himself, physically crumpled by his illness.

16–23. In a final burst of grief, Job wrestles with the sheer pain of his disease as if it were objectively a terrifying monster, chewing at his flesh day and night. Instead of using the passive (AV), RSV makes *night* the agent (17, 18). But it is better to see this as the time (7:11–19), and God as the agent, especially if we accept the inference of RSV, which has added *God* as subject of the singular verb in verse 19.[1] Verse 18 can then be compared with 7:15 as another part of the nightmare sequence, so that the choking is not due to phlegm (NEB) but caused by the 'paws' (so I would read *kpy*) of the attacker. Some commentators have found the idea of defilement in verse 19 as well as verse 18, interpreting the difficult Hebrew 'disguised'. We need not spend time on the result, seen for instance in Guillaume or NEB, for 11QtgJob now supports LXX *seizes*, preferred by RSV.

In the light of the plurals in 11QtgJob, verses 16–19 might

---

[1] NEB is even more emphatic, with 'God himself'. But 11QtgJob reads plurals until we reach verse 20.

be connected with verses 11–15 as Job's description of how he feels about the hostility that society is now displaying, the rough treatment he is receiving from men. But verses 20–23 are undoubtedly addressed to God. The *not* in verse 20b is lacking in MT. But MS support is not needed to supply it, because *not* in verse 20a does double duty, by a well-known poetic principle. But God's refusal to *heed* Job's outcry is not the main cause of his distress. While *stand* could betoken the formal posture of a suppliant or litigant ('I take my stand'), it could equally imply persistence, since 'stand' sometimes means 'continue' in Hebrew. God has become *cruel* (21), and once more the imagery of the *storm* (22) is used to bring out the violence of the attack and Job's helplessness. But AV 'dissolvest', nearer to MT than RSV *tossest*, might point to a quite different figure, and NEB admits to guessing its way through 'unintelligible' Hebrew. By contrast, verse 23 is perfectly clear. Death may be personified, but this does not make it a god outside the Lord's sphere. Sheol is vividly called 'the meeting-house for all mankind'. The certainty of Job's knowledge on this point gives a finality to his remark. This is the climax of his speech. The remaining strophe (24–31) is a counterpoise to the opening lament, and highlights once more the contrast between his 'days of affliction' (27) and his 'autumn days' (29:4).

24–31. In 29:18ff. Job outlines his former expectations. His present circumstances are as different as *darkness* from *light*. He *looked for* ('expected')[1] *good*, but *evil came*. The words chosen take us back to 2:10. His *heart* (literally 'intestines', organs of the most visceral emotions) is in ceaseless *turmoil*. The main cause of his distress is the unaccountable injustice of his present plight. Although the meaning of verse 24 is quite obscure, in the light of verse 25 it could present the picture of a person 'in ruins' stretching out a hand for help which no common humanity would deny. Certainly Job had never ignored such an appeal; indeed, *my soul grieved for the poor*. Verses 28–31 enlarge on his plight. Only the wild animals offer him hideous company (29); his appearance is repulsive (28, 30); his voice harsh and hoarse (31). On the rule 'you reap what you sow' Job should now be treated as he treated others (chapter 29, especially verses 12–17). His cry, unheeded by God (verse 20), is ignored by men also (28). The meaning

[1] The use of this important verb, and its parallel *waited*, supports our interpretation of Jb. 13:15.

of *blackened, but not by the sun* is not understood, and something parallel to verse 28 has been tortured out of it (as by NEB) only by recomposing the line. Although a different root is used in verse 30, there is probably some connection. The word translated *sun* in verse 28a means 'heat' and the (different) word *heat* in verse 30b suggests drought or desolation. Job ends his lamentation on the physical agonies of his illness, unrelieved by a kind word or friendly touch. His friends sat with him (2:13), but they did not weep with him.

iii. Job's ultimate challenge (31:1–40). This priceless testament is a fitting consummation of 'the words of Job' (verse 40). It is an oath of clearance in the form of a negative confession. The procedure was well known in ancient jurisprudence. A crime could be disowned by calling down a curse on oneself if one had committed it. Take stealing, for example. In pleading 'Not guilty' the accused did not simply say 'I am not a thief', or 'I did not steal the ox'. To repudiate an unfounded allegation, one might demand that the person wronged come forward, lay charges, and submit supporting evidence. So Samuel asks: 'Whose ox have I taken?' (1 Sa. 12:3) and similar questions, following them up with an undertaking to pay the appropriate penalty if the needed proof is supplied.

The negative confession worked differently. Although made in the interests of one's public honour, it was addressed to God in an appeal against human judgment. Charges have already been made (Jb. 22:5–11), but no supporting witnesses have come forward. Job has given a blanket denial (23:10–12) and left his vindication to God (27:2–6). Chapter 31 completes the protest which began in chapter 29 with insistence on his unblemished record and continued in chapter 30 with a complaint about the injustice of his present treatment at the hands of men and God.

Job 31 lists specific crimes, denying them all. The form Job uses is, 'If I have done X, then let Y happen to me!' X is the crime; Y is the penalty. Since Job is handing everything over to God, not to a human court, there is no call for man's testimony, since God sees everything (28:24). And the sentence is not a statutory penalty, such as a commensurate fine or reparation. It is some act of God. Its character as punishment for a particular sin takes the form of poetic justice. God arranges for someone else to do the same thing to the culprit by way of retaliation. Job fully endorses the *lex talionis* and affirms the doctrine that you reap what you sow. Thus he expects that the price he would pay for committing adultery with his neighbour's wife would be that Job's neighbour would commit adultery with Job's wife (31:9, 10).

The list of crimes in Job's negative confession is neither systematic nor complete. It was not drawn up by an articled clerk. It is a poem, recited by a miserable outcast on the city rubbish dump, not by a prisoner in the dock. It is Job's last passionate outburst, and the author has given it an earnestness and a torrential quality by composing it with a measure of incoherence. This effectively conveys Job's persistent indignation. This effect is lost when the loose ends are tidied up and the speech is made like a page from a barrister's brief.

The simple form outlined above is not followed in every instance. Sometimes it is incomplete; the 'if' clause is a sufficient denial, and a suggested consequence of guilt (to which would be added perjury) is not given. Sometimes the oath is augmented with positive assertions that Job had, in fact, done the right. Sometimes questions are added or observations are made about the seriousness of the fault. Once or twice it would seem that the pieces of a single oath are not all together in the same place. The sequence or grouping of the individual crimes does not show much order, as in a well-written code. This has annoyed the tidy minds of scholars, some of whom have recomposed the chapter to remove such faults. They are dissatisfied in particular with the addition of a final oath (verses 38–40) at the tail-end, after the whole has been rounded off by Job's 'signature' (verse 35). NAB, to give an extreme example, has sliced the text into seven bits and stuck them together in a different order to give a better result. NEB is similar, and *AB* has shuffled the pieces in its own way. We have no right to ban such work; indeed we have reason to be grateful for every attempt to throw light on real problems in the text. But such drastic measures seem to us to be not only unproductive, but also harmful to the living art of the whole poem. The reorganization has no textual support, since ancient versions, including 11QtgJob, support MT, except that LXX has a few typical omissions. It is hard to imagine by what mechanical process a text which began like NAB or NEB, *etc.* could have become like MT, as if a page had been accidentally torn and the pieces put together wrongly. Nor can we imagine any mental process by which a scribe would have deliberately rewritten the orderly NEB into the disorganized MT. On the other side of the argument we have already met in Job many examples of speeches in which strophes or periods dealing with the same theme are not continuous, but separated, often in balancing structures with patterns of introversion or the like. The same applies to chapter 31. The placement of the central idea away from the end (verses 35–37) so that the last lines (38–40) are not the climax, but an echo of a point made earlier in the poem, is a common device.

It is not clear how many specific sins are itemized. Fohrer (pp. 429ff.) finds ten strophes of variable length. Nine of them (the tenth is verses 35–37) deal with twelve failures, sometimes one per strophe, sometimes two, but hard-heartedness towards the poor (16–23) occupies two strophes. This is, perhaps, over-nice. On a full count, there are sixteen concrete sins in 'if' clauses. But, as already pointed out, some of these are not followed by 'then' clauses; they are grouped together as if they are facets of a single fault. The number sixteen could be increased when it is recognized that a single 'if' might embrace two or three successive clauses without having to be repeated in each.

The speech is not a handbook of personal ethics. Connections with ancient lists, such as the Decalogue, can be traced, but direct dependence on any one of them has not been demonstrated. Although ample, Job's selection is too brief to be called a code. It illustrates the codes of Israel. Selective, it nevertheless highlights matters considered by Job as supremely important for an index of character. The additional comments reveal the foundations of Job's morality. While all but one of the failures he disowns are crimes against his fellow men (the exception is idolatry in verses 26f.), such acts are odious because they are offensive to God (23), not just injurious to society. An act of injustice against the meanest slave would be heinous in God's sight because each and every human being is precious to Him (15) and under His immediate protection.

1-4. Lust. Job plunges into the oath without preliminaries. The eye as the first instrument of sin is mentioned more than once. Job begins, not with the normal form of the negative confession, but with a statement of fact. He had *made a covenant*. If Job appears over-scrupulous in avoiding even the occasion of possible temptation, it is because he is so sensitive to what is at stake. The translation *how* in verse 1b, though literal, does not seem to fit. Since the import of the following idiom is made clear by Ecclesiasticus 9:5, Dhorme prefers to take *māh* as negative. He may be right. So NEB. Job is cautious, because the question he habitually asked about every action was, 'What will God think?' Since God observes *all my steps*, all that matters is one's *portion* and *heritage* with Him. The idea of a reward, if not a future punishment, is present. The main point is the certainty of divine retribution on the wrong-doer (3). The strength of Job's convictions on this point should be noted. The justice of God is his paramount belief, and is a further answer to scholars who have removed similar statements from Job's earlier speeches as a scribal concession to the friends' point of view that Job would not have made.

On the assumption that sexual sins should all be dealt with in the same place, the verse has either been moved, or the reference to lascivious looks has been changed by altering *virgin* to 'folly' or the like.

5–8. Dishonesty. Job denies falsehood and deceit. That he thought of *integrity* as inward is shown by his marvellous definition of covetousness as the heart following the eyes (7). The self-curse of crop failure (8) suggests that verse 5 refers to shady business practices. While *falsehood* and *deceit* are abstractions which might be personified as Job's companions, it is possible that the nouns are used as collectives for the concrete 'false' and 'deceitful' associates.

9–12. Adultery. We commented above (see p. 239) on the appropriateness of the penalty invoked. While *grind for another* may refer to the lowest servitude (Ex. 11:5), a euphemism for sexual intercourse may be hidden in it, in view of the parallelism. The seriousness of the offence is indicated by the solemn language. If the *judges* in verse 11 are human, this is the only place in the chapter where they are recognized. This is insufficient reason for removing the line. Verse 12b is unclear, but verse 12a parallels verse 11b, indicating that adultery is a sin punished by both men and God, in this life and the next. But references to fire as a destructive agent in Sheol (*Abaddon*) are rare in the Old Testament.

13-15. Oppression. This section embodies a humane ethic unmatched in the ancient world. Job lived in a society of slaves and owners (1:3), as everywhere in the ancient East. But in his valuation a slave is not a chattel, but a human person with rights at law, rights guaranteed by God Himself, their specially active Defender. Verse 13 shows that Job believed that a slave had the right to initiate a suit against his master. Several times Job has boasted that he would win any lawsuit that God might bring against him. He has invited such indictment. But he would have nothing to say (14), no claim on God as His 'slave' (1:8; 2:3), if he had treated with despite *the cause* of another. Females had equal rights with males in this matter. Job's reason for these enlightened views is the fundamental fact he has already affirmed in 10:8-13. Common humanity as God's creatures levels or rather elevates all (Eph. 6:9).

16-23. Miserliness. In 22:7ff. Eliphaz accused Job of inhumanity towards the poor and helpless. In chapter 24 Job castigated the wicked for such conduct, and in chapter 29 insisted that he had no part in it. Here he repeats his disclaimer. The care of widows, orphans and other destitute, defenceless people was one of the most sacred obligations in Israel, near God's heart. Here Job had been most assiduous, generous with alms of food (17) and clothing (19, 20), kept alert by his wholesome fear of God (23). In verse 18 MT reads 'from my youth' // 'from my mother's womb' and 'I guided her', the last a reference to *the widow* (introversion). It all yields sense so long as we do not fuss about the impossibility of anyone caring for widows and orphans from the moment of birth. All that need be intended is life-long practice.

If the reference to *the fatherless* continues in verse 21 (some make a slight change to read 'perfect'; *cf.* NEB 'innocent')[1] then the gesture of raising the hand could involve a fraudulent business deal or a miscarriage of justice *in the gate*, the place of public business, or even physical violence. The reference to 'help' is less clear. NEB interprets plausibly as 'knowing that men would side with me in court', an abuse of the influence of powerful friends common enough. The form of the auto-imprecation is clearer here. The arm that struck would be destroyed. The precise anatomical references, especially the meaning of *socket* (literally 'reed', a unique usage), has

[1] See note to the comment on 6:27, 28 (p. 133, n. 2, above).

aroused much inconclusive discussion, but the general idea is clear.

24, 25. Avarice. In 22:24f. Eliphaz urged Job to make God his treasure. Here he denies placing any confidence in his wealth. There is no apodosis (curse) attached to this protasis (denial). Completion of the form is not necessary. But the avoidance of cupidity might be linked with idolatry (verses 26f.), with verse 28 as the common guilt.

26–28. Idolatry. Because verse 11b characterized adultery in similar terms (*this also* would then link the two public crimes and capital offences: *cf.* Dt. 17:2ff.), the severity of the language does not single this out as the superlative sin. Social wrongs are just as bad in God's sight. In view of the continuity of the strophe, *sun* and *moon* might continue the theme of avarice.

In verse 27b the Hebrew is actually 'my hand kissed my mouth'. While throwing kisses with the hand as a gesture of adoration might be intended, such a ritual was not a part of Israel's known worship, illicit for any god but the Lord. The hand could be placed before the mouth in greeting.[1] While the statement does not actually say that the sun and the moon are being reverenced as gods, the act would have been a denial of God (28b).

29, 30. Vindictiveness. From here on there are several 'if' clauses without following penalties. Some have found the thread hard to follow, and RSV isolates some parenthetical material. In verse 29 Job's ethics reach their noblest height. The emphasis is on inward integrity, the hardest of all virtues to develop and sustain. Its reality is known only to God. With our endless ingenuity for self-deception when it comes to thinking of ourselves more highly than we ought to think, it is not likely that any such boast would bear God's scrutiny. Job is amazingly confident. It is impossible for even the most spiritual to avoid a momentary surge of pleasure at the ruin of an enemy, sanctified by gratitude to God for His justice. Though at once suppressed, its poison is always there. A person who attains the standards of Jesus (Mt. 5:43–48) has to be as perfect as God. Not even in his heart did Job wish the most wicked men harm. To claim this is a most

[1] A. Goetze, 'The Laws of Eshnunna', *AASOR*, XXXI, 1951–2, p. 51. Illustrations in M. A. Beek, *Atlas of Mesopotamia* (1962), pp. 78f.; D. J. Wiseman, *Illustrations from Biblical Archaeology*[2] (1963), pp. 26f., 77.

daring invitation for God to search him to the depths for wicked ways (Ps. 139:23f.). Here then is either a very clean conscience or a very calloused one.

31, 32. Parsimony. If these verses continue the theme of Job's attitude to his enemies, the word *tent* is being used in the broad sense of 'settlement', not just household. The reference to *the sojourner* in verse 32 fits neither group, since the stateless, homeless *wayfarer* was generally linked with widow and orphan as an object for compassion. In any case Job's hospitality was widely known. Verse 31b seems to apply universally, and to feed an enemy is to make an inviolable reconciliation (Pr. 25:21f.). Job's generosity with food and board reminds us of Genesis 19, but there is no need to derive from this an unsavoury meaning for the word 'flesh', although Pope writes an elaborate note in support of Tur Sinai's discovery of a reference to sexual abuse here.

33, 34. Hypocrisy. Job has never dissembled, attempting to conceal his sin 'like Adam'. Not all commentators have accepted this apparent reference to Genesis 3. Job never pretends to be sinless, and is unconcerned about men's opinions in this regard. Job has elsewhere maintained that fear of God was his only motive for right conduct. NEB translates rather freely 'the gossip of the town'. Verse 21 may be compared. Job's candour in admitting to *transgressions* in verse 33 is a bit startling in view of his claim to virtual sinlessness sustained through the rest of the chapter.

35-37. This is the final challenge. Job demands a hearing. He signs a document. Job 19:23 and 31:35 should be brought into interplay. Because the Hebrew *tāw* is the last letter of the alphabet, JB makes the fanciful suggestion that Job means, 'I've had my say, from A to Z.' The letter was shaped like a cross, and meant 'mark', hence *signature*. The following reference to *the indictment written by my adversary* takes us into the terminology of legal proceedings. Job would be proud to carry such a document on his *shoulder*, wearing it *as a crown, like a prince*. Far from being abashed, Job is belligerent to the last, eager to have the case settled, confident of the outcome. He is capable of giving a full *account* of all his steps.

38-40. Exploitation. The concluding paragraph deals with the responsible use of land. Recapitulation in the main style of the oath of clearance is an echo that sustains the mood of the whole speech beyond its proper end in verses 35ff.

The land is personified as the chief witness of the crimes committed on it, such as eating the produce *without payment* (more likely to be the wages of reapers, or the share of tenants, than purchase from owners), or illegal seizure (1 Ki. 21). Job is prepared to accept the primaeval curses on Adam (Gn. 3:17) and Cain (Gn. 4:11). As in verse 8, poetic justice would then be done, and seen.

b. Elihu (32:1 – 37:24)

See the Introduction (pp. 49–52) for a discussion of the authenticity of the Elihu speeches and their place in the structure of the book.

i. Introduction (32:1–5). 1. The new speaker is introduced by a paragraph of narrative prose. Some editors connect the conclusion in 31:40c, marking the termination of Job's speeches, with the opening observation that *these three men* (their designation elsewhere – 2:11; 19:21; 42:10 – as 'friends' in relation to Job is not inconsistent) stopped replying to Job. The implication is that they thought it was futile to reason with a person *righteous in his own eyes*.[1]

2. Only Elihu is given a patronymic and a clan name as well as tribal membership (*Buzite*). No identifications have been made, although many have been proposed. The names are transparently West-Semitic, but Buz has both Aramaean (Gn. 22:21) and Arabian (Je. 25:23) connections, just like Uz (Jb. 1:1).

It is noted four times that he became *angry* about the stalemate between Job and his friends. His reason for being *angry at Job* was different from the withdrawal of the friends from debate. Elihu thought that 'Job had made himself out more righteous than God' (NEB). While some soften the preposition 'from' to mean 'before God' (the ancient versions have already done this), the plain meaning is that Job thought himself to be in the right in his dispute with God, and that God was correspondingly in the wrong. Elihu's opinion, of course, and an obvious inference. Since Job has not indicted God, except to insist on the fact that it is God who has done these things to him without justification, Elihu

---

[1] 11QtgJob leaves a line blank at this point.

has already joined the friends in his estimate of Job as self-righteous. No-one can yet see a solution in which both Job and God are shown to be in the right.

3. Job can prove his point by showing that God is in the wrong. The friends can prove theirs by showing that Job is in the wrong. Neither has succeeded. According to scribal tradition, the Hebrew text originally read 'and they declared God in the wrong', presumably by their failure to answer Job, not by any statement they had made. By conceding that Job's position was irrefutable, they left the field open for that inference. Both conclusions – Job's that he is right, the friends' that God is wrong – are inferences drawn by Elihu, who is proud of his logic. The scribes, out of reverence, changed the text to what is now in RSV, but NEB has reinstated the censored original. In any case RSV *although* is a rather adventurous translation of *waw*-consecutive. Rowley's explanation, that they found no answer and (so) showed Job to be wrong, has some merit. But it is more likely that the one negative covers both clauses: 'they didn't find an answer and (didn't) prove Job wrong' (*cf.* NEB mg.).

4. This failure Elihu will now rectify. Hitherto he had held back out of respect for their age. Now he joins in with a combination of deference and cocksureness that captures the pose of youth that sees a little, but sees it clearly.

ii. Elihu's first speech (32:6 – 33:33). This is quite a rigmarole. The speech proper does not begin until 33:1, where Job is addressed by name. The rest of chapter 32 (verses 6–22) is Elihu's self-introduction and *apologia* for intervening. He is very wordy. When he finally attempts to refute Job point by point (33: 8–28), his remarks are framed by opening (33:1–7) and closing (33:29–33) exhortations directed to Job personally.

6, 7. Elihu had given age the first say; but he had been disappointed. The friends have already appealed to their seniority (15:10). Elihu does not think he will merely contribute another *opinion*. The word means 'knowledge' (NEB).

8, 9. Where this knowledge comes from is not clear. Verse 8 suggests that it is *the breath of the Almighty* that gives understanding. But if this is in men by creation, why are so few wise? While not claiming special inspiration, Elihu does refer in 33:14f. to a dream revelation rather similar to Eliphaz's

(4:12ff.), where the same word *spirit* is used. But here it is feminine.

Elihu is able to make only the negative point. The Hebrew 'Not many are wise' has been changed to *the old* to achieve closer parallelism with the next colon. The result is not good, since Elihu would be going too far with a categorical assertion that no old people are wise. By leaving the adjective and combining it with the following noun, we obtain a holistic statement that 'not many old men are wise'. At least Job and his friends are not, as Elihu will soon demonstrate.

10–12. This is repetition. The author has made Elihu pompous.

13. This may match verse 9. The connections with chapter 28 should be noted. Verse 13b is not clear. NEB makes it a statement to the effect that only God can rebut Job. But why, then, does Elihu essay to do just that so confidently? RSV attaches this to verse 13a as part of the deluded 'wisdom' of the friends. But they did not come to the conclusion that Job had a wisdom that only God could handle.

14. The connection is not clear, unless Elihu means that so far Job has not included him in the discussion, but, if he did, he certainly would not go about it the way the friends did. The irony is that his position is much the same as theirs.

15. The change from second person in verse 14 to third in verse 15 suggests that at this point Elihu turns to Job, whom he mainly addresses. But he does also speak to the friends from time to time as he goes along (compare the opening words of 33:1 with 34:2).

16, 17. Once more bombast. We expect something impressive after such a build-up.

18. *I am full of words.* Rowley comments laconically: 'None would dispute this' (p. 267). For *spirit*, cf. verse 8.

19, 20. Elihu measures his irresistible impulse to speak with the help of a fancy image. The word *wineskins* is found only here, so the meaning arises from the context. No convincing alternative has been proposed.

21, 22. Elihu has not yet given his qualifications, except that he is bursting to speak. Job warned the friends against the dangers of being one-sided in their assessment of his case, even if they took God's side (13:7f.). Now Elihu abjures *partiality*, but by speaking about *flattery toward any man* he seems to be saying no more than that he will speak plainly,

247

not giving titles to anyone. He has already excused himself from the respect he might have been expected to show to his elders. Nevertheless his reason for disregarding distinctions of age or class is a good one that Job has already used (31:14f.) to abolish social distinctions. God would punish him; and this would apply as much to insult as to flattery.

33:1-7. This stance is borne out by Elihu's opening words to Job. We are back to the courtesy which the friends forgot very quickly once the temperature of the argument rose. But it is overloaded with Elihu's continued prolixity, and although he assures Job that the latter has nothing to fear (7), he is so self-important that he cannot avoid ruining the effect by being patronizing. He protests too much about his sincerity (2f.). He repeats himself (verse 3). The absence of a verb in the first colon of verse 3 (RSV supplies *declare*; but NEB is quite different) need cause no worry, since the verb in the next line will do for both. With verse 4 compare 32:8. The reference to creation is so simple that it is not clear whether Elihu is claiming special inspiration, as Rowley thinks (p. 269). In verse 6 he assures Job that they are both on exactly the same footing, so far as God is concerned. Their common humanity is traced to creation.[1]

8-12. Elihu gives a fairly extended summary of Job's position, his claim to innocence (9-11). Although the words *You say* are not present in the Hebrew of verse 9, it is clear from verse 8 that Elihu considers that he is reproducing what he heard Job say. It is not a verbatim quotation, although some lines are similar to 13:24-27. But the word translated *pure* is found nowhere else in the Old Testament. We need to ask, therefore, whether Elihu is fair. To some extent, he is. Job has repeatedly claimed to be *clean* and *pure*, whatever the words he used (9:21; 10:7; 11:4 (Zophar, quoting Job); 16:17; 23:7; and all of chapter 31). But, side by side with this, Job has often admitted to being a sinner. It is harder to find a source for the negatives, *without transgression* and *no iniquity*. Verse 10b is quoted from 13:24, but there the parallel question is: 'Why do you hide your face?' In 13:23, which could be the origin of verse 10a, Job asks what his

---

[1] For the imagery of working clay or dough, which makes 'nipped' a better translation than 'formed' in verse 6b, see Jonas C. Greenfield, 'The Root "GBL" in Mishnaic Hebrew and in the Hymnic Literature from Qumran', *Revue de Qumran*, No. 6, T. 2, 1960, pp. 155-162.

transgressions are, as if to imply that they are imaginary; in order to have a pretext for punishing him, God had to invent sins. But the meaning of the word *occasions* is not clear here. In any case, Job had never gone quite this far in explicitly accusing God of malice, dishonesty or injustice, although he often came so close to this that it could seem to the listener that he had. Like the friends, Elihu was shocked by the sound of Job's words, but he had not grasped the essential point as Job experienced it. This is why it is so easy for him to give the answer: 'You are wrong' (NEB).

His reason for this conclusion is the first big disappointment in his speech. The truth that *God is greater than man* (12b) is so obvious as to be banal. No-one denies this. Job and all the friends have continually affirmed it, none more eloquently than Job himself. Elihu must be making some inference which invalidates rather than answers Job's contention. If so, he does not spell it out.

13–18. Another of Job's complaints was that God did not answer when he called. Hence, although the word *saying* is not present in the Hebrew, it is probable that Elihu is quoting Job in verse 13b.[1] Verses 14ff. are his counter-argument: 'But God does speak. . . .' A double speech by God is mentioned in Psalm 62:11, and the duplication of a dream is seen by Joseph as proof of its divine origin (Gn. 41:32). Elihu recognizes the same medium of revelation in verses 15f. We remember that Job has been having terrifying nightmares. Elihu believes that a spoken message can be given during a dream (16a). But the content of the revelation is again a disappointment. All that God says, after all that trouble, is a warning against the dangers of sin. Who needs a revelation to discover that? And that is not the kind of communication that Job has been asking for. Because the verb translated *perishing* (18) means 'pass through', it is better to adapt the word *sword* to it, rather than the reverse, and to find a parallel to *Pit* (see 17:14). Pope (p. 250) has a solid defence of an identification of 'the river of death' (NEB).

19–22. Men are also warned by God through the more everyday experience of sickness. Job is not unfamiliar with this also. No hint of a spoken oracle goes with this revelation. Elihu's list of horrible symptoms ends with another reference

[1] But NEB makes it the enunciation of another truism: 'No one can answer his arguments.'

to death confronting the sick man. Verse 22 affords a parallel to verse 18. The word *mmtym*, 'killers', while it could mean *those who bring death*, is not a very good designation for the denizens of *the Pit*. Pope's reading 'the waters of death' (p. 251) has a lot to be said for it, in spite of Rowley's rather amused comment: 'a King Charles's head to some Ugaritic enthusiasts' (p. 273).

23-28. The third reference to *the pit* in verse 30 marks the end of the section, and completes the 'one, two, three' pattern (*cf.* 14, 29). This section, however, does not record a further mode of revelation, but rather a response which a man might learn who makes right use of dream or illness as a message from God. He will entrust his cause to *a mediator*. Rowley, with some cogency, thinks that this is another act of God, sending the angel. NEB is neutral. As a messenger from God, the angel would *declare to man what is right for him*, which suggests instruction on the right means to remedy the sin or sickness. Since the word *mediator* means 'translator' (in 16:20 it is generally taken as 'scorner'), and is not the Vindicator of 19:25, an agent of revelation speaking for God could be in mind. But verse 23b could be referring to a 'spokesman . . . to vouch for a man's uprightness' (Gordis, p. 289). It is this being who is *gracious* and finds the *ransom* (24) or means of atonement (*kōp̄er*). But some commentators think that 'God' is the implied subject. NEB brings out clearly the mediatorial role of the angel. The designation *one of the thousand* rules out the idea that there is one angel who is a specialist in such negotiations. It implies rather that God has a large team available for such a task. RSV continues verse 25 as part of the angel's prayer. NEB makes the cure the outcome of the prayer. In either case the rescue from *the Pit* is a restoration of health. In verse 26, according to RSV it is the sick man who now prays to God (not to the angel); but in NEB it is the angel who entreats God's favour on behalf of the man. We think that the latter is a little strained. The activities described here resemble the traditional thanksgivings of the healed man who joyfully praises God for his cure, and *recounts to men his salvation* in public testimony. The Psalms afford many examples. In view of the way the theme of forgiveness of sin is part of the healing (27), there is no need to tidy up the sequence of thought the way some commentators and translations have done.

29-33. This is the kind of thing God does. Verse 30 is

almost a repetition of verse 28. Job is invited to listen, and, if he wishes, to comment. Verse 33 is almost a repetition of verse 31. Elihu gives the impression that he knows best, and that he has Job's justification (32) under control.

iii. Elihu's second speech (34:1–37). In Israel the ban on idols placed restrictions on the decorative visual arts. The prohibition of ritualized myths was another part of the campaign against paganism and prevented the development of drama in Israel. As a result the prime media for artistic expression were music, with song and dance, and the spoken word. In all these Israel excelled. Nothing was esteemed more highly than a word fitly spoken (Pr. 25:11). It was savoured by the ear *as the palate tastes food* (Jb. 34:3). Such art could easily become decadent, when the form was prized for its own sake, rather than as an expression of truth. Elihu's speeches tend to come under this condemnation. In his second one he repeatedly appeals to the wise men. He is no longer reasoning with Job with a view to helping him; he is attacking Job in order to score a point. For all their lucidity, his words are devoid of pastoral concern. They have become an exercise in rhetoric. It is not that they are overloaded with florid decoration. On the contrary, Elihu's theological axioms are pronounced with less adornment than any other speeches in the book. This gives them a cold, detached quality.

God's justice and Job's right have collided. The friends have defended God by condemning Job. Job has defended himself by appealing to God's justice, but it appears to everyone that Job is questioning God's justice, if not denying it outright. Elihu is now caught in the same logic as the friends. By affirming that God's ways cannot be questioned, he is forced to denounce Job's opinions as impious. By linking God's omnipotence as a further reason for blind submission to all His acts, Elihu advocates a course of prudence which leaves God's morality in doubt, unless conscience can be submerged in agnosticism. As we have seen, this Job will never have.

Elihu's defence of the justice of God, which blends the themes of His power, knowledge and impartiality (10–30), is flanked by open attacks on Job for impiety (2–9) and folly (31–37).

2–9. Job is impious. Elihu addresses the *wise men . . . who* *know*. These could be the friends and, since he expects them to agree, he has taken their side. But a larger audience could be intended. It is less likely that readers are being appealed to.

3. Quoted from Job (12:11).

4. By switching to the first person, Elihu ranges (all) wise men with himself as capable of working out what is *right* and *good*. The friends are probably excluded, because Elihu is 'angry' with them (32:3); so the verb *choose* probably means decide which of the two parties in argument (Job and the friends) is in the right.

5, 6. Elihu represents Job's position by means of a mixture of identifiable quotations (such as 27:2) and summaries which are harder to trace to Job's reported words, and which, perhaps, distort his views. The difficulties in verse 6 are due to the fact that it has no source. RSV takes *I am . . . a liar* as a false accusation attributed to God by Job, an affront scarcely less shocking than LXX 'He (God) is lying', which many scholars accept as the original, toned down by MT. In any case Elihu is exaggerating, for Job has never accused God of branding him a liar, and thus telling a lie. His complaint has been that God has not lodged any formal charge at all. Many emendations have been proposed to get rid of the reference to 'lie' altogether. *My wound* (6b) is literally 'my arrow'; *wound* is the result of an emendation. In view of recent studies of divination by arrows, the suggestion of I. Eitan that here it means 'luck' has a new plausibility.[1] Comparison with Job 6:4 suggests 'his (God's) darts', for which Pope is able to find supporting arguments.

7. Elihu repeats Eliphaz's insult, replacing 'iniquity' with 'scoffing', enlarging it with the wholly groundless accusation that Job is a companion of *evildoers* (verse 8).

9. Since a new beginning is made in verse 10, with a fresh address to 'intelligent men', this further saying attributed to Job might be linked to verse 6, and refuted in verses 7f., or rather branded there as impious, with verses 10–30 as a broad demolition of Job's general position. In either case, the sentiment expressed in verse 9 cannot be found in Job's speeches in as many words. Chapter 1 showed Job profiting greatly by his religion. In all his subsequent trials Job never

[1] I. Eitan, *JQR*, N.S., XIV, 1923–24, pp. 41f.; S. Iwry, *JAOS*, 81, 1961, pp. 27–34. *Cf.* NEB.

said this was a waste of effort. On the contrary, he said again and again that he would stick to his integrity to the end. What, then, is Elihu getting at? Job has made two observations: first, that the expected judgment often does not fall on the wicked (21:7–34); secondly, that trouble comes to good and bad alike (9:22). Incidentally, the latter remark shows that Job had not adopted a one-sided view that the good suffered, while the bad were let off. The attitude that Elihu portrays is precisely what Job finds in the wicked in 21:14f., as they encourage themselves in their evil deeds. It is quite unfair for Elihu to claim that Job thinks this himself, even if he believed that this would be the next step in Job's thought.

10–15. Elihu repeats the self-evident truth that God can do no wrong. He attaches three thoughts to this proposition. First, he infers from God's supremacy as Creator that He is not accountable to anyone (13). This takes us to the edge of a dangerous cliff. For, if everything God does is right, by definition, and if, because He is Sovereign, God does everything that happens, it follows that everything that happens is right, and the category of evil disappears. Secondly, verses 14 and 15 specify that every living thing depends on God for its being, so that He may, indiscriminately or universally, withdraw this gift of existence and do nothing wrong. This is a fine acknowledgment of God as owner of all, and a fine tribute to His might. But it leaves no grounds for saying that any act of God is 'good' rather than 'bad'. 'Might makes right' is the upshot of Elihu's doctrine, and in this emphasis he approaches rather closely to Job's contention. But he wriggles out of the difficulty by falling back on the doctrine that God requites every person according to his behaviour (11), stating it in crass individualistic terms. But this is the very thing under debate, and no answer to the problem.

16. Since the verbs are singular, the following questions are addressed to Job. NEB supplies the name.

17–30. The references to *nation* and *reign* in verses 29f. seem to complete a strophe that begins in verse 18 with parallel references to *king* and *nobles*. If the government of human monarchs cannot be questioned or opposed, it is inconceivable that the universe should be governed by one *who hates justice* (17). This is a mere assertion. Why should not the ultimate power be demonic (by our standards)? Or an Absolute 'beyond good and evil', a thought irresistible to many modern minds, and one that often threatens Job's confidence in God's goodness. Can this never be more than a blind affirmation of faith, or is it reasonable to expect some kind of explanation of the rightness of acts of God which seem, to our moral judgment, to be wrong?

Elihu's answer to this problem is not altogether clear. He emphasizes that God's knowledge is complete and infallible (21, 22, 25a, 28b), so His actions are beyond human comprehension. We are already familiar with such attempts to forbid human enquiry. In 24:1 Job wanted to know why God did not hold regular public sessions of judgment, so that justice might be seen to be done. Elihu replies that God's judgments are inflicted without warning and without trial (20, 24 (*without investigation*), 25b). This response is stimulated, not so much by indignation against the wicked, as by concern for *the cry of the poor* (28). And it is done publicly (26) to the notoriously wicked (27), all without partiality (19). But oppressive rulers seem to be the particular objects of God's destruction, and the fact that they can be broken suddenly without human help (20) seems to Elihu to be sufficient evidence that God is at work.

29, 30. No explanation is necessary, so Job has no grounds for complaint because God has been silent to him. God is not beholden to any man for explanations, which, in any case, a man might not grasp because he sees but a few of the facts, whereas God sees all. But verses 29f. are not satisfactory, and some have found in them a darker and more disturbing thought. Even if God is quite inactive, leaving evil unchecked, *who can condemn?* If He chooses to hide His face, who can make Him show it? The only possible explanation, brought out by NEB, is that 'he makes a godless man king' to punish 'a stubborn nation'. The prophets were able to entertain the thought that the Assyrian was the rod of God's anger (*e.g.* Is. 10:5), and Habakkuk could think the same about the Babylonians. But they always added that these nations, despite such use by God, were fully accountable for their evil deeds, and would in due time pay for them. But this involves a historical stage, group guilt, and long spans of time, which are not used in the book of Job. This keeps the problem focused on the apparent injustice of God's treatment of one man, Job.

31-37. The last strophe seems to be addressed to Job

personally. It is full of difficulties and we must take what guidance we can from the clearer passages. Verse 37 is pretty blunt in its accusation. Earlier Job's irreverence was attributed to stupidity rather than to wickedness. The former might be cured by instruction in wisdom. The cure of the latter is more difficult, especially when it is wilful and repeated. Like the others, Elihu is locked in to the inevitable conclusion: Job is to blame. And his guilt is to be measured by the scale of his sufferings. To his *sin* (which could be a minor fault, failure or missing the mark) he has added *rebellion* (open and deliberate disobedience to God's known law, or treachery). This is proved by the way he *multiplies his words against God*. Once more we see that communication broke down at its most vital point. Job's earnest words, which grasped the heart of the issue and which could have led them all into the truth, are rejected as blasphemous by Elihu, just like the rest. Consequently he can only do what they did, and urge Job to repentance. Job has spoken *without knowledge . . . without insight . . . like wicked men* (35, 36). He is urged to renounce such dangerous talk (31b, 32b). It is a pity that verse 33 is so unclear. There is no clear promise of forgiveness, unless some mitigation of his well-deserved punishment is all he can hope for. NEB suggests that Job's 'rejection' of God has gone so far that it is doubtful if restoration is possible. Much depends on whether the word *requital* (payment, satisfaction of a debt) means 'retribution' (God still hasn't paid him for 'his endless ranting against God', 37b, NEB) or 'recompense' (God must now make it up to Job for the unfair treatment he has received). This leaves it unclear what it is that Job *must choose* (33). But even the repentance Elihu prescribes in verses 31f. does not seem to carry with it any happy prospects of renewal. If 'requite' in verse 33 means what it does in verse 11, then Elihu has paid the price which all moralists must pay whose defence of God's justice is the slogan: *according to the work of a man* (11a). Justice is safe; but there is no forgiveness.

iv. Elihu's third speech (35:1-16). This speech deals with two questions (1-3). In 34:9 Job, according to Elihu, has asked: 'What is the use of being good?' Elihu does not have a sufficiently personal understanding of God to believe that God can be delighted with a good man, and grieved by sin. As the impartial administrator of justice (34:19), He applies the law to all alike. So when Elihu puts in Job's mouth the opposite question: 'What do I lose by sinning?'[1] he is caught in his own trap.

His answer is given in verses 4–8. His claim to be able to answer everybody (4) is not borne out. What he says in verses 5ff. is largely drawn from earlier speeches, and affirms commonplaces about the greatness of God not in dispute. With verse 5 compare 9:8–10; 11:8f.; 22:12; an opinion shared by all. With verse 6 compare 7:20, a question Job has already asked God. With verse 7 compare 22:3. Since these are all identifiable quotations, perhaps only verse 8 should be taken as Elihu's own reply to them. In any case, the answer is not profound. Nothing that a man does either hurts or helps God; its repercussions are felt only among his fellow-men. This thought is so similar to the position that Elihu purports to be refuting, that there would seem to be something wrong, either with the text or with the usual interpretations. A solution will probably be found by tracing a closer connection between verse 8 and verses 2f. The parallelism invites this, and the grammatical difficulties in verse 8 might be helped out if it completes the statement begun there. As it is, Elihu seems to have finished up in a corner, affirming that God is quite unaffected by human wickedness or righteousness. If he is saying that God's intrinsic righteousness is perfect, not capable of being augmented by human goodness, not capable of being diminished by human wickedness, then the idea is a very abstract one, and an evasion. If it means that God couldn't care less about human conduct either way, then he is echoing the opinions quoted in verses 6 and 7 and has undermined his whole case, saying in effect that justice means nothing to God. Beginning with impartiality, he has ended with indifference.

His reply (9–16) to the second problem is equally callous. The question is, 'Why doesn't God answer prayer?' In particular, 'Why has He not heeded Job's sustained appeals for some kind of response, any kind of response?'

It is always possible to think of a reason for unanswered prayer. The trite explanation, which we hear all too often, is that 'You didn't have enough faith', or 'You prayed from the

---

[1] It is not certain that this is the meaning of verse 3b. The Hebrew is cryptic: 'How do I profit from my sin?' But 'from' is comparative; hence the paraphrase in RSV is to be preferred to the more literal NEB.

wrong motive', or 'You must have some hidden, unconfessed sin'. This diagnosis is always applicable. Everyone who prays is aware of the weakness of his faith; everyone with a scrap of self-knowledge knows that his motives are always mixed; everyone who searches his conscience can find no end of fresh sins to be dealt with. If no prayers could be offered and none answered, until all these conditions were satisfied, none would ever be offered and none answered. The Elihus of this world do not care about the cruelty of their perfectionist advice and its unreality. Their theory is saved; that is what matters.

We notice that, by taking this line, Elihu has changed the focus from *the multitude of oppressions* (9a) which should arouse the anger of a just God, irrespective of the spirituality of those who *call for help*. According to Elihu, the suppliants disqualify themselves by defects of their own. In his universe, answers to prayer are just as automatic as judgments on the wicked, provided the conditions are satisfied. *God does not hear an empty cry* (13a). The word *empty* implies a vain, indeed profane, prayer. In verse 12, then, *the pride of evil men* probably describes the wrong attitude of the person praying and the reason why God does not answer, rather than the reason why *they cry out*. This prepares the way for accusing Job of such pride in verses 14f. In verses 10 and 11 Elihu does suggest a suitable prayer, which, however, the oppressed are not willing to use. Just why such a prayer should be effective is not clear. As a plea for justice, it is surprising that God is addressed as *my Maker*, not Judge or Saviour. And the attributes of God, for all their expressions of appreciation,[1] do not seem as pertinent as appeals to His power or justice. Man's superiority to brute creation is a key thought in Job, and it is remarkable that Elihu uses it here. To remind God of one's capacity to receive divine instruction is evidently not the kind of pride that ruins prayer.

What Elihu seems to be leading up to is a stern denunciation of Job's prayers as abundant but ignorant (16b). He applies to them the epithet *empty*, which Job has applied to the

[1] That *God . . . gives songs in the night*, when the disconsolate tend to be particularly cheerless, as Job well knew, is one of the most beautiful tributes to our kindly Father in Scripture. There is no compelling need to change 'songs' to 'protection' as some have done, even though the thought is still appropriate.

friends. Since verse 15 is quite obscure, we are left to guess that it means that Elihu is accusing Job of completely misunderstanding God's unresponsiveness as heedlessness, whereas in fact God is holding His anger in. Job is guilty of despising God's longsuffering (Rom. 2:4, AV). Verse 14 suggests that it is Job's posture as a litigant that Elihu finds objectionable, and a barrier rather than a means of access to God. To complain *that you do not see him*[1] is an impertinence, when the fault lies with Job. Elihu, who thinks that he is 'perfect in knowledge' (36:4), has a manageable, predictable God. Job, all too conscious of the sovereign freedom of the Lord, lives in the suspense of faith, praying without guarantees.

v. Elihu's fourth speech (36:1 – 37:24). Elihu's last word falls into two parts so distinct in tone and content as to give the impression that they are independent compositions and could have been separate speeches. The first section (36:1–21) continues the themes of the preceding chapters. The second (36:22 – 37:24) introduces a new line of argument. It begins to move in the direction of the Lord's speeches that follow and so serves as a transition to the concluding cycle (chapters 38–42). In a similar manner, Elihu's opening speech had two parts, the first of which (chapter 32) took off from the preceding debate. This connective tissue is evidence of the planned dramatic unity of the Elihu speeches within the whole book. Even if they are the last part to be written, they were built in, and not just dumped in, as some critics suggest.

This concluding statement contains Elihu's best and most distinctive ideas. Up until now he has been treading on familiar and conventional ground, repeating largely the ideas which Job and his friends have already expressed. The harsh tone that Elihu had adopted in his second and third speeches is here softened. Job 36:1–21 is a more mature and engaging statement of orthodox theology than anything found elsewhere in the book. Its presence is one of the main reasons why some scholars have found Elihu's contribution so pleasing. While it does repeat some arguments that have already failed to carry the day, they are diffused by a deeper analysis and a more humane sensitivity that brings them

---

[1] But *cf.* NEB: 'He does not see me.'

nearer to Job's condition. God's dealings with men are seen not simply in terms of rewards and punishments; they are also remedial, or at least intended to be so, if rightly used. Life teaches through 'discipline' (the key word of Wisdom teaching, introduced by Eliphaz at the very beginning; *cf.* 4:3; 5:17). Every experience, good or bad, brings fresh opportunities to learn more about God. The wise man rides the wave; the fool is drowned by it. Perhaps this is what Elihu was getting at when he said to Job: 'The choice is yours' (34:33). The meaning of suffering depends on the spirit in which it is 'received' (2:10). Since 'discipline' is imposed on a child by a parent or on a pupil by a teacher, it is intended to be beneficial. The recalcitrant and unteachable, of course, can deprive or even injure themselves by struggling against the yoke; but, correctly worn as an instrument of honourable work, it enables greater achievement and actually lightens the load.

The full answer to Job's suffering cannot therefore be found in questions about justice. Beyond justice there is a benevolence in God that calls men to trust Him. More simply stated, the issue is whether a person can continue to believe that God is really good. Then he will be able to sing in the dark (35:10), no matter what happens. The search for an explanation by tracking Job's sufferings to their origin and cause has failed. More light will be gained in the search for their outcome and goal.

1-4. Elihu begins his final speech with a renewed plea for patience. He still has 'words concerning [or from] God' (2b) to say. But his vanity spoils it. The truth he is about to reveal is not accessible to ordinary men. It comes 'from' (*l-*) a distance, even 'from' (*l-*) God himself (3). The parallelism in verse 3 is against the usual interpretation *I will . . . ascribe righteousness to my Maker.*[1] *I will fetch* (3a) parallels 'I will give'. Job, rather than God, is the object of this gift, the recipient of knowledge. So *from afar* parallels 'from my Maker' (same preposition, with the same meaning). Hence *knowledge* (3a) and *righteousness* (3b) are also parallels, constituting a single phrase: 'authentic knowledge', a common attributive use of *ṣedeq.* A similar claim is repeated in verse 4a, *šeqer,* 'falsehood', being the antonym of *ṣedeq,* and *knowledge*

---

[1] 'I defend the justice of my Maker' (NEB), or 'prove my Maker just' (JB).

(plural in verse 4b) makes an *inclusio*. Elihu is so confident that he can claim to be *perfect* (the same word, or at least root, is used for Job in 1:1) *in knowledge*. This is a claim to accuracy, not omniscience. But, although an almost identical attribute is given to God in 37:16, and 1 Samuel 2:3 indicates that only the Lord is 'God of knowledge', it seems as if Elihu is giving himself such a certificate of genius, as if the brash young man is all unaware of its astounding presumption. Elihu does not think that God is with Job, and he has just claimed to be bringing knowledge from God who is at a great distance. This all sounds so vain that one wonders if the author is being ironical at this point. But, if the author is serious, we must look in what follows for 'sound conclusions' (4b in NEB).

5–12. God sends troubles to test and to train people. The emphasis once more is on God's irresistible might, backed up by *strength of understanding*. But verse 5 is very difficult. The verb *despise* has no object. *Any* in RSV has been supplied in translation. We would expect something like 'he does not despise the afflicted, or the pure in heart' in parallel with verse 7a. NEB has given up the negative. Verse 6 is clearer. It is a flat contradiction of what Job has observed, namely, the denial of rights to the oppressed and the prolongation of the life of the wicked. If Job and Elihu cannot agree on the facts of life, they cannot begin to discuss their significance.

The example Elihu chooses is reminiscent of the Joseph story, in spite of the plural *kings* (7), which has worried some scholars. Certainly Joseph is another classic case of a person treated unjustly, and that more than once. Furthermore his experience provided, not only the occasion for his own character to develop, but also the means by which God brought him to great power for the benefit of his whole family. This helps us to see that *the righteous*, on whom God keeps His eye (7a), are not necessarily sinless in relationship to God, for verse 10b expects them to repent. The righteous are the afflicted, wronged by men, and so with a just claim on God's help. Elihu's point seems to be that this help is not immediately forthcoming. God watches to see whether the victim will find the uses of adversity sweet. This is stated succinctly in verse 15 (*q.v.*, below). Elihu develops the theme of the two ways set before every man. In this instance, men who are *bound in fetters*: they can either listen and prosper (11) or not listen and perish (12). But Elihu does not seem to be altogether sure that a righteous person would ever find himself in fetters. Verse 9 implies that such humiliation is God-sent punishment for pride, weakening his point considerably, at least in its applicability to Job. Imprisonment is intended as a corrective discipline (*mûsar*, 10), aimed particularly at arousing a consciousness of sin. The Wisdom teachers recognized that there was always room for improvement, even when there were no faults to be eliminated. But Elihu does not concede quite this much to Job.

In the contrast between verses 11 and 12 there is a play on the words '*ābad* and '*ābar*. Taking the latter ('cross') literally, Dhorme found a parallel to the idea of death in verse 12b, and a contrast to the promise of long life in verse 11, by identifying *šlḥ*, not with *the sword* (12a), but with the Canal (of death); *cf.* NEB. This possibility was discussed in the commentary on 33:18; but it should be noted that 11QtgJob clearly supports 'sword'. To *die without knowledge* does not mean that 'death comes on them unawares' (JB), but that they pass ignorantly into the region where there is no knowledge to be gained, they go to Hell having learnt nothing in this life. This conclusion suits the general drift of Elihu's argument that the purpose of life is to learn what God wants to teach us through the things He does to us.

13, 14. These verses complete the sketch of the person who refuses to pray when in trouble (13b). He comes to an untimely (14a) and shameful (14b) end. The word translated *shame* means 'male prostitutes' (NEB), but it is hard to see what such an allusion is doing in the present passage.

15. Although somewhat sententious, this seems to sum up everything. There is a subtle play on the sounds of the roots here, impossible to capture in English. Instrumental *by* is favoured, although 'from' is another possible meaning. In any case, the idea of the poor man being saved by his poverty (Dhorme prefers this nuance rather than *affliction*, RSV, or 'suffering', NEB) is paradoxically stated. It is God who saves; adversity provides the occasion, if the right advantage is taken of it.

16-25. This strophe, in the singular, seems to be addressed to Job. The text is full of problems, so that even its form (accusation, warning, encouragement?) is not clear. It lacks concreteness, and this is a handicap. Some editions, instead of following through verses 22-25 as a final exhortation to piety, join them to the following passage as part of Elihu's recitation on the greatness of God. Because the problems are insoluble, we shall illustrate by a few examples how divergent the translations can be. TEV develops the thought that Job is only getting the punishment he deserves and that 'it will do you no good to cry out for help'. JB heaps accusations on Job: 'You did not execute justice on the wicked, you cheated orphaned children of their rights; . . . led astray by riches, or corrupted by fat bribes.' NEB simply warns Job against such dangers in a far more friendly tone. RSV, making a more honest attempt to remain close to the Hebrew, has left us with a translation almost as unintelligible as the original.

26–33. We have already noted the difficulty of finding the boundary between the two major sections of this speech. The phrase *from afar* at the end of verse 25 is the same as that in verse 3, and could be an *inclusio* completing the section. But verses 22 and 26 both begin with the same words, *Behold, God . . .* , and could introduce closely-related strophes. Fortunately the text continues to improve as we move along, until the theme of God's power is unfolded with a brilliance surpassed only by the Lord's own speeches.

Elihu's first clear pronouncement was that 'God is greater than man' (33:12). He repeats it now (verse 26), using a different adjective. Elihu has, in fact, steered the argument away from the justice of God to His wisdom, using His power as the bridge. There is a gain here, for the rightness of an action may be justified by its wisdom, even if it does not satisfy the canons of justice. But there is also a danger which Elihu, and perhaps even the book of Job as a whole, does not entirely avoid. To take refuge from undemonstrable justice in inscrutable wisdom might be no more than to hide God away in a cloud of mystification. We have already seen that chapter 28 does not do this. So far as the world is concerned, God's wisdom is seen in its variegation and in its order. So far as man is concerned, God's wisdom is expressed in his moral conduct. Somehow the book is moving towards a synthesis of these two by ascending to God as the common Creator of all, not by descending to the dull aphorism that the 'good' is what is 'according to nature'. The questions which begin to appear in verses 22 and 23 dominate the rest of the book. They all point from different directions to the greatness of God, bringing it into the view of all men (25a), even if they see it only 'from a great distance' (25b). A man's proper response is to sing in praise (24). Since no-one has put God in charge of this 'realm' (a possible alternative to 'way' in verse 23), no-one can call Him to account and suggest that there might be something 'wrong' with what He has done. The earlier discussion has already made us acutely aware of the dangers in this kind of talk; nevertheless Elihu has struck out on a profitable line, and our respect for him is restored when he says things like this about God.

Elihu first directs Job's attention to the splendour of God in nature, in the storm (26–33). As the discourse continues, he will elaborate on what happens in winter (37:1–13) and on the beauty of the sky when the storm is over (37:14–24).

26. The agnosticism of the usual translations is uncalled for, in view of Elihu's tribute to God as an incomparable teacher in verse 22. The object *him* is lacking in MT. As the parallel shows, God's eternity is conceivable, but not comprehensible. We know that God is great. That is an enormous amount of positive knowledge. But we can never know just how great He is. Yet this perceived limitation does not invalidate what we do know, especially when that knowledge is grounded, not in transcendental speculation, but in contemplation of God in His manifold works of creation.

27–33. The clouds and the rain display God's astonishing control of the world in operations of such delicacy and strength that men can neither understand nor imitate them. If twentieth-century men appeal to the science of meteorology by which we predict our weather and plan our times, in order to reduce the weight of Elihu's wonder, our superiority is quickly moderated because our expanded knowledge of the universe only projects Elihu's questions all the more unanswerably on a screen of cosmic size. The word *mist*, which occurs only here and in Genesis 2:6, has no etymological support, although NEB clings to the tradition. Albright's demonstration that it is a borrowing from Sumerian[1] is as complete as one could hope for in such cases, notwithstanding residual difficulties in morphology and continued debate as to its exact denotation. Pope (p. 273) has made the helpful observation that the suffix *-ô*, troublesome in Hebrew, reflects the original Akkadian ending, thus removing partly a difficulty

---

[1] *JBL*, LVIII, 1939, pp. 102f.

felt by Speiser.[1] But, in our opinion, Pope has left too much mythological connotation in his translation 'flood', whereas the evidence adduced by Speiser points to a more everyday association. His narrowing of the denotation to an outbreak of subterranean waters certainly fits the occurrence in Genesis 2:6. Here, however, the collocation with *rain* and the uncertain meaning of the verb *distils* (which is translated 'refine' in Jb. 28:1) oblige us to suspend judgment. The unresolved question is whether two sources of water – the sky and the underworld, as in the Flood story – are in mind, or only one, both sea[2] and groundwaters yielding the moisture *which the skies pour down* (28a).

The language of the whole poem is poetic in any case, and exact science is not likely to provide the needed clues. Since the sky is sometimes spoken of as God's tent, the cloud surfaces we see might well be the carpeting of the floor (*cf.* NEB), but the modern reading is intended to get around the puzzling phrase *the thunderings of his pavilion* (29b). But this is not the usual word for 'thunder' any more than the word translated 'lightning' in verses 30 and 32 is the usual word for that phenomenon. What is meant by *the roots of the sea* is another enigma (30b). The picture of hands covered with lightning (32) might be compared with representations of the storm-god with flashes leaping from his hands.

Even though so many details escape us, the general effect is clear and forceful. God's power in the thunderstorm is particularly terrifying, an expression of *anger against iniquity* (33b) and of judgment (31a). Yet it is also the means by which he *gives food in abundance* (31b). The one act of God can be destructive and beneficent.

37:1–5. There is no break between the chapters, except for a sudden ejaculation by Elihu, who is startled into mixed terror and admiration at the awesome spectacle of God's power in the thunderstorm. The parallel in Habakkuk 3:6 indicates that it is the perception of the living presence of God Himself in such events that makes men *tremble*. The Bible contains some magnificent descriptions of the thunderstorm. Psalm 29 is the best of these, but Elihu's poem comes a

---

[1] E. A. Speiser, *Oriental and Biblical Studies* (1967), pp. 19–22.

[2] The word 'sea' is readily produced in verse 27a by reading *m* with the preceding word, instead of 'water'. The preposition *l–* in the next colon is then 'from', and mythological imagery recognized, without going all the way with Pope.

close second. The request to *hearken* is plural, addressed to Job and his friends, if not to the bystanders as well. We can almost imagine that Elihu gives his description while a tremendous storm actually breaks over them all. While thunder and lightning are both mentioned, prominence is given to the deafening sounds, identified quite simply as God's *voice*. There is a considerable amount of repetition, and some rare words are used to refer to thunder. Since verse 5 is a well-formed bicolon, with 'marvels' and 'prodigies' in parallel, and since the new beginning in verse 6 marks verse 5 as climactic, we should recognize verses 2–4 as a heptacolon flanked by the symmetrical verses 1 and 5. The structure of these seven colons then emerges with similar symmetry. A single colon dealing with 'lightning' (the simple word 'light' is used as in chapter 36) is placed midway between a pair of tricolons, both of which deal with the *voice*. The completeness of this heptacolon is indicated, not only by its inner symmetry, but by the return to the word 'hear' in verse 4b as an *inclusio* for verse 2a. This analysis clears up some problems. Misled by a narrow search for two-line units, which has already influenced Massoretic punctuation, some scholars (*e.g.* Rowley, p. 302) identify *it* in verse 3a with 'lightning' (3b) for the sake of parallelism. Pope (p. 278) completes this by translating 'flashes it'. His impressive Ugaritic parallel disqualifies the Aramaic verb which we have used up till now to supply a cognate. But, by incorporating the suffix into the root, he solves one problem only to create a new one. The review of the problem in *Ras Shamra Parallels* (pp. 24f.) should be studied before final judgment is given. NEB translates the verb 'roll' in line with our suggested analysis. *Lightnings* in verse 4a is not in MT. RSV *we cannot comprehend* (5) supports our remarks on agnosticism in the commentary on 36:26, where the identical words were translated 'we know him not'.

6–13. The boundaries of this strophe are marked by clear grammatical signals. It deals with the rains of winter, accompanied by snow and freezing cold, which keep men indoors (7; but the Hebrew is far from clear, and NEB has probably carried its guesswork a bit too far) and drive animals into their lairs (8). With the return to *ice* in verse 10 the outline of an introverted structure may be discerned; but it is not as clear as in the strophe in verses 1–5. Elihu draws two conclusions as men watch helplessly. God is in complete control of all these events (12), even though their 'whirling around' might suggest aimless, chaotic forces. NEB brings this idea to clearer expression. Secondly (13) *he causes it to happen* for any one of several quite diverse reasons. Three possibilities are mentioned, each introduced by 'if': 'if for rod, if for his earth, if for *ḥeseḏ* (the great word for covenanted loyalty, used in 10:12)'. Because the reference to *land* does not seem to fit, commentators have either changed it or thrown it out (so NEB). But 36:31 has already made the point that rain water can be destructive or beneficial. Here the same contrast is secured by the word 'rod' (hence AV 'correction') and *love* (RSV). The most dramatic events in Israel's history were occasions when God used the most destructive storms to give His people the victories promised in His covenant, that is, to do *ḥeseḏ* (Jos. 10; Jdg. 4; 1 Sa. 7:10; Ps. 18; *etc.*). These reasons for sending storms have to do with men, and have a moral justification along familiar lines: to punish the wicked or to rescue the just. The third reason is the most interesting, for it has nothing to do with men, and opens up a completely new line of thought. God does a great number of things in His vast universe which find no explanation by reference to mankind, just as the Lord's own speeches will remind Job that He has many creatures besides men to look after. Sometimes He might have a storm, just 'for Himself'. Although it was suspected long ago that the root *rṣw* is hidden in the word *his land*, the arguments of Dahood (which could have been stated much more strongly by Pope, whose translation 'for grace' is not as good as something like 'for pleasure') have opened the way for the recognition of many more supporting examples.[1] God is free to do what He pleases without having to explain everything as part of His purpose for mankind.

14-20. Elihu now addresses Job more directly by name. He launches into a string of questions, somewhat in the mode that the Lord Himself will use when He eventually speaks.[2] Reviewing once more the marvels of the sky, he asks

---

[1] To give but one which, so far as I know, has not yet been reported: *'arṣāh* in Gn. 38:9 should be translated 'deliberately, wilfully', thus eliminating the absurd circumstance of having intercourse on the bare ground.

[2] This anticipation does not spoil the impact of the divine encounter, as some critics feel who wish to remove the Elihu speeches altogether. Almost from the outset the dialogue included poems in this vein (5:8-16; 9:5-10; 12:7-12; 26:5-14; 28; 35:11). The Lord's speeches are thus a *crescendo* of themes already announced.

Job if he knows how God does such things as *balancing* the
clouds (16) and spreading out the heavens (18). Since the
sky seems firm and solid to a viewer on earth, the poetic
comparison with *a molten mirror* should not be spoilt by intro-
ducing quarrels about its 'scientific' accuracy. The Hebrews
were fully aware that the structure of the heavens was much
more complex than that of an 'inverted bowl'.

Verse 17 seems to be contrasting the sultry summer weather
with the conditions described in verses 6–13, but why he should
highlight Job's personal discomfort – 'sweating there in your
stifling clothes' (NEB) – is not clear, unless it is to drive home
the point that man has absolutely no control over the weather,
unlike God, who changes it at His will. It then prepares for
verses 19f., which, although far from clear,[1] apparently chide
Job for wanting to 'dictate to God' (NEB) even in such an easy
and everyday matter as the weather, let alone in the moral
ordering of human affairs. A comparison of various translations of verse 20b restrains us from attempting any comment.

21–24. Elihu's speeches end on a note of awesome tranquillity. The storm has abated and sunlight streams through
the breaking clouds. Some commentators are unhappy about
the position of verse 21 at this point, for Elihu returns to
a description of nature after he has begun to moralize. But
there is no need to shift verse 21 to another place, as some do.
We have seen this kind of thing several times before. A final
acknowledgment of God's *terrible majesty* (22) prepares for
final affirmations of His greatness.

It is a disappointment to discover that the beautiful rendering of verse 22a in RSV, *Out of the north comes golden splendour*,
has such a precarious foundation in the Hebrew. The *gold*
(*i.e.* the ordinary metal) referred to by the Hebrew might
refer to the afterglow of a rainstorm, but this would not be
in the north. If it is the aurora borealis, a suggestion which
many scholars find attractive, then we have brought in a
completely different feature of the night sky, unrelated to the
storms which have dominated Elihu's speech thus far.

Blommerde's[2] identification of the title Most High God in

[1] We don't know why Elihu suddenly starts saying 'we'. Does he mean
that he and Job might jointly submit to God a request for clement weather?
Verse 19b is equally opaque. Does it mean that God is concealed in darkness,
or that we are in the dark?
[2] A. C. M. Blommerde, *Northwest Semitic Grammar and Job*, p. 132.

verse 22b deserves to be taken seriously. Verse 22a should be joined to verse 21 to make a tetracolon and verse 22b joined to verse 23 to make a six-line strophe of two-beat colons, full of memories of ancient hymns, a fitting climax to Elihu's grand recital.

Verse 24 is then the finishing touch, the application to men, especially Job. It resembles other verses which conclude speeches in this book by having a succinct bicolon with tight parallelism. But translators have missed it. NEB has silently removed the troublesome negative (*not* of RSV), but loses the parallelism by translating the same word 'reverence' in verse 24a but 'look' in verse 24b. *Yr'h* is repetitive parallel of *yr'whw* with defective spelling, according to a principle pointed out by the author.[1] In parallel with *lkn*, *l'* must be assertative:

> 'Therefore men fear Him,
> Surely all wise of heart fear Him!'

We have come full circle to Job 28:28.

V. YAHWEH AND JOB (38:1 – 42:6)

The Lord Himself finally breaks silence, speaking 'out of the whirlwind' (38:1; 40:6). Although not altogether un-prepared for (see above, p. 266, note 2), what He says is quite surprising in both content and style.

His speeches are addressed exclusively to Job, a late response to a request that Job had repeatedly made, a request that was his final word (31:35). But they are not what Job has asked for. He has requested either a bill of indictment, with specific charges which he is prepared to answer, or else a verdict from his Judge which he confidently expects to be a declaration of his innocence. Neither is forthcoming, although the form of cross-examination might sound at times like an accusation that Job has been foolishly darkening counsel 'by words without knowledge' (38:2).

Even so, God's two lengthy recitals are not replies to the questions that have tormented Job and which his friends have failed to answer. At least, on first inspection, they do not seem to have anything to do with the central issue of why Job

[1] *JBL*, LXVIII, 1970, pp. 343f.

has suffered so severely when he has done everything humanly possible to maintain a good relationship with God. The Lord apparently says nothing about this. Indeed, He makes very few positive statements or affirmations. His speeches are not oracles; He answers Job's questions with a deluge of counter-questions. This sustained interrogation is not just a formal peculiarity. The function of the questions needs to be properly understood. As a rhetorical device, a question can be another way of making a pronouncement, much favoured by orators. For Job, the questions in the Lord's speeches are not such roundabout statements of fact; they are invitations, suggestions about discoveries he will make as he tries to find his own answers. They are not catechetical, as if Job's knowledge is being tested. They are educative, in the true and original meaning of that term. Job is led out into the world. The questions are rhetorical only in the sense that none of them has any answer ventured by Job. But this is not because the questions have no answers. Their initial effect of driving home to Job his ignorance is not intended to humiliate him. On the contrary the highest nobility of every person is to be thus enrolled by God Himself in His school of Wisdom. And the schoolroom is the world! For Job the exciting discoveries to which God leads him bring a giant advance in knowledge, knowledge of himself and of God, for the two always go together in the Bible. This change in his mind is so radical that it could be called a con-version; but not at all like that first conversion, unavoidable for anyone who wishes to enter God's family, in which a penitent sinner renounces his evil ways and receives forgive-ness. Such a repentance is not required of Job; he is not asked to disown his claim to be in the right.

The very fact that God does not come forward (as the friends did) with a list of Job's sins is itself sufficient proof that this was not needed. That God speaks at all is enough for Job. All he needs to know is that everything is still all right between himself and God. Knowing that, he does not care what happens to him. It is this assurance that is restored by the Lord's speeches. To that extent it does not matter much what they talk about. Any topic will do for a satisfying con-versation between friends. It is each other they are enjoying. But this does not mean that the content of the Lord's speeches is irrelevant; by some indirect and more subtle route they lead Job to complete satisfaction.

The universal admiration of readers for the superb poetry of these speeches is often mingled with puzzlement over their quite unexpected content. They consist almost entirely of 'nature' poems. There is very little about God's moral government of human affairs, His dealings with men. On first reading, the speeches seem to side-step the issues which have dominated the book up to this point. There is no reference to Job's experience or his problems. There is no debate with any of the things that Job and the other speakers have said. The obvious resolution, to tell Job at long last what was really behind it all, by disclosing to him the fact that doubt had been cast on his character by the Satan and that the Lord had confidently put Job into a test – none of this is ever revealed.[1]

Many frivolous readers have found God's response not only puzzling, but irrelevant, evasive, even insulting.[2] There is no hint that God despises Job as unworthy of divine companionship; far from it. He invites Job to meet Him almost as an equal, standing up 'like a man' (38:3). There is no hint of that irritating cant that silences the honest seeker with the reminder that it is not for us to question the ways of the Almighty. Part of our inhibition is caused by a long-standing tradition in western Christian thought that belittles the knowledge of God gained by thinking about the world. 'Natural theology' was kept within bounds by the scholastics, and denied altogether by Neo-orthodoxy. The book of Job does not take this discouraging attitude. Just as Jesus invited us to 'consider the lilies of the field', so the Lord is like a

---

[1] It is one of the many excellences of the book that Job is brought to contentment without ever knowing all the facts of his case. In view of the way in which the Satan brought up the matter, something had to be done to rescue Job from his slander. And the test would work only if Job did not know what it was for. God thrusts Job into an experience of dereliction to make it possible for Job to enter into a life of naked faith, to learn to love God for Himself alone. God does not seem to give this privilege to many people, for they pay a terrible price of suffering for their discoveries. But part of the discovery is to see the suffering itself as one of God's most precious gifts. To withhold the full story from Job, even after the test was over, keeps him walking by faith, not by sight. He does not say in the end, 'Now I see it all.' He never sees it all. He sees God (42:5). Perhaps it is better if God never tells any of us the whole of our life-story.

[2] George Bernard Shaw, in *The Adventures of the Black Girl in her Search for God* (1932), has her call the Lord's speech 'a sneer' (p. 12). In the preface found in the Penguin edition (which is entitled *The Black Girl in Search of God*) Shaw says that God 'jeers' at Job (p. 19).

friend who asks you to join Him in a walk around His garden. God enjoys His world, and He wants us to enjoy it with Him. But it is only when God Himself conducts the tour that the excursion is profitable.

The selection of creatures which the Lord parades before Job's eyes is remarkable, especially when we notice some of the phenomena which have not been included: the sun, for instance, which men have always found one of the most impressive of God's works and the one which often comes first to mind as a symbol of God Himself, blinding but beneficent. But any creature will serve the purpose, for all speak about the power and wisdom of their Creator, saying at once that God is marvellous and mysterious, observable and elusive.

There is a kindly playfulness in the Lord's speeches which is quite relaxing. Their aim is not to crush Job with an awareness of his minuteness contrasted with the limitless power of God, not to mock him when he puts his tiny mind beside God's vast intellect. On the contrary, the mere fact that God converses with him gives him a dignity above all the birds and beasts, assuring him that it is a splendid thing to be a man.[1] To look at any bird or flower – and how many of them there are! – is a revelation of God in His constant care for His world.

In this sharing of a common life in the same world, God and Job both find the vindication that neither received in the discourses of the friends. The whole story became a test of both God and Job. Here is the answer to the Satan's cynicism. Here is the proof that Job has clung to God when stripped of all else. Here is the proof that a man can love God simply for being God, not for reward. Here the lack of a formal answer to the moral question, indeed the narrowing of the spotlight of the book to one individual, is positively instructive. Job is vindicated in a faith in God's goodness that has survived a terrible deprivation and, indeed, grown in scope, unsupported by Israel's historical creed of the mighty acts of God, unsupported by life in the covenant community, unsupported by cult institutions, unsupported by revealed knowledge from prophets, unsupported by tradition and contradicted by experience. Next to Jesus, Job must surely be the greatest *believer* in the whole Bible.

[1] The theme of Kierkegaard's lyrical discourse *Consider the Lilies* (Eng. tr. 1940).

But Job's faith is not exercised blindly, in a vacuum. He still finds God *in the world*. This is very important, indeed it is vital for understanding the Lord's speeches. These charming poems about goats and ostriches are not at a tangent to the rest of the book. It is as a man in the world, as one among all these creatures, that Job stands before God. He is not called to a flight of pure thought into the transcendent Beyond. He is not called to plunge into the depths of his own being to find the Ground of all. It is by looking at the common things with God that Job is able to exclaim in the end: 'Now I'm satisfied; I've seen You with my own eyes' (42:5). This is more than enough to answer his questions, or rather it liberates him to live with joy even when the questions are not answered.

a. First round (38:1 – 40:5)
As in a folk-story, the same formulae are used over again in each of the two exchanges between the Lord and Job. The narrative here thus resembles the opening chapters in style.

i. Yahweh (38:1 – 40:2). After a few opening words (38:1-3), the Lord begins to ask Job questions about His world. The first speech gives rapid sketches of some twenty creatures. Both inanimate and living things pass in review, expanding our amazement at the range and complexity of the works of God. To suggest that God's governance is obscure is to speak in ignorance (38:2). The list is but a sample: the earth (38:4-7), the sea (8-11), morning (12-15), the underworld (16-18), light (19-21), snow (22, 23), storm (24-27), rain (28-30), various constellations (31-33), clouds (34-38), the lion (39, 40), ravens (41), the ibex (39:1-4), the wild ass (5-8), the wild ox (9-12), the ostrich (13-18), the horse (19-25), the hawk (26), the falcon (27-30). The list is assorted, with no strict order. It begins with some cosmic elements, moves to meteorological phenomena and ends with animals and birds. The horse seems to be the only domesticated animal mentioned, and it is his majesty, not his servility, that is stressed.[1] With this exception, all the creatures men-

---

[1] This kind of Wisdom poetry has an affinity with hymns (the Psalter contains several) which can grow to a catalogue of the size of *Benedicite omnia opera*. Making such lists was an early exercise in science (*cf.* 1 Ki. 4:33). Genesis 1 reflects and stimulated this tradition (see W. Schmidt, *Überlieferungsgeschichte der Priesterschrift Gen. 1:1 – 2:4a, WMZANT*, VIII, 1964).

tioned are beyond the control of men. Yet all are among God's pets. He cares even for the sparrow. Somehow this discourse arouses in Job a sense of awe at the beauty and order of the world. A sense of mystery too, for some of these animals seem ugly, repugnant, useless to men. And some of the things mentioned are remote from men, and some are a danger to him.

It has been suggested (*e.g.* by Gordis, p. 297) that these glimpses of nature hint at a moral order of similar complexity, beauty and mystery. They are a kind of allegory. It is certainly part of the method of Wisdom teachers to talk about human conduct by means of similes drawn from natural history. The book of Proverbs contains many examples. But if such analogies are intended here, they are concealed. No morals are drawn, unless perhaps in 40:8–14. The descriptions are remarkably objective, as if the Creation should be enjoyed for its own sake, or rather as God's artistry, and not for the lessons it can teach us about ourselves.

1–3. Job's troubles began when a great wind killed his children (1:19). The Lord was in that storm, and now He speaks from the tempest (*cf.* Ezk. 1:4). Some commentators think that Elihu's concluding words are a description of the onset of this storm, but this cannot be so if 37:22 describes the calm as the storm abates. Job is first rebuked (but not derided) for speaking *without knowledge*. The Bible does not consider ignorance to be either sin, or the root of sin. *Darkens counsel* has become a celebrated expression, but, as commonly quoted, it is applied to muddled talk that obfuscates issues. This is not its meaning here. It does not refer slightingly to the inconsequential debate between Job and the rest. *Counsel* usually refers to the 'plan' of God ('design', NEB; 'Providence', Dhorme). But since in the end God will say that Job spoke the truth about Him, it introduces a serious contradiction if here He accuses Job of obscuring the divine purpose.[1] But *counsel* often refers to the 'advice' dispensed by a wise man. As such it is a good parallel to knowledge. This suggests that the negative *without* does double duty. Robbed of its object, the verb (participle) becomes absolute and elative. Job is

---

[1] This discrepancy does not worry critics who assign the prose Epilogue to a different author from the poetic Dialogue; in fact they adduce it in support of this multiple authorship.

completely in the dark because he lacks counsel and knowledge. These God now supplies.

4-7. Knowledge of the origins of the world is inaccessible to men. Man, the latest arrival on the scene, never observed the beginnings. Creation is a hypothesis, reasonable, but not verifiable. The result is seen, but not the act, nor the Agent. Here then is a vast mystery, and the Bible views it in many different ways. The Old Testament contains at least a dozen creation 'stories' which use almost as many different images, casting God in the role of builder, potter, weaver, *etc.*, drawing the illustrations from the crafts of men. The book of Job contains several of these, or at least what look like fragments of forgotten creation stories of more ample scope. Some have no clear parallels either in the rest of the Bible or in its background literature. Here, as in Job 26, lost Canaanite sources may be suspected. As in Psalm 24, Isaiah 40, and other passages, the world is described as a vast edifice whose designer and maker is God, who *laid the foundation*[1] *of the earth*. The figure is developed with material details, including a trench for footings, cornerstone, *etc.* This makes it possible that *bînāh* in verse 4 is not *understanding*, but a noun based on *bānāh*, 'build'. The *when*-phrase in verse 7 links with the *when*-phrase in verse 4 to complete the strophe. God was not solitary when He started this world. His world was already populous with creatures: 'divine' beings (literally *sons of God*), the angels of later theology, whom we have already met in assembly in chapters 1 and 2. They celebrated with songs and cheering the achievement of God. Unless parallelism points to *the morning stars* as an alternative name for *the sons of God*, these might be pre-eminent beings in the retinue, probably to be associated with the twin gods of Dawn and Dusk in Canaanite lore, or Venus as Lucifer and Hesperus in classical. It is noteworthy that 11QtgJob has completed the demythologizing, making the stars shine instead of sing, and calling the *sons* 'angels'. Here already the exultant reaction of such superior creatures, so much nearer to God, is a call to Job to be amazed and to rejoice with them.

8-11. The origin of the *sea* is described by vivid use of the metaphor of child-birth. It is idle to make this yield a scientific

---

[1] The author has discussed the architectural and geological meaning of this word in *Australian Biblical Review*, VI, 1958, pp. 1–35, and in *Biblica*, L, 1969, pp. 393f.

cosmology, since any Israelite knew as well as we do that poets go in for such fancies and do not expect us to believe that God makes rain by pouring water from tilted waterskins (38:37).

The questions continue. The imagery is again quite concrete. The translation *shut in* (8), abandoned by NEB, suggests the restriction of the sea to its present bounds as described in Genesis 1:9 and in verses 10 and 11 below. But the first stage is the gestation of Yam in the womb of an unnamed mother. The verb does not have the meaning of 'shut' anywhere else, but it occurs in an exactly equivalent phrase in Psalm 139:13, 'belly' corresponding to 'double doors' here, making them a specific reference to the labia. The commentary on 3:10 above supports this result.

> 'Who constructed the sea within the doors?
> Who delivered[1] [it] when it burst from the womb?'

Translations correctly continue the questions, supplying *Who?* (not in the Hebrew); but it needs to be added to the next line also.

The comparison of the swirling clouds with the *swaddling band* of the new-born ocean is very picturesque. As in Genesis 1, the primal abyss is under *thick darkness* at first, but some interpret this as 'fog' (NEB) in the interests of parallelism. But this gain, if allowed, is offset by calling the fog the baby's 'cradle', a change which has little support from the lexicon.

The picture in verses 10 and 11 is different, and more naturalistic. Although the sea is still personified, it is not a babe, but a threatening element that must be kept in place. Here the double door and the safety bar, typical defence works of a city, are more likely to be a barrier to keep the sea out than part of a prison to keep it in. The *bounds* ('my bound' or 'decree' in Hebrew) can mean either a rule to be obeyed ('statute') or a line inscribed, as if God drew on the earth's surface a limit for the sea's encroachment (*cf.* verse 5). Only this context can justify RSV translation of 'broke' by *prescribed*, but no solution to this problem is in sight. If we have the picture right (and verse 11 is entirely in line with it) then *'ālāyw* is badly translated *for it*. 'Against it' should be read, and it should operate in both colons. Identical usage

[1] Reading *yôṣîʾ*, spelt defectively. An act of God is much more suitable than a natural process.

in Psalm 24:2 (where 'upon' should be abandoned) adds further proof, as the writer first pointed out in 1958 (see above, p. 274, n. 1).

The majestic rendering of verse 11 in AV has never been improved upon.

12–15. When speaking about the sea (8–11), God moved from its birth to its present state. It is not the original creation of *the morning*, treated as an entity as distinct as night and day, but the miracle of its daily appearance that is now described in highly fanciful language. Here is another thing over which Job exercises no control. The allusions in verse 13 are harder to grasp, and the conflict of translations betrays underlying difficulties. NEB has found another astronomical reference to the 'Dog-star' rather than *the wicked*. The traditional interpretation seems to describe the sunrise as a removal of the dark robes of night from the world, exposing *the wicked* who had sheltered beneath its cover. But *it* in the last word refers to *earth*, not to *skirts*. The imagery of verse 14 is quite different. The tinted rays of the early morning sun bring the earth's surface into sharp relief like soft clay under a seal. But the figure is lost in verse 14b, unless the colour refers to the pink hues of dawn. But the mention of *a garment* and the return to *the wicked* in verse 15 suggests that we have picked up once more the theme that evil-doers are restrained by daylight.[1] The shattering of the arm upraised for violence (15b) hardly allows us to call the sun *their light*. In view of the annoyance of some scholars over the proposal of new examples of enclitic *mem*, I hesitate to suggest that there are two of them in verse 15a, translated *from* and *their* in RSV. But since the Massoretes were unsure of the word *wicked* in both occurrences, there are too many unknowns to permit control. We note that G. R. Driver suggests that the *uplifted arm* is another constellation ('the Navigator's Line')[2] which has been adopted by NEB, thus eliminating all references to human beings from the passage.

16–18. Another realm beyond the reach of men is the vast subterranean region. Here are found the abyss of waters, Yam and Tehom of the old myths, and the land of death.[3]

---

[1] Since the Hebrew reads 'they take their stand' (*cf.* AV), the verse obviously needs more work. Comparison with Jb. 24:13–17 may help.

[2] *JTS*, IV, 1953, pp. 211f.

[3] *Earth* (*'ereṣ*) of verse 18 is certainly the underworld.

These Job never explored, but the Lord rather banteringly invites him to make a report, *if you know all this*.

19-21. In the story of creation in Genesis 1 light is the first thing made in contrast to the primaeval darkness. Here *light* and *darkness* are personified and associated as mysterious beings whose *place*[1] is beyond man's reach. They need a guide to help them find their way home. God can do this, but Job cannot. NEB brings this out much better than RSV. Although there is no interrogative particle in the Hebrew, verse 21 probably continues the questions: 'Do you know ... ?' In Genesis 1 God separated light from darkness, that is, He assigned to each a distinct realm. If Job were old enough to have been *born then*, he might know how it was done. Since Job had never pretended to have such knowledge, he is quite undeserving of the sarcasm which many commentators find in this verse, which, as a statement of fact, is ridiculous. But, as a question in line with the rest, it is a not unkind invitation to Job to accept his limitations and to let God be God.

22, 23. The creation of snow and hail is not described in biblical cosmologies. Here it is supposed that God has them stored in His treasuries (the Lord thinks about snow the way a man thinks about gold!), ready for use in wartime (*cf.* Jos. 10:11; Jdg. 5:20f.; 1 Sa. 7:10). Job has never inspected this arsenal.

24-27. As it now reads, verse 24a is almost identical with verse 19a. But the rest of this section deals with a rainstorm, so that the word *light* has been doubted. Since no convincing emendation has come to hand, we might remember, before discarding the word, that 'light' was used more than once in Elihu's fourth speech to refer to lightning in connection with the thunderstorm. Perhaps the same connection exists here. The language is fanciful, and it is surprising to have a shower brought by *the east wind*. NEB is encouraged by our knowledge of the kind of weather usually caused by such a wind to read 'heat' in verse 24a. If so, verses 24f. and verses 26f. refer to quite different phenomena.

Up to this point God has shown Job regions of the cosmos to which he has no access. But he is quite familiar with rain. So the curious point is made that rain falls on uninhabited wasteland. The repetition of *no man* underscores this. God is

---

[1] Because of the parallelism, we think that *drk* means 'realm', not *way*.

up to something which has nothing to do with man. In fantastic words, the streams are described as flowing down a sluice. As a result, God makes green sproutage grow in the most unpromising place. Why should He bother? Perhaps He enjoys clothing the ground with flowers, if only for a few days. This is marvel enough, and there is no need to look for a moral.

28–30. The *rain*, *dew*, *ice* and *hoarfrost* are not little gods with father and mother, as the old myths tell it. So far as Israel is concerned, such puerilities have been so long forgotten that a polemic is no longer needed, although these questions may be the last echo of it. Their purpose is not to discredit long-abandoned gods, but to impress Job with God's superb control of all such things. If a process of birth describes the making of ice (the same language was used in verse 8), the poetry is obvious, and the sole point to be taken is that the Lord made them all. There is also the continued reminder that Job understands little of such matters, and certainly cannot imitate these acts. The phrase *hoarfrost of heaven* compares with 'the dew of heaven' used in other parts of the Bible. Nothing is gained by quibbling over whether the author believed that dew and frost actually fell from the sky rather than condensing directly from the atmosphere. It is not easy to draw a line between such moisture and mists, fogs and low clouds. More to be wondered at is the quiet power of the winter's cold, which can turn water to stone, freezing the entire *face of the deep*. Since we have here again the name of the great ocean, it is interesting to ask where our author travelled to observe freezing on such a grand scale. Yet he speaks of it as if his listeners would all know that such things occur.

31–33. It is a little surprising that the panorama does not include the sky, the most venerable item in most cosmologies; and sun and moon, so conspicuous in man's experience, so alluring for his reverence, are not discussed.[1] Avoiding the obvious, the Lord turns to the constellations. The references to *Pleiades* and *Orion* (31) are clear (*cf.* 9:9), but there is less certainty about the identity of the stars mentioned in verse 32. Compare the various translations. Whatever they are, the

---

[1] Gn. 1 includes an oblique polemic against the worship of sun and moon. Not only is their creaturely status made plain, but they are belittled by calling them rather contemptuously 'lamps'.

point is clear: they are all bound and fettered by God, who leads them around the sky as He pleases, a thing no man can do. The memorable phrase of AV, 'the sweet influences of Pleiades', must regretfully be abandoned, savouring too much of the lingering influence of mediaeval astrology on the translators. Some of this still remains in the RSV translation of verse 33, which implies that the stars exercise some rule over events on earth, even though Job does not know how this works. It is more likely that verse 33 is not a continuation of the questions about the stars, but a more general question about the *ordinances* which God has made for heaven and earth, which, in Hebrew terminology, comprise the universe, for which they had no special word. Although NEB has modernized the thought too much by speaking of 'the laws of nature', it is an improvement.

34–38. Nor does any man understand the movements of clouds. Once more we have the familiar reference to thunder as the voice of God, which no man can imitate, shouting to the clouds so that *a flood of waters* may cover Him. Lightning flashes are fiery missiles hurled by God, another feat that no man can emulate (35). The writer's fancy is at its best in this little touch of the ridiculous, as if Job could marshal the lightning to report to him with the words: *Here we are.* RSV goes too far in verse 36 by supposing that wisdom has actually been conferred on things like *clouds* and *mists*. This cuts across the Bible's emphasis on God as the exclusive holder of wisdom, except in so far as He shares it with favoured men. Occurring in the middle of the strophe dealing with clouds and rain, one would expect in verse 36 a reference to some aspect of the weather. But the words translated *clouds* and *mists* are unique, and have stimulated scholarly debate that has raged for nearly two thousand years without resolution. Identification with Egyptian gods, Thoth and Sekwi, has gained considerable favour in recent research.[1] Birds have long been suspected, and TEV settles for ibis and rooster. Constellations have also been tracked down (Rowley, p. 316), while RV located wisdom in the 'inward parts' and 'mind'. NEB, more abstract, adopts 'darkness' and 'secrecy'. The placement of this well-formed bicolon so symmetrically between two tetracolons, each of which deals with clouds and rain, makes it less

---

[1] Ample discussion, with references, in Pope, p. 302.

compelling to find the same topic here. A more general reference to *wisdom* and *understanding* would be in order, but it is less likely that the thought would jump to birds (unless they have something to do with the weather, a connection which TEV has succeeded in making), and highly improbable that pagan gods would turn up in a book so ruthlessly monotheistic, and in naturalistic poems which, for all their adornment with mythic imagery, are thoroughly purged of mythological thought. *Non liquet*.

The effect of rain on the soil is realistically described in verse 38, but verse 37 contains the quaint picture of God making rain by tilting water-bottles in the sky. Moderns betray a dull imagination if they think that anyone in antiquity took such language literally, any more than the conduits in verse 25.

39, 40. The survey of selected[1] natural phenomena ends at 38:38. The rest of the Lord's first speech, and most of the second, are devoted to living things closer to man's observation. These extraordinary creatures are hard to relate purposefully to men. Although placed in charge of the world, no man would hunt prey for a lioness! Yet God supplies such an animal with food. Explain that!

41. This little poem about the *raven* has been subjected to doubt, coming as it does between lions and goats. Such an argument has little force. The raven's *young ones* are described as imploring God for food, just as a hungry man does in need. Placing these helpless birds next to the rapacious lion brings out the benevolence of God towards all His creatures. A man may then learn to take his place beside these other children of God.

39:1–4. Since the creatures that God talks about are nearly all untamed animals, the one referred to here is the wild *mountain goat* or ibex. The point that is made is simple, but quite marvellous. Removed from men, who supervise the breeding of their own flocks, these animals have their young unobserved and unsheltered. Job is invited to reflect on the mystery of instinct (the Bible would more truthfully call this a wisdom of divine origin implanted in animals) by which mother gives birth and kid quickly learns self-preservation.

---

[1] Seismic events are not included, nor dramatic celestial occasions such as eclipses. These might have served the author's purpose well, but the almost random assortment gives the impression of only touching the fringe.

If the 'wild doe' and her 'fawns' (NEB) are another species treated along with the wild goat, the point is the same. It does, however, have a bearing on the meaning of *bār*, their natural habitat: 'corn' (AV), 'the open' (RSV), 'the wilds' (TEV), 'the open forest' (NEB), *etc.*

5–8. The thought is not far off that the Lord has His own rich flocks and herds (Ps. 50:10). It comes into clearer light in this charming vignette of *the wild ass*, who lives in the land that God gave him (6). He has his own life, wide-ranging (8), and his place in the purpose of God is not to be explained by the service he renders men (like his domesticated cousin). He scorns civilization (7), and the poem seems to express a certain envy of his freedom, notwithstanding the hardship of the rough terrain, *steppe* and *salt land* he lives in. In spite of this contrast, however, the animal does not seem to be represented as a brumby. He has not escaped; he has been released. There is no rebuke of man as a hard task-master, as if God is accusing Job of abusing the trust of Genesis 1:26ff. It is God who has set this beast free, forgoing the legitimate claims He might have on its services.

9–12. Rowley (p. 319) draws attention to the association of the tame ass and ox in the Bible. The *wild ox* contrasts even more sharply with his servile cousin, even though his superlative strength makes him all the more desirable as a draught animal. The beast in question is the aurochs, not the fabled 'unicorn' of AV. Extinct since 1627, this enormous animal was the most powerful of all hoofed beasts, exceeded in size only by the hippopotamus and elephant. It is the standard symbol of strength in the Old Testament, where it is mentioned nine times. It is ludicrous to think that it would willingly *spend the night* with more docile cattle in a stall. It could not be trusted to bring in the harvest. What is Job to make of such a creature? Is there a hint that its Creator might be more fearsome and unmanageable?

13–18. From the sublime to the ridiculous. It is hard to argue that this hilarious sketch of the ostrich serves any solemn didactic purpose. It is what it is, a silly bird, because God made it so. Why? This comical account suggests that amid the profusion of creatures some were made to be useful to men, but some are there just for God's entertainment and ours.

The poem presents a crop of difficulties. It breaks the chain of questions and turns to quite factual description. It refers to God (17) as if He were not the speaker. It is missing from LXX, but whether omitted by the translator or lacking in the Hebrew original we cannot say. For such reasons many scholars regard it as an interpolation. The difficulties we still encounter in the text could be the reason why the Greek translators abandoned it. Verse 13 is unintelligible, and we shall resist the temptation to try our hand on it, since more than enough guesses are already available. Since all the other creatures are spoken of with undisguised admiration, it is a problem to some that here the ostrich seems to be disparaged. While her speed is an asset (18), her treatment of her young is considered stupid and cruel (14-16). Pope brings together a lot of information about the odd behaviour of this bird, and also documents its reputation for foolishness, already well established in antiquity. A sensible discussion of the problems of this passage can be found in G. S. Cansdale's *Animals of Bible Lands*.[1] Complaints that the author's knowledge of the facts was defective are trivial, and Dahood[2] has defended the bird against the charge of irresponsibility as a parent. The essential point is made in verse 17. If God is pleased to create a bird deficient in wisdom, so what? Is Job being reminded that some of his behaviour might be equally lacking in *understanding* (the same word as in 38:4, but see the commentary there), unless he receives it as God's gift? *Cf.* Psalm 49:12, 20.

19-25. This living portrait of the *horse* is perhaps the most brilliant of all the poems. It is a spirited account of vitality and action. Although the last word in verse 19 is a *hapax legomenon*, NEB is probably right to replace RSV *strength* with 'mane'. The same root occurs with $g^e b\hat{u}r\bar{a}h$ and reappears in verse 25 below (*thunder*), but a synonym is not required. The idea of agitation suggests the flowing mane, and the idea of 'quivering' (NEB) rather than 'leaping' (RSV) is continued in verse 20a. The difficulty of the next cryptic line can be appreciated by comparing the versions. In general the nervous energy of this mettlesome steed can be felt more effectively when the poetry is arranged in short staccato lines:

[1] G. S. Cansdale, *Animals of Bible Lands* (1970), pp. 190-193. This reliable book should be used for additional information about all the creatures mentioned in Job.

[2] *JBL*, LXXVIII, 1959, pp. 307ff.

'His shrill neigh terrifies;
He paws violently;[1]
And exults mightily;
He charges the foe;
He laughs at fear;
And is never daunted;
And never shies at the sword.
Beside him quivers rattle,
Spear and javelin flash.[2]
He shakes with excitement;[3]
He swallows the ground.[4]
He can't stand still[5] when the trumpet sounds.'

Verse 25 brings the horse's response to the battle-call to a climax. The tricolon should be retained, although NEB discards the last line. Although the din of horn and battle-cry ends the poem, the horse's reaction is to 'smell the battle in the distance'. Anyone who has been carried away watching the performance of a magnificent charger might feel that the impact of this incomparable poem is quite enough, without searching for a lesson in it. But two questions are applicable to Job. Can you make such an animal? Can you control him? Even the well-broken and best-trained mount might break from the restraints of the most skilled rider, so that even the one domesticated animal included in the list is not completely under the control of man. And is man, more free than

---

[1] MT traditionally *in the valley* (RSV). Blommerde (*Northwest Semitic Grammar and Job*, p. 135) assembles an impressive alliance of experts to support this new interpretation which is gaining wider acceptance. The parallelism supports it.

[2] Whether throwing or stabbing spear, sabre or scimitar is the subject-matter of an extensive literature.

[3] This rendition is admittedly free. The Hebrew has nouns: *fierceness and rage* (RSV). The latter, in 3:26, could mean either external commotion or internal agitation. We are guided in part by belief that the poetry here is constructed in epic two-beat lines.

[4] Quotations from Arab poets are brought as evidence that this means 'he races swiftly'. Perhaps it does. But, in view of evidence that '*rṣ* sometimes means 'wilfully' (see commentary on 37:13), we suspect here a reference to the horse's impulsiveness. The parallelism of the next line supports this.

[5] Commentators are undecided as to whether to adopt this (RSV) or to retain the more literal 'he doesn't believe' (*cf.* AV). The latter is taken to mean that the horse is so delighted with the call to battle that he can hardly believe his good fortune – surely a fanciful idea, even for our extravagant author. 11QtgJob lacks this difficult verse.

any beast, to be understood as struggling against the reins of God when stirred up as Job was? If so, we have an allegory.

26. This verse gives a brief glimpse of the *hawk*, spreading its wings towards the south, probably in his instinctive migration. The question to Job is whether the bird does this *by your wisdom* (the word is actually 'discernment', as used in 38:4, 36). Does God ask if Job endowed the creature with this instinct? But this would mean that Job was the Creator, which is not the issue. Does God ask if the bird's movements are under Job's control? The immense difference between a man's limited mastery of his environment and God's total sovereignty is certainly one of the themes of these speeches. Or does God ask Job a more intellectual question (suggested by the word 'understanding'), whether he comprehends *how* the bird responds to the seasons and flies so gracefully? Perhaps the last two are interwoven in the idea of knowledge which enables a man to control nature.

27–30. This is borne out by the final question about the *eagle* (or 'vulture', NEB).[1] Is it at Job's *command* (literally 'mouth') that this bird flies higher (the *hip'il* is elative) than any other, and builds its nest so high? The ability is God's gift; the performance is outside Job's wishes. For once the vivid picture of the vulture's way of life is free from difficulties in the text. The parallelism in verses 26, 27 and again in verses 29, 30 is clean and classical. Furthermore these are unified by common themes into well-formed tetracolons. This leaves verse 28, symmetrically in the middle, as a distinct bicolon which affirms the central fact. Its structure is unusual, since each colon is not a complete clause (although NEB makes them such). Instead of a text-book construction:

'On the cliff he dwells
And spends the night on the crag,'

the parallel verbs are both in the first colon and the parallel nouns are both in the second colon.

40:1, 2. The conclusion of the Lord's first speech is a repetition of His challenge to Job, in the light of all that He has now said. Job has had his request. God has spoken. What has Job to say now? The meaning of *yswr* at the end of verse 2a has been much debated. 'Yield', that is, capitulate, is

---

[1] Many species of hawks, eagles and vultures are known in the Holy Land.

widely favoured. But is the Lord trying to beat Job into submission? NEB casts Job in the unpleasant role of 'stubborn' and 'answering back'. But the verb *answer* does not imply impertinence; it is a fitting response as discussion continues. Job is invited to speak and he does so. If parallelism is any guide, *yswr* must be a synonym, for 'he who disputes with the Almighty' is the same as 'he who argues with God'. We think that *yswr* can be added to the examples already pointed out by the writer[1] as a byform of *ysr* with its usual Wisdom meaning of 'instruct' (so as to correct). If Job understands any of these matters better than God, God is willing to learn from him. The question is ironical, of course; but in view of the friendly tone of the speeches, it is not at all snide.

ii. Job (40:3-5). Job's response is subdued, humble. He rates himself as 'light', but hardly 'contemptible'. But is it correct to say, as Rowley does (p. 326), that Job 'confessed and submitted'? Job has nothing to say. But does declining the invitation admit 'defeat'? Misunderstanding at this point has made it difficult for some commentators to see why a second speech from God should be needed. Quite apart from the artistic requirements pointed out in the Introduction, we suggest that Job's reply is somewhat evasive, and not at all a satisfactory end to the matter. The gesture of placing the hand over the mouth could be a mark of respect (*cf.* 21:5; 29:9) or a sign of silence. Job admits that he cannot answer, but he still does not admit to any sin, so there is no 'confession'. Nor does he retract any of his former statements, so there is no 'submission'. On the contrary, he seems to be sticking to his guns. He has already *spoken once*, and need say no more. Indeed he has already repeated himself (*twice*) and will not 'add' anything.[2] This suggests that Job has nothing to say that he has not already said. But it would be going too far in the other direction to find defiance here, or even a complaint that God has still not answered his questions. But even if that were so, the words of God which immediately follow supply this lack.

---

[1] F. I. Andersen, *ZAW*, LXXXII, 1970, pp. 270-274.

[2] Neither RSV (*I will proceed no further*, which suggests giving up) nor NEB ('I will do so no more', which suggests the renunciation of an admitted fault) quite catches the meaning of the Hebrew verb which means to 'continue' or 'repeat'.

b. Second round (40:6 – 42:6)

The same introductory formulae are used as in the first round.

i. Yahweh (40:6 – 41:34). Even though Job is now in a more subdued frame of mind, this is evidently not enough. God speaks again, but this time new things are said. There are two more nature-poems, but they are different in mood from the light and charming little sketches of the first speech. They are much longer, especially the second, which takes up one quarter of the total space allotted to God. But, even more strikingly, they are quite fantastic, so different in fact as to raise doubts in some minds as to whether they come from the same pen. (See the Introduction.) The writer's fancy goes to extremes, his imagery so far-fetched that we are not sure what he has in mind, whether some animals we know, like the recognizable birds and animals of the first speech, or some monsters of myth-lore.

8–14. The two poems about animals are prefaced by a passage which deals more directly with the moral issues that Job has raised. As such it may be the heart and pivot of the Lord's reply, as befits its central placement within the contrasting nature-poems. This does not mean, however, that it is unrelated to them. It will be part of our task to search for that relationship. But here the personal issue between Job and God is more directly dealt with. The problem, as seen by the friends, is whether Job has been forced to put God in the wrong in order to maintain his own integrity.

> 'Dare you deny that I am just
> or put me in the wrong that you may be right?' (8)

Then God takes the dispute beyond right and wrong by going behind such questions to the matter of responsibility.

In Israelite society the judge who gave a verdict was obliged to see that justice was done. As adjudicator he passed sentence; as vindicator he secured the right for the injured party. It was only indirectly, in connection with restoring things to rights, that wrongdoers were punished.[1] Job has rightly appealed to God to maintain his cause. In verses 8–14

---

[1] It is in keeping with this pattern that God never does anything about the criminals who despoiled Job.

Job is reminded that he does not have the ability to secure his own vindication. Hence the emphasis on the power of God. The contrast between the two has not been rubbed in to humiliate Job, to convince him that he cannot hope to succeed in an unequal contest with God. The point made now is quite different, and we suddenly see what all those apparently irrelevant excursions into nature were leading up to. Job now must realize that he is no more able to exercise jurisdiction in the moral realm than he is able to control the natural. Hence the question:

> 'Have you an arm like God,
> And can you thunder with a voice like his?' (9)

To take over the management of the universe, Job would have to be as splendid and majestic as God (10). These are the great attributes of Psalms 21:5; 93:1, 96:6; 104:1; *etc.* Is he equal to the task of bringing down the wicked (11–13), the thing that everyone has been looking for as proof of the presence and justice of God? There is an introverted structure here, shown by the repetition in verses 11b and 12a. Can Job take up the responsibility of bringing about, or even wishing, the death of any wicked man, as described in verse 13? (This matches verse 10, leaving verse 14 to complete the thought of verse 9, with 'arm' and 'hand' as the *inclusio*.)

In spite of its aggressive tone, this speech is not really a contradiction of anything that Job has said. In many respects it is very close to his own thought, and endorses his sustained contention that justice must be left to God. But it brings Job to the end of his quest by convincing him that he may and must hand the whole matter over completely to God more trustingly, less fretfully. And do it without insisting that God should first answer all his questions and give him a formal acquittal.

Here, if we have rightly found the heart of the theology of the whole book, is a very great depth. There is a rebuke in it for any person who, by complaining about particular events in his life, implies that he could propose to God better ways of running the universe than those God currently uses. Men are eager to use force to combat evil and in their impatience they wish God would do the same more often. But by such destructive acts men do and become evil. To behave as God suggests in 40:8–14, Job would not only usurp the role of

God, he would become another Satan. Only God can destroy creatively. Only God can transmute evil into good. As Creator, responsible for all that happens in His world, He is able to make everything (good and bad) work together into good. The debate has been elevated to a different level. The reality of God's goodness lies beyond justice. This is why the categories of guilt and punishment, true and terrible though they are, can only view human suffering as a consequence of sin, not as an occasion of grace.

15-24. This climax, to which the earlier and gentler poems led, is now enforced by two rhapsodies on monstrous animals altogether beyond man's power to tame. They are Behemoth (40:15-24), the fiercest land animal, and Leviathan (41:1-34), the most terrifying sea creature.

It is not easy to tell whether these creatures are real or fabulous, and, if real, what they actually are (hippopotamus, crocodile or whale?). If mythological, can we find them in some of the old myths? A general conclusion on this point at the outset shows up in the slant of the resultant translations. If real beasts are described, then the fanciful language (such as breathing fire) is a licence agreeable to poetry, but out of place in a zoology textbook. If, however, they are mythological, the translator will take the fire quite literally – it is a veritable dragon! – and allow the language to move even further into the realm of the fantastic.

Although great names can be quoted in support of the mythological theory, we think that a naturalistic interpretation is better. And, without trying to count votes, we think that a majority of scholars incline to this view.[1] Reasons for excluding the fabulous are, first, that the poems, although longer and put into a separate speech, are not essentially different from the earlier ones, which deal with familiar but fascinating birds and animals that the reader is obviously expected to know. Secondly, quite fanciful imagery has already been used in these earlier poems; we are no more required to believe that Behemoth's bones were made of metal (40:18) than that God has water-bottles in the sky (38:37). Thirdly, allowing for such poetic fancies, the book

---

[1] It is worth noting, in favour of the mythological theory, that later apocalyptic writers were greatly fascinated by Behemoth and Leviathan, definitely cosmic monsters, and came up with all kinds of bizarre notions of the part they would play in the end of the world.

of Job is realistic throughout. God is the only supernatural reality; the Satan is quite minor, and the angels even further in the background. Finally, and this would seem to be quite conclusive, Job 40:15 states explicitly that Behemoth and Job are equally God's creatures.[1]

Behemoth is the plural of the Hebrew word for 'beast', here used as a proper name. The details given, allowing for exaggeration and also for many obscurities in the text, fit the hippopotamus best. His habitat is the water (21ff.), his diet grass (15). His immense strength of bone and muscle is highlighted (16, 18). It is hard to see how *his tail* can be compared to *a cedar*, for the tail of the hippopotamus is small and short. There is something complacent in his indifference to the weight of swirling waters (23), and, since *Jordan* is explicitly named as his home, there is no need to go outside Palestine for the background, although many scholars locate it in Egypt. The reference to *the mountains* (20) presents some difficulty, although hippopotami do venture to forage. Verse 24 emphasizes the difficulty of capturing him, even though it is hard to see why one would try to *pierce his nose with a snare*. This point reiterates the theme of the first speeches.

As we have seen so often, a statement of special significance is embedded in the middle of more descriptive material. Verse 19 is different from the rest. It accords Behemoth the place of honour as *the first of the works of God*. AV (*cf.* NEB) interpreted this as 'chief', but the statement could be a reflection of Genesis 1:24. Verse 19b is the despair of all commentators; the innumerable conflicting solutions offered do not encourage us to accept any of them.

41:1-34. *Leviathan* is the name of a seven-headed sea dragon in the old myths, particularly those of Canaan before the Israelite occupation. Scraps of this ancient literature survive in the Old Testament, and are undoubtedly the source of the name used here. The abundant proof supplied by Pope (pp. 329ff.) settles this point. But it does not prove that Leviathan is still a mythological monster in this poem. The extravagant picture fits the crocodile well enough, but other identifications have been proposed, some of which involve dividing the poem into smaller portions. NEB has settled for

---

[1] NEB has unfortunately adopted G. R. Driver's emendation of this line to read 'Consider the chief of the beasts, the crocodile'. Once the identification is made, the whole translation can be adjusted to suit.

the whale, at least in verses 1–6, which it transfers to the end of chapter 39.

The style of the first speeches is more prominent here, since the discourse begins with a string of questions, aimed at convincing Job how helpless he is in the presence of such a frightening creature. How could you catch him (verses 1ff., balanced by verses 7, 8 by an introverted structure)? And, even if you could, what would you do with him? The suggestions are silly. Make him a servant (4) – but what use would he be? A pet (5)? Sell him (6)?

After this introduction is completed by the introversion we have already pointed out, verses 9–11 dwell on the folly of tackling him. Since the rest of the poem (12–34) is devoted to a detailed description of the animal, we suspect that the vital point being made is to be found in this embedded material. Unfortunately the text is very difficult. While verse 11b makes a fairly clear assertion that God owns everything in the world, and therefore Leviathan, the import of verse 11a quite escapes us. (NEB has brought it into line with verse 10 as part of the warning against attacking him. But in doing so it makes the whole refer to Leviathan, altering the reference to God preserved in RSV. But this variant does have support from MSS and versions.) It is a pity to be left in uncertainty on this point. Assuming that RSV is generally correct, the argument runs like this. If even the most courageous man would not be so insane as to *stir up* Leviathan, how could anyone be so foolhardy as to *stand* up against God, as Job has done? We can feel the force of this as a warning against irreverence. But in the dialogue it was always the friends who tried to warn Job off his enterprise with reminders about how much stronger God is than he. Job has never challenged God to a trial of sheer strength, as a man would who hunted a crocodile. The argument to the superior strength of God is made, not to discourage men from trying to have dealings with God, but to enhance God's capability of managing the affairs of the universe so that men will trust Him.

Space does not permit detailed commentary on all the whimsical things that the Lord says about Leviathan: his *strength* (12); his skin, described as a *double coat of mail* (13); his mouth, fancifully called *the doors of his face* (14); his scales, each of which is like a warrior's shield (15–17; verse 15b is difficult; it could describe rock-like hardness, *cf.* TEV); his fiery *breath* (18–21);[1] his *neck* (22); his impenetrable hide (23); his solid *heart* (24); his contempt for every weapon (26–29); his spectacular movement through the water (30–32). Our poet can hardly write a line without including a simile, a habit which many critics censure as artistic over-kill. Considering the conventions of Wisdom writing, we suspect that Israelites would have found it delightful according to their own canons. And as for its length, which has also evoked complaints from modern readers, we think that the longest poem about the most terrifying animal was deliberately left until last to provide a terrific climax. The dread that Leviathan inspires was noted in verse 10, mentioned again in passing in verse 25, and forcefully driven home in the concluding lines (33, 34).

ii. Job (42:1–6). Job is satisfied. His vision of God has been expanded beyond all previous bounds. He has a new appreciation of the scope and harmony of God's world, of which he is but a small part. But this discovery does not make him feel insignificant. Just by looking at ordinary things, he realizes that he cannot even begin to imagine what it must be like to be God. The world is beautiful and terrifying, and in it all God is everywhere, seen to be powerful and wise, and more mysterious when He is known than when He is but dimly discerned. The Lord has spoken to Job. That fact alone is marvellous beyond all wonder. Job has grown in wisdom. He is at once delighted and ashamed.

His first spontaneous outburst, so different from the reserve of his reply to the first speech, is an expression of unrestrained admiration:

> 'You can do everything!
> None of your plans can be frustrated!'[2]

In verse 3a Job repeats the question that the Lord had asked him in 38:2. Now he answers it. He admits that he spoke out of limited knowledge, speaking too confidently about things *too wonderful* for him to understand. This is the

---

[1] Taken naturally, this is the steam we observe in our own breath on a frosty day; mythologically the fire is considered real.

[2] Verse 2; modern versions are to be preferred to AV.

cry of a liberated man, not one who has been broken and humiliated.

In verse 4 Job quotes the words that the Lord had spoken twice (38:3; 40:7) and to which he had declined to respond at the end of the third speech. Now he answers, and his reply is positive. It has two sides, as inseparable as the sides of a coin. He has gained knowledge of God and of himself. God comes first, and fills his vision: *now my eye sees thee*. The hope of 19:24–27 has found its first fulfilment.[1] Since what Job says about himself in verse 6 is all-important as the last word on the whole matter, it is a pity that ancient versions, including the new Qumran Targum, show considerable deviation at this point. There seems to be contrition, for Job says *I despise* (and translations usually supply *myself* as the object not found in the Hebrew). This does not go as far as the abject self-loathing of that radical repentance that requires admitting known sins. If we are to connect it with verse 3, Job could be expressing regret at his foolish words, uttered hastily and in ignorance (this is how TEV takes it) – a fault deserving correction, but not a wickedness deserving punishment. Job never says: 'Now, at last, I concede that I deserved that punishment.' If he is sorry about what he said, such behaviour after the catastrophe cannot be the sin it was intended to punish. Such a discovery could, however, be the spiritual growth it was intended to promote, and Job now recognizes this. Many alternate renditions of the word *despise* have been proposed. It is equally important not to misunderstand the word *repent* by reading into it too many conventional connotations of penitence for sins which weigh on the conscience. The whole story would collapse if this is the outcome. Job would have capitulated at last to the friends' insistent demand that he confess his sins. Job confesses no sins here. And, even if this is implied, it is one thing to repent before God and another thing to disown one's integrity before men. Job's reference to *dust and ashes* reminds us of Abraham's words when he was praying to God (Gn. 18:27). As a humble suppliant, he knows his status. But, next to Job, Abraham is *the* righteous man of the Old Testament, and to kneel thus before God is an honour that exalts him above other men.

---

[1] We still think that its ultimate fulfilment comes through physical resurrection after death.

VI. THE OUTCOME (42:7–17)

Now poetic justice is done and the story is quickly ended. The Lord gives His verdict (7–9) and Job is reinstated (10–17).

a. Yahweh's verdict (42:7–9)

Only when the issue with Job is settled does God turn to the friends. Although they are condemned, God does not deal with them according to their folly. Job is clearly pronounced to have had the better of the debate (7). We have rested a great deal of our interpretation on this result. Job's vindication over against them is made public. Their roles are reversed! In the course of their speeches, not one of them even hinted that they, not Job, might be the object of God's *wrath* (7) and in need of His grace. Now they discover (it is a delightful irony) that unless they can secure the patronage of Job (the very one they had treated as in such need of their spiritual resources), they might not escape the divine displeasure. The effective prayer of a righteous man to turn away God's anger from the wicked (*cf.* Gn. 18) adds another meaning to Job's suffering that no-one had thought of.

b. Job's restoration (42:10–17)

Job ends his days in full enjoyment of all the relationships in which a person is fully human. His reinstatement is not the result of his repentance in verse 6, but of his intercession in verses 8 and 9. It was when Job prayed for his friends that the Lord restored his own fortunes (10). His relations and all his acquaintances came to him with their consolations (11). It is worth dwelling on the fact that, even when everything is set right, Job still feels the hurt of his losses, and needs human comfort for them. The significance of their gifts of money and jewellery (11b) is not clear. It is more likely that they are to honour a rich man than to succour a poor one. It is a wry touch that the Lord, like any thief who has been found out (Ex. 22:4), repays Job double what He took away (10b). His flocks and herds are twice as big as they were before the disasters. The strange numeral in verse 13 could mean 'twice seven sons'; but the number of daughters is the same. Analogy has suggested from his additional *hundred and forty years* (16) that Job was seventy when the story began, but this is a speculation.

The disclosure (14) of the names of the daughters, which have meanings that seem strange to us but for which no hidden symbolism has been found, while the sons remain anonymous, is probably intended to go with the remarkable fact that they shared the inheritance with their brothers (15). No explanation is given for this arrangement, which was not required by law, but lay in the father's discretion. (According to Nu. 27, daughters inherited only when there were no male heirs; this need did not arise here.) Job's gesture might have been an additional expression of gratitude for his replaced family, or a further proof of his restored wealth which provided plenty for all. The simple, dignified ending (17), which reminds us of the peaceful deaths of the patriarchs in Genesis, completes the fulfilment of the Israelite ideal.

Some scholars have complained that the story is ruined by the happy ending, as if the author had slipped back into the crude theology of punishments and rewards which it was his aim in the discourses to discredit, or had been unable to expurgate this feature from the basic folk-story, even though it contradicted his thesis. But his point has been made so firmly that these final touches cannot harm it. God does what He pleases. It would be absurd to say that He must keep Job in miserable poverty in order to safeguard the theology. These gifts at the end are gestures of grace, not rewards for virtue.[1] It is an artistic, indeed a theological fitness, if not necessity, that Job's vindication be not just a personal and hidden reconciliation with God in the secret of his soul, but also visible, material, historical, in terms of his life as a man. It was already a kind of resurrection in flesh, as much as the Old Testament could know.[2] Job's complete vindication had to wait until the resurrection of Lazarus, and of a Greater than Lazarus.

[1] We have suggested, however, in the comment on verse 10, that there is compensation for the unwarranted wrongs that God had done Job.

[2] C. H. Gordon, in a public lecture, has suggested that Job's children in chapter 42 are identical with the ones in chapter 1, raised from the dead. This is building too much on the minor difference in wording between 1:2 ('there were born') and 42:13 ('he had').